Alternative Shakespeares 3

This volume takes up the challenge embodied in its predecessors, *Alternative Shakespeares* and *Alternative Shakespeares 2*: to identify and explore the new, the changing, the radically "other" possibilities for Shakespeare studies at our particular historical moment.

Alternative Shakespeares 3 introduces the strongest and most innovative of the new directions emerging in Shakespearean scholarship—ranging across performance studies, multimedia and textual criticism, concerns of economics, science, religion, and ethics—as well as the "next step" work in areas such as postcolonial and queer studies that continue to push the boundaries of the field. The contributors approach each topic with clarity and accessibility in mind, enabling student readers to engage with serious "alternatives" to established ways of interpreting Shakespeare's plays and their role in contemporary culture.

The expertise, commitment and daring of this volume's contributors shine through each essay, maintaining the progressive edge and real-world urgency that are the hallmark of *Alternative Shakespeares*. This volume is essential reading for students and scholars of Shakespeare who seek an understanding of current and future directions in this ever-changing field.

Contributors include: Kate Chedgzoy, Mary Thomas Crane, Lukas Erne, Diana E. Henderson, Rui Carvalho Homem, Julia Reinhard Lupton, Willy Maley, Patricia Parker, Shankar Raman, Katherine Rowe, Robert Shaughnessy and W. B. Worthen.

Diana E. Henderson is Professor of Literature at MIT.

IN THE SAME SERIES

Alternative
Shakespeares 3

Edited by
Diana E. Henderson

Routledge
Taylor & Francis Group

LONDON AND NEW YORK

First published 2008
by Routledge
2 Park Square, Milton Park, Abingdon, Oxon OX14 4RN

Simultaneously published in the USA and Canada
by Routledge
270 Madison Ave, New York, NY 10016

Routledge is an imprint of the Taylor & Francis Group, an informa business

Typeset in Joanna and Scala Sans by
Florence Production Ltd, Stoodleigh, Devon
Printed and bound in Great Britain by
The Cromwell Press, Trowbridge, Wiltshire

British Library Cataloguing in Publication Data
A catalogue record for this book is available from the British Library

Library of Congress Cataloging in Publication Data
Alternative Shakespeares 3/edited by Diana E. Henderson
  p. cm. — (New accents)
 Includes bibliographical references and index.
 1. Shakespeare, William, 1564–1616—Criticism and interpretation.
I. Henderson, Diana E., 1957–
PR2976.A644 2007
822.3'3–dc22   2007018248

ISBN10: 0–415–42332–5 (hbk)
ISBN10: 0–415–42333–3 (pbk)
ISBN10: 0–203–93409–1 (ebk)

ISBN13: 978–0–415–42332–8 (hbk)
ISBN13: 978–0–415–42333–5 (pbk)
ISBN13: 978–0–203–93409–8 (ebk)

CONTENTS

GENERAL EDITOR'S PREFACE

No doubt a third General Editor's Preface to *New Accents* seems hard to justify. What is there left to say? Thirty years ago, the series began with a very clear purpose. Its major concern was the newly perplexed world of academic literary studies, where hectic monsters called "Theory," "Linguistics," and "Politics" ranged. In particular, it aimed itself at those undergraduates or beginning postgraduate students who were either learning to come to terms with the new developments or were being sternly warned against them.

New Accents deliberately took sides. Thus the first Preface spoke darkly, in 1977, of "a time of rapid and radical social change," of the "erosion of the assumptions and presuppositions" central to the study of literature. "Modes and categories inherited from the past," it announced, "no longer seem to fit the reality experienced by a new generation." The aim of each volume would be to "encourage rather than resist the process of change" by combining nuts-and-bolts exposition of new ideas with clear and detailed explanation of related conceptual developments. If mystification (or downright demonization) was the enemy, lucidity (with a nod to the compromises inevitably at stake there) became a friend. If a "distinctive discourse of the future" beckoned, we wanted at least to be able to understand it.

With the apocalypse duly noted, the second Preface proceeded piously to fret over the nature of whatever rough beast might stagger portentously from the rubble. "How can we recognise or deal with the new?" it complained, reporting nevertheless the dismaying advance of "a host of barely respectable activities for which we have no reassuring names" and promising a program of wary surveillance at "the boundaries of the precedented and at the limit of the thinkable." Its conclusion, "the unthinkable, after all, is that which covertly shapes our thoughts," may rank as a truism. But in so far as it offered some sort of useable purchase on a world of crumbling certainties, it is not to be blushed for.

In the circumstances, any subsequent, and surely final, effort can only modestly look back, marvelling that the series is still here, and not unreasonably congratulating itself on having provided an initial outlet for what turned, over the years, into some of the distinctive voices and topics in literary studies. But the volumes now re-presented have more than a mere historical interest. As their authors indicate, the issues they raised are still potent, the arguments with which they engaged are still disturbing. In short, we were not wrong. Academic study did change rapidly and radically to match, even to help to generate, wide-reaching social changes. A new set of discourses was developed to negotiate those upheavals. Nor, as new additions to the series demonstrate, has the process ceased. In our deliquescent world, what was unthinkable inside and outside the academy all those years ago now seems regularly to come to pass.

Whether the *New Accents* volumes provided—and provide—adequate warning of, maps for, guides to, or nudges in the direction of this new terrain is scarcely for me to say. Perhaps our best achievement lay in cultivating the sense that it was there. The only justification for a reluctant third attempt at a Preface is the belief that it still is.

TERENCE HAWKES

Contributors

Michael Boyd	Artistic Director, Royal Shakespeare Company
Rui Carvalho Homem	Professor of Anglo-American Studies, University of Oporto
Kate Chedgzoy	Professor of Renaissance Literature, University of Newcastle
Mary Thomas Crane	Professor of English, Boston College
Lukas Erne	Professor of English, Université de Genève
Diana E. Henderson	Professor of Literature, Massachusetts Institute of Technology
Julia Reinhard Lupton	Professor of English and Comparative Literature, University of California, Irvine
Willy Maley	Professor of English Literature, University of Glasgow
Patricia Parker	Professor of English and Comparative Literature, Stanford University
Shankar Raman	Associate Professor of Literature, Massachusetts Institute of Technology
Katherine Rowe	Professor of English, Bryn Mawr College
Robert Shaughnessy	Professor of Drama and Theatre Studies, University of Canterbury at Kent
W. B. Worthen	Professor of Drama, University of Michigan

Acknowledgments

In an act of transatlantic benevolence, Terence Hawkes entrusted this volume to me; I have benefited from his wisdom, wit and great spirit at every stage, and thank him both heartily and humbly. The diligence, receptiveness and integrity of my fellow contributors have been remarkable, making my work most often a pleasure. And throughout the process, the professionals at Routledge have been patient and supportive. I am grateful for the cheerful assistance of Amanda Finkelberg in compiling the bibliography, and to my sister Joyce Henderson for her help with the index. Finally, to my family, my colleagues at MIT, and to Shakespeareans far and wide who have supported me at every turn of a career, my enduring gratitude and affection.

D. E. H.

1

INTRODUCTION

Diana E. Henderson

"Can there still be an alternative Shakespeare?" muse some skeptical colleagues. Can there not be? The very success of the first two volumes in this series, and the radically progressive impulse within Shakespeare studies for which they stand, conjures such questions. So do the remarkable range and freedom of Shakespeare in performance during these decades, both live and on screen, which have brought the plays to larger audiences and new cultural locations. With these expansions of possibility, both in practice and method, Will Shakespeare has attained a new kind of pop celebrity even as the Bard remains in some quarters the last bastion of community and inherited values. Thus if we take the title as descriptive, it is assured that any representative collection of Shakespeare essays today will indeed be about alternative Shakespeares.

But of course, *Alternative Shakespeares* and *Alternative Shakespeares 2* had more edge than that and defied the simple celebration of pluralism or variety: their contributors knew from the start that more television channels would not necessarily entail more significant choices, that the structures of consumption were as much the issue as the particulars of representation with which they were involved. The alternative agenda was overtly political, anti-individualist and subversive both within the British academy and in regard to the power relations of Anglocentric discourse and society. Shakespeare, clearly embedded within those structures, had to be debunked, re-formed and re-placed within the semiotic and cultural debates of the here and now. Twenty years on, the reformation proceeds apace, and so we must ask anew, in and for our moment: alternative to what?

The question can be addressed most directly within the terms of the contemporary academy and scholarship, but brings with it more paradox. When the first *Alternative Shakespeares* appeared, the influence of poststructuralist theory and cultural materialism was just beginning to be felt within Shakespearean circles: trumpeting the importance of these critical methods and a "collective commitment to the principle of contestation of meaning" (Drakakis 1985: 24), the volume was clearly alternative to the dominant academic practice within this sub-specialty in English studies. It buoyantly aimed to "liberate these texts from the straightjacket of unexamined assumptions and traditions" (1985: 25). A decade later, queer and postcolonial studies were likewise emergent fields of contestation and perceived sites for liberation. But in many ways these once-alternative visions have now become the dominant practices, accompanied by an archive fever that followed from the critique of historical master-narratives and was later abetted by a backlash against the less accessible (and sometimes more philo-sophically challenging) forms of theory. This overarching paradigm shift testifies to the intellectual force and social value of the alternative critique. Within university classrooms and the minds of scholars, close poetic and psychological analysis has been challenged, if not supplanted, by sociopolitical contextualization and linguistic decenter-ing. It is hard to locate a meaning now that is *not* contested.

Yet it is not so clear what effects on the wider world have followed, and indeed whether the radical import of the original critique has in fact been realized: if the dominant academic practice is more like a politically denuded version of alternativity, can more assertions of progressive critique avoid the same fate? Moreover, is the very desire for the new and "the next big thing" so thoroughly enmeshed within the logic of global capitalism that alternativity has itself become merely a sign of the status quo? Is it (to use a vocabulary more current in those heady paradigm-shifting days) an empty gesture at demystification or a space of delusory freedom within the hegemonic logic of commodification? If it is, claims of liberation and making a larger cultural difference would smack of naivety or even bad faith, and a bit of humility would seem in order.

To say so is not to deny the value of the thinking process itself or its local consequences. But it does require some rigorous scrutiny of the gap between scholarly practice and political claims. As Alan Sinfield has recently remarked, the move from cultural materialism to the merely material results in "a kind of textual anthropology" producing valuable work, but "the political edge is blunted" (Sinfield 2006: 4). Arguing that the "unfinished work" is to continue challenging hegemonic critical traditions that shape our reading of texts by (among other things) recovering the subordinated voices audible only "through the frosted screen of textuality," Sinfield's tone nevertheless marks a historical difference between the revolutionary defiance of 1985 and the dogged pragmatism of 2006: "Yet ideology functions not, in the main, through spectacular breaks, but by processes of steady drip, in which no one can be sure that his or her efforts will not tilt a local balance, in one direction or another" (2006: 25). Undeniably true and true to the continental theoretical traditions upon which cultural materialism was built, Sinfield's doubly negative construction and lack of specified direction as to the effects of one's efforts must nevertheless give one pause.

Indeed, this passage oddly recalls for me the sardonic voice of Julian Barnes in a memorably contesting but inconclusive novel, describing another kind of steady drip:

> The history of the world? Just voices echoing in the dark; images that burn for a few centuries and then fade; stories, old stories that sometimes seem to overlap; strange links, impertinent connections. We lie here in our hospital bed of the present (what nice clean sheets we get nowadays) with a bubble of daily news drip-fed into our arm. We think we know who we are, though we don't quite know why we're here, or how long we shall be forced to stay. And while we fret and writhe in bandaged uncertainty—are we a voluntary patient?— we fabulate. We make up a story to cover the facts we don't know or can't accept; we keep a few true facts and spin a new story round

them. Our panic and our pain are only eased by soothing fabulation; we call it history.

(Barnes 1989: 240)

Unfair though my associative connection may be, it captures a nagging truth that has haunted Anglo-American modernity for as long as artistic and critical manifestos have announced our collective liberation. Nor is its skepticism a sign of weakness so much as strength: it shows a willingness to look hard at the gaps in our stories, the places (to revert to the earlier vocabulary) where ideological hegemony is ripe for contestation. It is no mere coincidence that Barnes's novel confronts terrorism and religion head-on and, with them, the ways we contort living beings into the clean and unclean, the saved and the damned. This is secularism at its muscular core, even if Barnes would confine us to a hospital; less grim in his imagination, Sinfield is right to acknowledge both the limits and the necessity of ongoing advocacy even if all we have are those obscured (darkling) voices. To say that the Real may be inaccessible or delusory is not to lessen the force or energy of our project in this time and place: it may be less likely to inspire the troops, but that is precisely why it is less likely to lead in the direction of another Spanish Inquisition.

It would be absurd to claim to have definitive answers or a blanket solution to the paradoxical situation reigning in the first decade of the twenty-first century, although I can confidently assert that alternativity in and beyond Shakespeare studies has produced meaningful effects in our classrooms by enlarging the range of perspectives and readings allowed, and has contributed to more social inclusiveness in higher education. This is a direction worth pursuing further, as several of the essays in this volume do. Moreover, addressing the debates about theoretical assumptions and the cultural production of meaning not only in interdisciplinary programs but at the very heart of the literary canon, in Shakespeare classes, has been crucial to their effectiveness more generally. Here too, *Alternative Shakespeares* 3 continues the unfinished work. For those who read criticism—be they students, artists, "common readers," or scholars—the *Alternative Shakespeares* volumes (and other Accents on Shakespeare that followed) have provided accessible routes to participation in some of the more intellectually rigorous and urgent critical conversations of our days, and have revealed ways in which the conglomerate known as Shakespeare participates in the ongoing work of culture. In fractious times, the work grows more urgent than ever.

What this volume (and I hope our field more generally) also attempts in the "here and now" is to keep sociopolitical progress within our vision without spending too much time polemicizing differences of method within the field—that is, without engaging in the kind of internecine squabbling and "us versus them" rhetoric that Virginia Woolf wishfully assigned to the "private-school stage of human existence where there are 'sides'" (Woolf 1989: 106). Or, to borrow Linda Charnes's updated metaphor, *Alternative Shakespeares* 3 by and large eschews the "Smackdown" approach to critical debate and the "ideological fantasy of some kind of critical holy Grail: in Lacanese, a methodological Big Other (the Critic-Supposed-to-Know) that will render our arguments authoritative and impregnable" (Charnes 2006: 14). Here the feminist contribution to theory may also model a critical way forward out of the Oedipal maze. For if (and only if) John Drakakis meant it when he said in the Afterword to *Alternative Shakespeares* 2 that the volume must "disown its filial obligation" to *Alternative Shakespeares* 1 as an "act of patricide" (never mind that Drakakis, as the first volume's editor, is also imagining suicidal prospects for himself and other repeat contributors), then *Alternative Shakespeares* 3 takes up its "path forward to yet further alternatives" not as the next generation but perhaps more like a third term (Hawkes 1996: 244)— or if still conceived generationally, like a collaborative daughter rather than a murderous son, not feeling quite such a need "to bite the hands that feed" her as she struggles to realize the liberatory potential of the parental legacy (Hawkes 1996: 244). That different positioning allows an entirely new set of contributors to appear here and speak perhaps less uniformly though no less collectively in their politics and method.

Thus in the essays written for *Alternative Shakespeares* 3, the reader will again find signs of truly new dimensions and potential for progressive, engaged forms of analysis in Shakespeare studies. Performance and media studies have made major advances in the past decade, and Shakespeare is perceived more than ever as a multimedia artist. Several contributors from these fields bring interdisciplinary breadth to the collection, and raise questions about the theories and institutional contexts involved in performing Shakespeare. The digital revolution and its multimedia consequences—which have allowed new production possibilities and have prompted allied explorations of print culture and the circulation of information—are only the most obvious of such territories. The first set of essays by Robert Shaughnessy, Katherine Rowe and W. B. Worthen draw respectively on theatrical, film, and digital vocabularies to consider the changing place of Shakespeare and our artistic and critical use of his plays within these new media contexts. Collectively, these essays move towards a more rigorously historicized sense of media and performance, refuting the pat dichotomization of "text versus performance" and false presumptions about the timelessness and self-evident quality of stage gestures and embodied interpretations. They show how twenty-first-century Shakespeare is shaped by contemporary forces such as information theory, theatrical realism and absurdism, and media convergence. Shaughnessy and Worthen refuse the self-congratulatory theatrical exceptionalism that would exempt live performance from recognizing its sociocultural interpellation, but they also reject the schematic subordination of the embodied particular characteristic of much cultural theory. Rowe similarly reveals the shaping power of media scripts as she challenges the medium specificity of much film studies discussion, which has heretofore inhibited the full incorporation of screen Shakespeare into the mainstream of Shakespeare studies. From Feuillade to Hytner, from stage to digitized screen, these three scholars take artistic form into account without falling into the anti-historicist traps of neoformalism or media studies triumphalism.

But it is not only in confronting modern performance that the material conditions and multimedia nature of Shakespeare's plays demand reconsideration. Awareness of new media as one dimension of a radically changing culture has also led to historically nuanced reconsiderations of old media and of Shakespeare's locations more generally in a "pre-literate" culture. The next, and largest, cluster of essays considers fundamental changes in the status of the book, the family, nations, and religions, and the basic communicative and epistemological vocabularies of words and numbers, in order to generate alternative readings of early modern culture as well as Shakespeare. Lukas Erne, pursuing a method Catherine Belsey has recently praised under the slightly tongue-in-cheek label "Intertextual Historicism," challenges the conventional *longue durée* description of Shakespeare's gradual medial transition from stage to page (although Worthen's redeployment of that history suggests its continued potency at the macro level). Erne recognizes the irrecoverability of past performance, but rather than lament or chase its chimerical traces, he finds in the stage directions of the earliest printed texts the potentiality for recovering—or at least hypothesizing—an early modern readerly experience. By focusing on the "extra-dialogic" dimensions of the text, he posits an alternative route through the page *versus* stage binary and explores traces of a differently reconstructed author. Patricia Parker extends Erne's challenge through her close attention to early modern connotations of words and names we may not discern and which subsequent editors have effaced. Her particular attention to lancets, lancelets, and the character now known as Lancelot Gobbo (a renaming that may be the unkindest cut of all) raises questions not only about material texts and graphic cutting but also about the complex representation of religion and race in *The Merchant of Venice*. Through scriptural citation, she reveals how the play interweaves its disturbingly abortive dramatization of bloodletting with skepticism about conversion and its capacity to produce a spiritual "circumcision of the heart."

The archive can too easily become a place of retreat, but in Parker's hands—as in the essays that follow—what Terence Hawkes calls "presentist" awareness leavens and helps reanimate historicist specificity (Hawkes 2002: *passim*). Significantly and appropriately, in both Parker's piece and Willy Maley's essay on *Cymbeline*, religion is considered not as an independent variable or a glib label (was Shakespeare Catholic?) but as a set of cultural texts and practices that is and was thoroughly enmeshed with sociopolitical and ethical assumptions. Building on the insights of postcolonial analysis of core and periphery but emphasizing the difficulty of unraveling the strands of internal colonialism and empire-building in amorphously bounded Britain, Maley emphasizes the symbolic and linguistic nexus of nationhood, religion, and ethnicity as it informs identity formation and

Shakespeare's seeming "hodge-podge" of a romance. Sexuality is another staple ingredient in Cymbeline's complicated "alphabet soup," and one that Maley reveals to be intertwined with nationalist attitudes (especially in responses to the Queen). As with religion, an adequate account of the narrative and cultural use of these social categories cannot be carried out in isolation. Thus Kate Chedgzoy, charting the queer and patriarchal strains within representations of Cupid, demonstrates how sexuality needs to be understood as part of a complex set of familial interrelations that involve gender and age as well as forms of desire. Focusing on Cupid's lability as differently deployed by the adult Shakespeare and fourteen-year-old masque author Rachel Fane, Chedgzoy attends to Sinfield's "subordinated voices"—but in this instance, the voices of early modern girlhood (or what we now call adolescence) for whom sexuality could figure a threat as often as a thrill.

Sociopolitical categories have been focal to the project of alternative Shakespeares, but there are other less obvious areas of contestation as well. Despite the theoretical currency of Foucault and Deleuze, Benjamin and Blumenberg, too often the "history of ideas" label still obscures the progressive contribution of those who look beyond concrete materiality to consider symbolic systems and epistemologies. Through attention to number (and grace) in The Winter's Tale, Shankar Raman reveals the cultural specificity and cross-cultural inheritance even of forms of knowledge as apparently divorced from the sociopolitical as mathematics. Whereas Lukas Erne's essay turns from the present of new media to reconsider old media in the light this new landscape encourages, so Raman's provides the pivot from interdisciplinary exploration within the early modern period to more direct consideration of its legacy and the need to roam further outside disciplinary boundaries in the present. Rather than focus on ingenious new readings alone, it is just as—perhaps more—important to resituate those readings within a larger, more deeply understood multi-disciplinary cultural landscape.

As scholarship extends our understanding of the importance of historicity in analyzing domains once thought "timeless" or transcul-tural (e.g. the senses, emotions, scientific analysis), we also recognize the need for renewed attention to the ethical significance and application of such knowledge. The final set of essays highlights the importance of renewed conversation beyond the literary or performance fields alone in order to analyze the cultural work of Shakespeare *post mortem*. Julia Reinhard Lupton draws upon a Greek dramatic forerunner and modern German interpreter of Hamlet's masculine "citizenship" not only to illuminate Shakespeare's idea of a prince but, more importantly, to glean the faint glimmerings (and struggles) of incipient constitutionalism at the heart of this royal's tragedy. Extending Lupton's attention to tragedy and political agency, Rui Carvalho Homem examines a cross-cultural translation of *King Lear*, showing how Portuguese Communist leader Álvaro Cunhal's political priorities and interpretation of history become his translation's ideological symptoms, signs of Cunhal's refusal to endorse tragedy as an individualist rather than collectivist genre. Carvalho Homem's analysis serves as a reminder (as will my discussion of Nahum Tate's *Lear*) that "Shakespeare"—even when understood as a specific set of play scripts or one play such as *Lear*—has become a varied, multilingual and multiply mediated text.

Shakespearean texts (in any language), performances, and their cultural contexts are not the only domains that still demand an alternative analysis. Drawing on the analogy with early modern print and manuscript circulation much studied of late, Mary Thomas Crane considers the interplay of patronage and market economics affecting publication of Shakespeare criticism today. Her own survey of a year's work in the field debunks certain common assumptions (for example, that fewer books are being published) and prompts her to demystify the "gold standard" and "benchmarking" rationales that dominate in debates over the value of scholarly monographs. Like the report of the Modern Language Association (MLA) (2006) urging a broader definition of "publication" for purposes of promotion and tenure, Crane's analysis reminds those in the academy that they are not only scholarly observers but implicated participants who might well desire and find alternative ways to study or contest Shakespeare. My own exploration of the epistemology and events shaping Tate's much maligned revision of *Lear* compared with its current academic use-value similarly suggests that we refocus our attention on our current institutional practices and labor. At the same time, I hope to suggest the value of looking anew at Shakespeare's earlier collaborators, the revisers and re-imaginers who are still too often deplored for introducing static into our direct connection with the early modern man. As has been true of all the works examined in these essays, larger political and philosophical assumptions inform the specific performance texts and are inseparable from our own considerations of quality, artistry, and technique.

In the alternative spirit, it seems fitting that the last word should go not to an academic but to a theatrical practitioner. Just as Nahum Tate's *Lear* kept the plays of Shakespeare in the public eye for 150 years, so too, for the past half century, has the Royal Shakespeare Company (RSC). In comments drawn from an informal interview, Michael Boyd reflects on the alternative potential of performance amid constraints as the artistic director of what remains known as the premier professional Shakespearean acting company worldwide. Rather than admire or chastise their productions, it would seem a better use of our scholarly time to engage in further dialogue informed by a practical as well as theoretical understanding of one another's professions and priorities. Perhaps this "Afterword," then, can also be an "early word" in the progress towards a more creative, congenial cross-professional collaboration.

Ideally such dialogue will embrace more perspectives and agendas than can be represented here, a further reminder that alternativity remains vital and open-ended as well as oppositional. Written in large part by those working within British and American university systems, *Alternative Shakespeares 3* does not aspire to capture the local variations across the globe theorized in its predecessor volume and in numerous other important recent collections: such a project now requires encyclopedic size or else risks replicating the kind of tokenism it decries. Nor can a single book include all the approaches and disciplines (ecocriticism, for example) that in recent years have influenced Shakespeare studies. No more than its predecessors does this volume try to capture or represent all the recent "isms": even were this desirable, the limits of its own material form now make that an impossible dream. As such, it provides another occasion to contemplate the potential of new media and digital forms in advancing our collective work, to consider alternative models of production that could be more conducive to radical change than the book can be, despite the persistent conservatism of humanities disciplines in assessing non-book contributions to our profession.

What are we professing when we teach and publish about Shakespeare? Who are we writing for and talking to? We still need to widen our gaze. All these essays call renewed attention to the importance of deep conversation beyond the boundaries of academic specialization, both within and outside the academy. Some look to those disciplines outside the "comfort zone" of most humanities scholars, and to methods involving quantification, science, and technologies in the service of something other than artistic production. At the same time, however, they endorse the value of certain traditional practices of literary analysis that have on occasion been set in opposition to alternative thinking unnecessarily: values of careful local analysis, textured reading, and nuanced, multilayered interpretation. Just as acknowledgement of the complexity of criticism's intervention in the broader political world may puzzle the brain, if not the will, and give pause to simpler actions or assertions, so too does attending to the potential contradictions or at least the multiplicity of allusive frames in shaping "meaning by Shakespeare". Perhaps in these early years of the twenty-first century, that is a good thing. I would even venture to say that it is devoutly to be wished: the resources of analytic attention and interpretive complexity are sorely needed in public discourse as I write, and the essays herein often combine such care with attention to the wider world and the implicit responsibility of criticism to engage with questions of fundamental importance and historical change. As such, they serve as better spurs and models for conscientious civil dialogue.

In his introduction to *Alternative Shakespeares 2*, Terence Hawkes writes, "An 'alternative' Shakespeare can . . . never be a 'finished'—and so diminished—Bard" (Hawkes 1996: 16). The past decade confirms that, as Hawkes predicted, the reverse continues to be the case. New approaches, technologies, and interdisciplinary fields have brought forth new versions of Shakespeare and new questions for academic study. But much in the world surrounding Shakespeare studies has changed as well, and not necessarily for the better. Post-9/11, in a world where "a coalition of the willing" conjures both violence and another sinister pun on the Bard's name, desire for security too often discourages a real search for alternatives. As scholars in the humanities feel increasingly marginalized and even imperiled, a sense of world-weary professionalism is undermining more ambitious attempts to look beyond narrow specializations and outside the academy. It is all the more important at this moment, then, to represent and mobilize the truly significant, forward-looking possibilities in Shakespeare studies.

Unlike the third offering in most trilogies, this volume does not seek closure for a now-familiar story (although perhaps it will be the last installment conceived as a print codex). Instead, it aims to take up the challenge embodied in the two ground-breaking essay collections from whence it derives its name: to identify the new, the changing, the radically "other" possibilities for discovery at our particular historical moment in the world with Shakespeare. It still collectively resists "assimilation into any of the dominant traditions of Shakespeare criticism" (Drakakis 1985: 24). At a time when even James Bond has been rehistoricized, perhaps Hawkes's concern about the "English fantasy of empire and espionage" being linked with the "shadowy, blank-faced British agent" known as Shakespeare is less concerning (Hawkes 1996: 14): on the other hand, Michael Wood, Stephen Greenblatt and others are still marketing the spy story (with a religious twist) to a fairly massive audience. And certainly we need to keep asking what the world needs from us, and to disdain answering only with professionally conventional answers.

To cite Linda Charnes's sardonic analysis once more:

> The competitive politics of institutional Oedipalism requires the invention of new "isms." If the sciences—with their endless vista of new discoveries—provide the benchmark for what intellectual "progress" should look like, then the humanities, including literary criticism, must keep up appearances.
>
> (Charnes 2006: 17)

This is a big "If-then" claim, and both the assumption and conclusion deserve the contentiousness we apply to Shakespeare; to make an effective counter-argument, however, alternative Shakespeareans need to understand what they are up against. The trumped-up Smackdown results in part because we speak predominantly to and about one another. We need to know more to make the bigger alternative case. What progress have we made? What do we and our students need to know? If we asked these questions more frequently and collectively, surely the practices of our profession (which remain recalcitrantly individualist in rewards and behaviors even if we have challenged such individualist assumptions philosophically and critically) would change. This would indeed be transforming the alternative critique from theory to practice.

Like Hamlet's language and the fundamental questions posed by modernity, the larger force of the first generation's approaches to alternative Shakespeares has not yet been exhausted, or even entirely confronted. Most of the essayists here explicitly take into account the radical instability and changing parameters of the topic so simplified by naming it "Shakespeare," even as they tackle a particular dimension of the territory. To take these challenges seriously is quite a different matter from learning a few theories in outline or adopting a few radical rhetorical gestures: it is to struggle with the purposes of the humanities, education, and political action—with what we are doing with our lives. In the pages that follow, we do our best to alter the landscape a bit more, and keep alternativity, like hope, alive.

2

"I DO, I WILL"

Hal, Falstaff and the Performative

Robert Shaughnessy

A MOMENT IN HISTORY

He really should have seen it coming. It is the play-within-the-play scene in *Henry IV, Part 1*, in Nicholas Hytner's 2005 National Theatre production, and, as long as Falstaff is in command, it seems to be going rather well. Perched precariously on a worn armchair, sporting a crimson cushion for a crown, brandishing a wooden dagger in one long hand as the other flutters delicately across his chest, Falstaff's, or Michael Gambon's, "utter joy at role-playing the king" (Merlin 2005: 105) is delightfully visible, incorporating camp theatrical lisping, sly mimicry of David Bradley's Bolingbroke, and an Olivieresque Richard III. The mood shifts a little almost as soon as Matthew MacFadyen's Hal takes his place, but this Falstaff, to start with, either does not notice or affects not to. As Hal, hardly bothering to conceal his disdain, reels through the catalogue of his abuses, Falstaff remains centre stage, back to the audience, his false belly, silken slippers and red pantaloon's trousers affording him a clownish pathos, swallowing each insult with a stoicism born of desperate neediness. Still he has his answer ready; his voice low, he implores Hal not to "banish plump Jack, and banish all the world". A long silence, then Hal leans ever so slightly forward, never closer to him than at this moment, and, matter-of-factly, issues the *coup de grâce*:

I do, I will.

It clearly hits Falstaff very hard indeed: Gambon's implausibly long, slender hand, so often in this production extended in futile entreaty towards the man he imagines as a kind of son, flies up in front of his face, clawing at the air as if it could reach the prince, as if it could catch the words and shield him from them. In the melee of knocking that follows, he looks forlorn and shell-shocked, trailing Hal around the stage like a puppy, desperate to erase the implications of what he has just heard. He will persist in this denial right until the end of the second play, when he reappears to gatecrash the new king's coronation procession, whooping with delight as he bounds round the stage, skipping, unforgivably, into the path of Henry's entourage to entreat a word with his "sweet boy". This time there is no mistaking the message: "I know thee not, old man" is a roar of exasperation that nonetheless carries absolute authority. Stock-still, facing upstage, Gambon waits for the King's train to exit before releasing a long, animal howl, and when he shambles off it is as a man on his way to his grave.

Still, it was not as if there were no warning signs. Even at their first appearance together, staggering out of the early morning mist down the centre stage ramp and splitting to either side for a comradely piss, each taking up station by a conveniently placed spigot, the distance, and difference, between Falstaff and the Prince was measured by the latter's fastidious washing of his hands; in the tavern scenes that followed, Hal usually sat well apart from his temporary companions, displaying an easy sense of superiority verging on outright contempt. If, for his part, Gambon's Falstaff was too thick-skinned or needy, masochistic or crafty to respond with anything other than gratitude, the spectator could hardly fail to sense the vitriol in Hal's accusations, and the force of his rebuff should be no surprise to anyone other than Falstaff himself, and perhaps not even to him. Had he known which play(s) he was in, he would have known that this is always the way the play extempore ends; as far as most theatre practitioners, theatregoers, Shakespearean editors and critics are concerned, the idea that Falstaff and Hal should sombrely rehearse the rejection that is enacted in earnest at the end of this play's sequel is well established and rarely questioned; and the unexpectedness (at least for Falstaff) of Hal's response is now thoroughly expected. Actor Simon Callow, for example, himself a notable Falstaff in the late 1980s, writes that "four of the most chilling words in all of Shakespeare" prompt a silence that is "broken by a loud knocking, which seems to dispel the highly charged atmosphere in which deep truths have been spoken, perhaps deeper than anyone intended" (2002: 58). T. F. Wharton, surveying the majority of modern stagings of the play, concurs:

> there is no doubt that Hal is not "playing". He is in earnest . . . The most obvious way of producing it in the theatre is to allow it to stop the show; to stop the actors in their tracks, reduce everything to silence, broken only by the knocking at the door. Falstaff looks at Hal, and realisation dawns that he means what he says.
>
> (1983: 41)

As the Arden 3 editor dissects Hal's line, "the first clause is present and all play; the second is future and all serious" (Kastan 2002: 234).

This is almost invariably how it has been played for half a century, but it was not always thus. During the eighteenth and nineteenth centuries, indeed, the whole play extempore sequence, now regarded as crucial both to Henry IV's exploration of the relationship between theatre and kingship and to the relationship between Falstaff and the Prince, was regularly cut, although the actors' poor opinion of the episode was not shared by their critics, and it remained a popular subject for illustration. Restored in the twentieth century, it was at first usually played purely for laughs, nowhere more typically than in the 1945 staging at the Old Vic, which rendered the riposte of Michael Warre's Hal to Falstaff as, literally, a throwaway line, as he accompanied it by tossing a cushion at Ralph Richardson's Falstaff: "it was all a game . . . there was no sign that he sees the future in this moment, no sign, indeed, that Hal was anything but a useful assistant in a big scene for Falstaff" (McMillin 1991: 30).

My concern in this essay is with how and when this shift occurred, so that Hal's rejection of Falstaff is not even played for the first time as farce, and, most importantly, why. Drawing upon terms proposed by W. B. Worthen, I am interested in what Scott McMillin calls the "weighted reading" (1991: 48) as an instance of "dramatic performativity" and in the relationships it articulates "between the verbal text and the conventions (or, to use [Judith] Butler's term, "regimes") of behaviour that give it meaningful force as performed action" (Worthen 2003b: 3). To excavate the history that lies beneath both this reading and the rhetoric of character it epitomises, I focus upon two Stratford productions (in 1951 and 1963) that mark its transformation from an intervention that one critic described as "unorthodox" and an "error of judgment" (David 1953: 137) to the accepted, even inevitable, way of playing the line.

The 1951 production at the Shakespeare Memorial Theatre (SMT) in Stratford-upon-Avon was directed by Anthony Quayle (who played Falstaff) and Michael Redgrave, and featured Richard Burton as Prince Henry. Offered as part of the nationwide network of cultural activities that formed the Festival of Britain, this *Henry IV* formed part of a cycle of histories that was as adventurous in its scope as it was conservative in its cultural politics. This was the first time since 1905 that the *Henry IV* plays had been performed together at Stratford with *Richard II* and *Henry V*; the conception of the event was also a pioneering instance of applied scholarship, in that the narrative history it engineered aimed to demonstrate the Tillyardian thesis that the "total sequence of plays dealing with the subject of Hal" express "a universally held and still comprehensible scheme of history: a scheme fundamentally religious, by which events evolve under a law of justice and under the ruling of God's Providence, and of which Elizabeth's England was the acknowledged outcome"—a vision that was explored in a scheme consisting of "the distortion of nature's course by a crime and its restoration through a long series of disasters and suffering and struggles" (Tillyard 1944 [1962]: 324–5). John Dover Wilson, writing in the volume published to commemorate the production, emphasised that the "serial presentation" was designed to afford

Richard II, the two parts of *Henry IV*, and *Henry V* "a measure of unity and coherence" lacking when the plays are performed separately; in this context, *Henry IV* traced Henry's progress towards "the ideal representative of order and security" that is seen in *Henry V*: "a Prince who, with the sceptre firmly in his grasp, could be the adored leader of a united and harmonious commonweal" (Wilson and Worsley 1952: 4, 22).

The 1951 Henry who reaches his apotheosis at Agincourt was thus "the true hero of the whole play" (Wilson and Worsley 1952: 24), but also a deeper, possibly darker figure than the "rousing patriotic hero" of stage convention: "we are more conscious than usual of the man behind the king, because we have fresher in our minds than usual the boy behind the man" (1952: 30). The cohesiveness of both the characterisation of Henry and the cycle's ideological project rests on the conviction that the rejection of Falstaff is necessary, inevitable and admirable: "we must get the impression from the Hal that, whatever comes in between, he is capable of his moment when the moment arrives" (1952: 30). Inscribed within a production scheme that conflated the Hal-narratives of the three plays in which he figures into the unified and coherent drama of Henry's journey towards maturity and legitimate, uncontested rule, Hal's mock rejection in the tavern scene was already marked with significance as an effect of the structure it inhabited, regardless of how the actor might opt to play it. The producers of the cycle seemed, at least initially, unaware of these implications; as McMillin points out, the evidence of the production promptbook, which "marks no pause in connection with 'I do, I will'" and "shows that the knocking on the door . . . came directly after the loud cheer on Falstaff's 'banish all the world'" (1991: 48), suggests that the scene was to have followed the playful and light-hearted tradition. The initiative came from Burton, who took the momentous decision "to take a moment to let the words have their full impact on the Prince, and then say to himself, 'I do, I will.'" (Bragg 1988: 72).

The "full impact", or force, of the words, in the context of Burton's overall conception of the role, consisted in their capacity to register his sudden, profound awareness of the weight of personal responsibility, and of his royal duty, and, correspondingly, the inevitability of his ultimate betrayal of Falstaff; it was a key moment in a performance that throughout was informed by what Ivor Brown called the "sense of destiny" of "every-inch-a-King-to-be" (quoted in Wilson and Worsley 1952: 69). Internalising its teleology of "order and security" as Stanislavskian superobjective, Burton was very much in tune with the cycle's ruling ideology, in effect its principal means of transmission—although he seemed far from cheerful about the destiny he anticipated. By addressing the key line to himself, rather than to Falstaff, Burton also rendered as inner monologue an utterance that had previously been a continuation of the play-game; this was typical of a performance that cultivated a Hamlet-like introspection at the expense of both youthful delinquency and conventional heroics, whose keynote was struck, as Richard David observed, on Hal's very first entrance, "slow, brooding, disillusioned", conveying "a deeper and more personal reflectiveness, it seemed, than mere animal sadness after a debauch" (1953: 136).

MASTERING SILENCE

It was, indeed, Burton's command of silence that seemed most impressive. For Kenneth Tynan, Burton's "shrewd Welsh boy" was "a still, brimming pool, running disturbingly deep", who "at twenty-five . . . commands repose and can make silence garrulous" (Tynan 1964: 103). Harold Hobson (writing in the *Sunday Times* [8 April 1951], quoted in Wilson and Worsley 1952: 68–9), saw in Burton a "suggestion of greatness" that was "as evident in the actor's stillness when other players are speaking as when he is sailing the full flood"; throughout, Burton "carried a quiet face whose repose was a constant dumb rebuke". Going further than Tynan, Hobson was also happy to speculate on what the silence and stillness harboured:

> Mr Burton looked like a man who had had a private vision of the Holy Grail, and was as determined to say nothing about it as he was incapable of forgetting it . . . Mr Burton offers a young knight keeping a long vigil in the cathedral of his own mind.
>
> (Quoted in Wilson and Worsley 1952: 68–9)

This is hyperbolic, maybe, but it indicates that Burton's technique of restraint not only demanded but, to a certain extent, actively helped to produce a new constituency of spectators willing to envisage interiority by reading inactivity as psychic action, passivity as reflection, and silence as being pregnant with significance. Silence was to become an increasingly important weapon in the postwar Shakespearean performer's armoury, and the weighted reading of "I do, I will" has often been most keenly felt in the spaces around and between the four monosyllables.

Yet this kind of silence, theatrically speaking, was only just beginning to become audible, indeed imaginable, at this moment; and as it did so, it brought with it some of the terms of reference of the contemporary theatre that modelled its use. There are, of course, silences and silences, and although the work of Burton and his successors to manufacture presence out of absence belongs to a history of modern actorly intervention, it can be traced back to the texts of *Henry IV* themselves, which tease us with the prospect of unexplained silence at this point. In the Folio (F) version of the scene, "I doe, I will" ("I do, I will" in the Quarto (Q) version) is followed by a stage direction marking an entrance for Bardolph ("Bardoll" in Q) "running"—but in neither text has a previous exit been specified. Textual editors from Malone onwards have resolved the crux by interpolating an exit for Bardolph and the Hostess and a sound cue for knocking within, thus plotting in a potentially extended sequence of gaps between the end of Falstaff's speech, Bardolph's exit and entry and Hal's reply (gaps that before 1951 had generally been filled in with the rough-and-tumble of comic business). As this essay seeks to demonstrate, theatre makers in their turn have not only accepted the implications of the interpolation but made them central to the play.

Not so, however, John Dover Wilson, the terms of whose scholarly endorsement of the 1951 production had been pre-empted both in his 1946 Cambridge edition of the play and in *The Fortunes of Falstaff*, published in 1943. Wilson spends little time on "I do, I will", but firmly rejects the possibility that Bardolph should exit and re-enter at this point because the implication that the stage might be "silent for several moments" was "absurd" (Wilson 1946: 155).

Wilson's position now seems anomalous but is worth pausing over, first, because it is informed by his larger political understanding of what the play is about, and, second, because it is conditioned by his acute sense of what was, in terms of his own theatregoing experience, either viable or tolerable, and thus is very much in accord with established stage practice at the time. In *The Fortunes of Falstaff*, Wilson gives the "mock-interviews" fairly cursory notice, stating that the scene "raises no problems that need disentangling"; if there is little scope for irony or ambivalence here, it is because the scene anticipates a conclusion to *Henry IV, Part 2* whose significance is equally clear-cut: "I cannot believe that members of an Elizabethan audience would have felt the 'sermon' anything but fine and appropriate" (1943: 56, 122). In his essay on the 1951 cycle, Wilson puts it even more bluntly:

the audiences for whom Shakespeare wrote the play, being accustomed to the "morality" tradition, no more thought of questioning or deploring the downfall and arrest of Falstaff at the end than their fathers would have questioned the spectacle of the Vice being carried off to Hell.

(Wilson and Worsley 1952: 21)

In the context of this authoritarian scheme a silence around "I do, I will" is not merely "absurd" in the sense of being silly or impractical or meaningless; because it creates a space for questions to begin to formulate, it is dangerously indeterminate.

Wilson probably intended the term "absurd" to be merely dismissive, but it is ironically prescient: the absurdity is that of a silent stage that he envisages as a void, a space of speculation or of awkward, embarrassing absence—or failure—of words and actions. Wilson could hardly have anticipated that an important strand within the theatre of the decade that followed would actively embrace the condition of absurdity both philosophically and formally; nor that, in this theatre, the spaces between verbal utterances would often be understood to communicate as powerfully as (often more powerfully than) the words themselves; still less that this sensibility would subsequently inform the performance of Shakespeare as well. The plays of Samuel Beckett were instrumental in introducing the technique to the English stage:

Peter Hall's 1955 Arts Theatre production of *Waiting for Godot*, with its pauses "lengthened to the point of embarrassment before being broken" (Knowlson 1996: 414) set a precedent. The idea that silence might be as significant (or, in absurdist terms, as insignificant) as speech would become axiomatic within both avant-garde and natural-istic drama by the end of the decade, although it could signify very differently: in Beckett's hands, the void between words was an existential one, whereas in the ultra-naturalist plays of Arnold Wesker, "slowness and silence", according to T. C. Worsley, formed part of a rich texture of "pointless reiteration, stubborn taciturnity, cowlike vacuity" (Worsley 1959). By the beginning of the 1960s, similar effects were becoming evident in Shakespeare at Stratford; for example, the first scene of Brook's 1962 *King Lear*, directed under the influence of Beckett and Jan Kott, recalled the glacial pace of Roger Blin's 1957 production of *Fin de Partie*.[1]

For the most part, however, the terms of reference were naturalistic rather than absurdist: reviewing the 1964 RSC season, John Russell Brown recorded that the eradication of "the glossy tones and meaningless pomposities" of traditional Stratford verse speaking, and the labour of emulating "ordinary speech" involved "a would-be impressive slowness", as "Long speeches are broken with pauses and far too frequently short speeches are prepared for with silent business, or followed by some such intervention" (1965: 151). The trouble with pauses and silences, vital as they were both to the reform of Shakespearean verse speaking and to the sustenance of depth charac-terisation, was that they were difficult to square with the RSC's ardent professions of fidelity to the text, and especially with the kind of metrical fundamentalism advocated by company supremo Peter Hall. As Hall acknowledged, there was no textual mandate for such interventions: "Remember, Shakespeare only uses silence this way once. Coriolanus answers his mother's great plea not to burn Rome with a stage direction: 'Holds her by the hand, silent'" (Lahr and Lahr 1974: 16). Hall is talking here about directing the work of Harold Pinter: Pinter was the dramatist who had by the mid-1960s done more than anyone, within the framework of a formal synthesis of the European absurd and the hard-edged realism of the English new wave, to elaborate the potential of pauses and silences on the British stage, and to devise a systematic, analytically precise means of notating them; and it was in Pinter's dramaturgy that Hall found an exact means of assimilating the newly discovered Shakespearean pause into RSC verse-speaking technique. As W. B. Worthen points out, tracing the new conventions of drama publication that both coincided with and facilitated Pinter's emergence as a major playwright, his attention to, and careful differentiation between the pause, the long pause and the silence, is "one of the features most characteristic of Pinter's dramatic writing, of his use of language"; and in order to be prepared to render them theatrically active, we have to be prepared "to read Pinter *as* poetry, New Critical fashion, to attribute 'the density of texture of true poetry' to his page", which means "reading the 'empty patches' as texture, the white spaces, and the *Pauses* that they hold, as significant, signifying, not merely as irrelevancies intruding into the dramatic dialogue" (2003a: 221).

Pinter's pauses were instrumental both to the aesthetics of menace and the poetics of inarticulacy, and combined within a dramaturgy that offered actors the resources to construct characters whose motivations, and histories, might well be unfathomable even to themselves: as Pinter put it in 1960, "the desire for verification is understandable but cannot always be satisfied . . . The more acute the experience the less articulate its expression" (Esslin 1980: 243). The implications of this position for the practice of acting are considerable, extending, for the purposes of this essay, to Shakespearean performance and to the relations between words, actions, stage presence and character. Hall recognised, and developed, the connection almost immediately: "Pinter is to me the most significant new English dramatist and one very relevant to Shakespeare . . . His writing has the balance, the inevitability, and the precision of poetry" (Hall 1964: 46). Prompted by his comment on the exceptional nature of the "pause" in *Coriolanus*, Hall's interviewer asks whether he held "special rehearsals for silences". Hall's response is revealing: "I did once have a dot and pause rehearsal. It drove the actors absolutely mad. I said, 'You don't remember the phrases.' Exactly as if an actor in Shakespeare had learned his text without knowing where the ends of the lines are . . ." (Wardle 1974: 16–17). The strength of the equation indicates that it is not at all incidental; the affinity between Pinteresque rhythms and phrasing and Shakespearean metrics is not merely an analogy but a deep, mutually enabling homology. It was his sustained work with Pinter that taught Hall how the pause could be designed with absolute precision, and how it could be clearly differentiated and categorised. The task of the actor, whether of Pinter or of Shakespeare, is not to search for intentionality or emotional truth but, to employ Hall's favoured operatic analogy, to find the exact rhythm and hit the right notes: "If you sing a Mozart aria correctly, certain responses begin to be necessary inside you . . . you're not improvising something of your own, you're singing some notes of Mozart" (Wardle 1974: 16–17). "Subtext", in this account, is an effect of technique, the converse of Stanislavsky's view of it. The approach pioneered by Hall (supported by the verse work of his co-director, John Barton) suggested that Pinteresque poetics offered a means of reconciling the formal imperatives of Shakespeare's text with a notion of subtext that was feasible and workable because it was so precisely scored.

TAKING THE PISS

Reflecting on his direction of the RSC premiere of The Homecoming, Hall recalled "the base of a good deal of Harold's work is the cockney game of taking the piss: and part of that game is that you should not be quite sure whether the piss is being taken or not" (Itzin and Trussler 2005: 137). That play, Hall observed, "doesn't take the piss in a light or flippant way. It takes the piss in a cruel and bitter way" (Wardle 1974: 14). Although the production of Henry IV that he co-directed with John Barton preceded the Pinter staging by a year, the sentiment seems very appropriate to Ian Holm's 1963 conception of Prince Hal. He played the role "as if the actor's main task were to prepare the audience for the 'rejection' of Falstaff" (Brown 1965: 151), and what Peter Roberts in Plays and Players (June 1964) called his "almost Puck-like high spirits" in the opening scene rapidly evaporated; Robert Speaight recorded that "the actor does not attempt to gloss over the hardness of the Prince's dealing with his social inferiors"; he made it clear that he "never liked" the fat knight "who was supposed to be his friend" (Speaight 1964: 384). An example of this, conveyed entirely through interpolated non-verbal business, came at Falstaff's exit to deal with the "nobleman of the court" at 2.4.288:

> As Falstaff disappeared up the stairs, Hal gave a little laugh, and then stopped. He looked at the others. They gave a little laugh, and stopped. Hal laughed again. They laughed again. Then, they clustered round him, to curry favour by excusing their own part in the cowardice and by ratting on Falstaff. Hal heard them with a mocking insolent smile.
>
> (Wharton 1983: 68)

This is a moment of piss-taking worthy of *The Birthday Party* (revived by the RSC the same year), *The Caretaker* or *The Homecoming* (a play specifically composed with the RSC in mind). It will come as no surprise, then, to learn that Holm's Hal was, in the play scene, already anticipating the climax of Falstaff's litany of pleas, "his reply already thought out. 'I do', then a long pause as he looked in the old man's face, then a pitiless 'I will'" (McMillin 1991: 63). The coldness and calculation of the reply, and the almost sadistic extension of the gap between the two utterances (a pause, in the Hall–Pinter sense, not a silence or a hesitation) epitomised Holm's characterisation. This can only have been reinforced when Holm, who played Lenny in *The Homecoming* at the Aldwych, returned to the role of Hal in the revived production of 1966. By now, his Hal had, according to the *Times* (7 April 1966) hardened into "a compelling study in cold-blooded self-interest: a character incapable of enjoyment (even in the Eastcheap charade he cannot enter into the game: his only reply to Falstaff is yet another string of insults)".

There is nothing new in the observation that the 1960s RSC directed its Shakespeare in the style of (or, sometimes, almost as) Beckett, Brecht, Pinter and so on. Hall, especially, was quite explicit about it: as he saw it, the stylistic and thematic continuities between Shakespearean and modern drama both legitimate and even compel this approach. As Alan Sinfield points out, this particular construction of "Shakespeare-plus-relevance" tends to assume a common ground of timeless, essentialised human nature, loosely characterised at the time in terms of "a sense of general violent destruction, proceeding both from uncontrollable political systems and from mysterious inner compulsions" (1985: 164). What merits further investigation, though, are the implications of this sensibility for the understanding of dramaturgic form and for the ways in which patterns of utterance in texts are, within the cultural situation occupied by these productions, construed as not only performable, but, in the sense adumbrated by Worthen, *performative*.

Let us turn again, then, to "I do, I will". In 1951, 1964 and in most stagings that have followed, there was no question that Hal was no longer playing when he delivered his reply to Falstaff; certainly, by 1966, if he was still taking the piss out of the old man, it was on Pinter's not-at-all light-hearted terms. But although the modern theatre invariably understands "I do, I will" to mark the sobering transition from play-acting to being, and from impersonation to plain speaking and psychological truth, it is not a reading that is necessarily mandated by the text. Intent on the task of developing a through-line capable of articulating the continuity between his eventual rejection of Falstaff and its proleptic surrogation in the play scene, actors from Burton onwards have tended to qualify Hal's involvement in the play extempore and, by means of the techniques that have been outlined above, make it unmistakeable that it is Hal as Hal, not Hal as Henry, who speaks its final line. It is obvious enough that, just as the Quarto and Folio neither authorise nor exclude the possibility of silence around this moment, there is nothing in the text to indicate definitively where the play extempore ends; what has less often been noticed is that this indeterminacy—which is characteristic of Shakespearean metatheatre—generates a plurality, and an instability, of meaning at a point where the modern tradition requires certainty, authority and singularity. Rather than constituting the point at which Hal becomes self-present, intensely aware of past, present and future and first-person singular in his own voice, "I do, I will" is the kind of Shakespearean moment where, as Catherine Belsey put it in an essay in one of this volume's predecessors, we are entitled to ask: "Who is speaking?" As with Rosalind/Ganymede/the boy player's epilogue to *As You Like It* (and many other key Shakespearean moments), we have a "comedy of uncertainty about whether a character is speaking from inside or outside the fiction" (Belsey 1985: 180–1). In Rosalind's case, Belsey proposes, this uncertainty interrogates "sexual difference itself . . . indicating that it is possible, at least in fiction, to speak from a position which is not that of a full, unified, gendered subject" (1985: 180). In Hal's, the ambiguity of whether or not he is still playing (to use a term far more appropriate to what is happening here than "acting"), and hence of who the "I" is in "I do, I will" effects a dispersal of the princely persona at exactly the moment when the modern Hal demands, and usually gets, coherence and closure.

To put it another way, the modern theatre's tradition of reducing the multiple possibilities of this line to confessional frankness reflects its determination to arrest what, after Derrida, might be called its "iterability" (or, after Hall's Pinter, its potential for piss-taking): radically uncertain of who it is that speaks, of how it is received, and of whether its import is sincere, ironic, mischievous or a combination of some or all of these, it offers itself as an utterance that both inhabits and generates "contexts without any center of absolute anchoring" (Derrida 1982: 320). Derrida's definition of iterability is occasioned by his reading of J. L. Austin's theory of the performative in language, and it is with reference to this, I suggest, that we may further refine our sense of the peculiar force that is attached to the line on the modern stage—a force which derives, moreover, not only from the ways in which it has been delivered, but from the words themselves: I do, I will. It is almost uncannily convenient for my purposes that Hal's line consists of the variant forms of the words used by the participants to signify assent in the Anglican marriage ceremony.[2] According to Austin (whose lectures on the topic were composed, delivered and posthumously published during the period between Burton's Henry and Holm's Henry), to say "I do" in this context is an exemplary performative act, in the sense that "the issuing of the utterance is the performing of an action . . . in saying these words we are *doing* something—namely, marrying, rather than *reporting* something, namely that we are marrying" (1962: 6, 13). When Hal, responding in deadly earnest rather than in play to Falstaff's plea, echoes these words on the modern stage, the rupturing of the metatheatrical frame shifts them from the realm of the performed to that of the Austinian performative: by meaning what he says, Hal does more than predict his act of banishment—effectively, he executes it on the spot. Over and above their affective capacity as plain statements of intent, the institutional authority and ceremonial solemnity of "I do" and "I will" underscores Hal's affirmation with a sense of absolute and irrevocable commitment. The words carry a powerful symbolic charge that is in excess of their immediate situation, not just in relation to the play extempore, but also to the scene in which it is embedded, to *Henry IV*, and to the larger cycles of performed history in which they are implicated; for in this convergence of past, present and future we are presented with an absolutely crucial moment of self-fashioning, as by symbolically banishing Falstaff, Hal authors himself into autonomous subjecthood. Hal appears really "real" at this moment because his silences and his speech alike evoke depth and presence, an illusion of agency that encompasses his and our awareness of both his own freedom to act, and the inevitable restraints upon that freedom.

That Austin's theory of language is also a theory of self, and as such is deeply ideological, hardly needs emphasising. Reflecting on Austin's use of the marriage example, Eve Kosofsky Sedgwick points out that the apparently volitional "I do" is uttered by a speaker who:

> gets constituted in marriage through a confident appeal to state authority, through the calm interpellation of others present as "witnesses", and through the logic of the (heterosexual) supplement whereby individual subjective agency is guaranteed by the welding into a cross-gender dyad.
>
> (1993: 3)

In short, Austin's notion of the performative misrepresents a situation in which we are at our most *subjected* as one in which we, seemingly free to speak and to choose, are sovereign. Applied to Hal's situation, we can see that he may be marginally less constrained in that he is, or he will be, the embodiment of the state authority that sanctions his decisions, but, in the guises in which he has appeared on the postwar British stage, he is as deluded as any of us if he believes that the traumatic but necessary repudiation of Falstaff is a matter of free personal choice. The stability of Austin's definition of the performative becomes even more unsettled when we recognise—as a number of recent performance theorists, following Derrida, have done—that it rests precariously on a number of strategic exclusions. Rejecting the idea that the success of a performative can be traced to the intentionality of the speaker, Austin distinguishes between "felicitous" and "infelicitous" speech acts on contextual and circumstantial grounds, specifically identifying theatrical performance as an arena in which infelicities proliferate: "a performative utterance will, for example, be in *a peculiar way* hollow or void if said by an actor on the stage, or if spoken in a poem, or spoken in soliloquy" (Austin 1962: 22, his italics). The point has already been made that the metatheatrical ambiguities surrounding Hal's piss-taking performative act hollow it out (or "void" it) in a variety of "peculiar" ways, but the process of evacuation does not stop there. According to Derrida, Austin's efforts to distinguish the spoken from the quoted, and the everyday from the theatrical, by excluding the latter "as anomalous, exceptional, 'nonserious', that is citation", represent "the determined modification of a general citationality—or rather, a general iterability—without which there would not even be a 'successful' performative" (1982: 325). Attempting to make Hal into a unified and coherent subject, self-present, real and true at this point, or perhaps at any point, is to deny not only the text but also one of the basic conditions of theatre, and of language, itself. It is the radical ambiguity of Hal's performative that renders it so seductive, so resonant, and so dangerous. Iterability may be endemic to all utterance, but some utterances are evidently more iterable than others, and, notwithstanding the modern theatre's determination to anchor it in character, "I do, I will" is one of them.

TRUE JACK FALSTAFF

We have seen how what has settled into a tradition of playing a specific, highly charged moment (which has become the "natural" and even obvious and inevitable way of doing it) is historically and culturally localised, and is the product of strategies for eliciting significance from Shakespeare's text that are informed in general terms by the sensibilities of psychological naturalism but more locally by the re-inflection of these within postwar English dramatic modernism. We can recognise that this (partial and selective) reading of the text in order to cultivate an angst-ridden subtext is an appropriative, perhaps manipulative, procedure, manufacturing a silence— to be inhabited how one will—that, objectively speaking, simply is not there, a classic micro-managed instance of the process that Terence Hawkes (1992) calls "meaning by Shakespeare". We may also suspect that the reduction of Hal's utterance to plain truth-telling, however psychologically plausible and however intense the reaction it produces, reduces the radical scope for Derridean play that the ambiguous metatheatricality of the text allows and perhaps encourages. And, perhaps dreaming of alternative modes of practice modelled upon those of the early modern stage itself, we might draw the conclusion that all this only confirms the modern, mainstream theatre's habit of misunderstanding, misrepresenting and abusing the Shakespearean dramaturgy with which it has been culturally entrusted.

While acknowledging the force and, indeed, the justice of these inferences, I end on a different, and hopefully more optimistic, note. If the work that I have been discussing can be seen as part of a larger project, initiated in 1951, of re-orienting the *Henry IV* plays so that they have been Hal-dominated rather than Falstaff-centred, and hence on the side of authority rather than licence, the evidence of performance history continues to suggest that audiences and practitioners have been far more willing to be seduced by the theatrical and ideological values associated with the fat knight than they have been eager to countenance the irresistible rise of Prince Henry. As an illustration of this, I want to return to the Falstaff with which this history began: Michael Gambon. As far as his director, Nicholas Hytner, was concerned, this was Gambon's, and Falstaff's, play: "every production of *Henry IV* should start [with Falstaff], because if you don't know who's going to play Falstaff there's no point in doing them" (Merlin 2005: 2). On the production posters and in the pre-publicity Gambon's ravaged, haunted face is central, foregrounded, with Bradley's Bolingbroke and MacFadyen's Hal behind him; the King meets our gaze over Falstaff's shoulder, his son inclines his head to look, not as his father, but at the turned back of the not-at-all fat knight. What this reflects in part is a star quality that, in this cast at least, is uniquely Gambon's own, in that it capitalises upon the pulling power of a face that is familiar even to the most casual of cultural consumers. Like the actors who flank him, Gambon is not in role, un-bearded, un-upholstered, dressed in neutral blacks, a star personality but not yet a character. As with any performer with a reasonably developed screen profile, Gambon's Falstaff was shadowed both on stage and off by the ghosts of his previous (and, in the context of their perpetual media re-circulation, ongoing) parts; but in this instance, the relentless multiplication of alter egos around the overdetermined, intertextualised figure of the actor had a peculiarly Falstaffian dimension, in that Gambon seemed wonderfully in excess of the play-world that was supposed to be containing him (see Hodgdon 2007). Indeed, he evokes a gamut of roles that runs from Albus Dumbledore in the *Harry Potter* movies to Hamm in *Endgame*, taking in Brecht's Galileo, Albert Spica in *The Cook, the Thief, his Wife and her Lover*, the Prime Minister in *Ali G Indahouse*, and more, and spans the full range of postmodern culture, popular and elite. Gambon has a reputation as a Falstaff figure: a prankster, raconteur, bon viveur and notorious maverick. He began his career in the theatre with a legendary encounter with Olivier, auditioning for the first National Theatre ensemble in 1962, for which he arrived prepared to offer Richard III: "I was thick as two short planks then and I didn't know he'd had a rather notable success in the part"; Sir Laurence's response was "You've got a fucking cheek, haven't you?" (Sher 1985: 124–5). He got cast, even so, but Gambon's insouciance, his apparently guileless capacity for cheek, and his image as a piss-taker (think of that spectacularly scatological first entrance as Falstaff) has stayed with him. Dubbed "the great Gambon" by Ralph Richardson, and described by Pinter as an actor of "enormous power, great depth, absolute expertise" who "goes for the heart of the matter, and does it most economically and totally without sentimentality" (Gussow 2004: 213), Gambon is in many ways at odds with the image of the classically "Shakespearean" actor, certainly in terms of his career trajectory. Prior to his acclaimed Lear and Antony for the RSC in 1982, for example, his last major Shakespearean role was as Coriolanus at the Nottingham Playhouse in 1969; the period between saw him mainly in the work of Ayckbourn and Pinter. Interviewed in 1990, Gambon responded to the suggestion that he might one day tackle Richard III with horror: "Oh, no. He says too much . . . he never stops talking. That's why Pinter is so good. None of his people say too much . . . that's what attracts me so much." Pushed to nominate a Shakespearean role that he still wanted to play, Gambon simply replied "I'd like to play Falstaff one day. But that's about all I can think of" (Gussow 2004: 71, 48). Although renowned as a consummate technician and craftsman, Gambon regards acting as, in the words of the director of his Lear, Adrian Noble, "just mucking about" (Gussow 2004: 213), an attitude that has led, in his Shakespearean performances at least, to a glorious volatility and unpredictability. Profiling Gambon in the *Guardian* (28 June 2006), Emma Brockes recorded that "cast members have likened acting on stage with Gambon to being in an unstable dinghy in the middle of the Atlantic". His Falstaff "came out differently every night, too— 'miles differently', says David Harewood, who played Hotspur in the same production. 'People were just coming off stage in fits of laughter, or looking at each other like, what on earth?'" (Brockes 2006).

What struck me, watching and listening to Gambon, was the extraordinary *range* of his performance: constantly switching and shuffling moods, personae and voices, this Falstaff was one moment a crisply spoken theatrical knight, the next a wheedling cockney, a living, vital embodiment of the production's social and geographical diversity. And in this, just possibly, he was also the embodiment of a kind of oppositional politics. Roaming the scene of a medieval– modern English landscape whose terms of reference were provided by the continuing war in Iraq (Hytner observed that the design reflected the recognition that "the big, unavoidable thing about these plays is that they're set against the backdrop of a catastrophic civil war" [Merlin 2005: 17]), Gambon was, according to Carla Power of *Newsweek* (20 June 2005) "a one-man anti-war movement, all tummy and red trousers . . . a bohemian cowardly lion, the opposite of force". In terms of the characterisation, this seems not right at all: as a liar, a fantasist, a profiteer and an opportunist, this Falstaff would be no more inclined to stop the war than he would have been capable of doing so. But in terms of what Falstaff represents within the scheme of the production, viewed in the light of the contemporary history it accesses, it seems deliciously apt. Effortlessly capable of fabricating a "monstrous" threat to his own security ("Eleven buckram men grown out of two!" [2.4.212–13]), which, once the fiction is exposed, he can then dismiss with a further twist of outrageous sophistry ("I knew ye as well as he that made ye . . . was it for me to kill the heir apparent?" [2.4.258–60]), Falstaff is both an ideal tutor for a king-to-be who will soon enough launch a war of his own on fantasy evidence and the Prince's most dangerous liability. Gambon's Falstaff is not only—perhaps not even—the antithesis of the values of the regime from which he has (probably corruptly) obtained his knighthood; he is also their monstrous, shaming, parodic incarnation. If it is a measure of the force, and the richness, of Gambon's portrayal that he made us happy to entertain his world of lies as a kind of truth, one thing was for sure: the silences that surrounded both his mock banishment and the real event were entirely Gambon's, and Falstaff's, own.

NOTES

1 See Kott 1964. As ever ahead of his time, Peter Brook had in 1948 directed a *Measure for Measure* at the SMT that incorporated "half a dozen long pauses . . . The thirty-five seconds of dead silence which elapse before Isabella decides to make her plea for Angelo's life were a long prickly moment of doubt which had every heart in the theatre thudding" (Tynan 1950: 151). Later productions would discover significance in Isabella's lack of verbal response to the Duke's proposal at the end of the play.

2 Austin's editors conceded that he "realized that the expression 'I do' is not used in the marriage ceremony too late to correct his mistake," but refrained from amending it "as it is philosophically unimportant that it is a mistake" (Austin 1962: 5). Since the change of tense alters the nature of the transaction from an undertaking *in the present* (the key to Austin's definition of the performative) to a promise that is also, perhaps, a deferral, the philosophical importance of this "mistake" seems to have been underestimated.

3

MEDIUM-SPECIFICITY AND OTHER CRITICAL SCRIPTS FOR SCREEN SHAKESPEARE

Katherine Rowe

This book might be called a diversion. Certainly it deals with a subject which is unconventional for an academic who has spent much of his life teaching English literature to college and university students and whose publications, until he began gathering material for the book, had little to do with films. It has been a diversion in another sense too, a distraction from other and more customary forms of research and writing, a recreation, and on the whole great fun ... Yet it is not so much a diversion as might be thought. I have been teaching Shakespeare for forty years and writing about the drama and stage for almost as long, and I have seen a great many films from the early days of cinema to the present.

Robert Hamilton Ball, *Shakespeare on Silent Film*, 1968

Shakespeare scholars have been moviegoers for more than a century but the barriers in our field taking this fact seriously as a contingency of our intellectual lives remain high. They are high enough that the division of spheres between scholarship and recreation, intellectual labor and fun, custom and errancy evoked by Robert Hamilton Ball should still seem familiar to anyone surveying a Shakespeare Association of America (SAA) program or scanning our leading journals to extrapolate their implied readership. The intellectual cross-pollinations of screen adaptation—like those of global appropriation more generally and also of performance—are pursued in separate seminars and panels, special issues, and dedicated anthologies and journals. Recent scholarship has put the study of screen Shakespeare on more theoretically supple and rigorous footing than earlier models of fidelity allowed. The teaching of Shakespeare on screen proceeds apace, especially at the secondary school level. And the revolution in textual studies has positioned adaptation, along with edition and collaboration, at the center of textual theory. No longer an epiphenomenon, adaptation is now understood as an essential condition of transmission for Shakespearean texts.[1] Yet in terms of the institutional structures of our field, we have not moved far from where Ball started forty years ago, with his first pass at a history of silent Shakespeare. And if one substitutes a more recent screen medium such as "television" for "film" in the epigraph above, things look considerably worse. It is still rare to encounter mid-career Shakespeareans who will disclose with the same frank cheerfulness that while they have been teaching and writing about Shakespeare for decades, they have also logged a great many hours in front of the TV.

As a field, Shakespeare studies still seeks the same separate peace between the spheres of the literary and the audiovisual that Thomas Leitch has argued characterizes adaptation studies generally. Indeed, the very fact that more than a decade of lively Shakespeare-on-screen criticism continues to dismantle that separation—on aesthetic, historical, and theoretical grounds—testifies that in our local arena of screen adaptations, as in the larger field, the structures of a separate peace remain in place and that they do so for institutional reasons. Leitch summarizes the interests served by this accommodation in adaptation studies more generally:

> to defend literary works and literature against the mass popularity of cinema, to valorize authorial agency and originality in a critical climate

> increasingly opposed to either, and to escape from the current
> orientation of film theory and from theoretical problems in general.
> (Leitch 2003: 168)

We can expand on Leitch's list by observing the different ways these interests are refracted in the three fields concerned with adaptation. In Shakespeare studies, screen adaptations inherit all the anti-theatricalism and suspicion of low culture that splits off the literary from the realm of the stage, intensifying a general iconophobia towards the translation of classic texts from print into audiovisual forms (Stam and Raengo 2005; Cartelli and Rowe 2007). Within performance studies—a leading edge in the study of adaptation as a cultural process—the idioms of stage and screen stand in an uneasy relation, with mass media of various kinds regularly linked to the death of theater. Within film studies, the logic of separate spheres has a long and complex history. From classical writings on film to the advent of the academic discipline, contradistinctions between film and the stage, and film and literature, have been enlisted tactically—serving to elevate cinema to the realm of high culture and to distinguish cinema studies as a separate discipline.[2] Thus, historically, formalist arguments about the specificity of film as a form have often served to maintain the autonomy of separate aesthetic and social spheres, and arenas of scholarly labor.

I will return to the institutional contours of this separation in Shakespeare studies in the second half of this essay. For the moment I want to use the historical lesson of film studies to observe that medium-specific rubrics have become especially prominent in our conferences and journals precisely at a moment when Shakespeareans are grappling with the phenomenon of media convergence in our daily lives. The remediation of familiar forms and practices (the essay, archival research) in new formats (web publication, relational databases)—and the tradeoffs this remediation involves—may be the most pressing facts of Shakespearean labor now, for journal editors, archivists, scholars, and classroom teachers. At such a moment, medium-specific rubrics (such as dedicated SAA seminars on "Shakespeare and TV," "Shakespeare and Film Theory," "Shakespeare and New Media") can have the paradoxical institutional effect of conserving intellectual boundaries that they are designed to dismantle.

The "alternative" tack to take in the arena of adaptation studies is thus to insist on the traffic, recycling, and cross-pollination between screen and other arts. This does not mean ignoring the specific demands of, constraints on, or opportunities offered by film or any other expressive medium. Nor does it absolve Shakespeareans of our responsibility to mine the significant bodies of scholarship, different vocabularies, and evidentiary protocols in the different branches of media studies. It requires us to be alert, however, to the history of specificity arguments about different media—and to the ways our local readings, grand narratives about adaptation, and institutional practices are all slanted by critical scripts based on such arguments.

These "media scripts" incorporate a host of unspoken meanings: codifying attitudes towards different media, communications strategies associated with them, and norms governing the way we handle them.[3] In the passage quoted at the beginning of this essay, for example, Ball navigates a number of such scripts: in particular the idea of film as light recreation, a diversion for buffs, not matter for real scholarship. Against this assumption Ball enlists the reassuringly stolid authority of print-based Shakespeare, evoked in an epigraph ("Dost thou love pictures?") addressed "To the Reader" rather than to lovers of motion pictures, and anchored by a citation (The Taming of the Shrew) (1968: 15). Then he works through the anti-film bias in an extended rhetorical play on the word "diversion" that reveals both the wit and seriousness of the scholarly mind at work in this study. My hypothetical Shakespearean TV buffs would face a similar tactical challenge in establishing that any real brainpower is required to study TV adaptations—for while media studies scholars seem to feel free to import Shakespearean references into their readings with little social cost, the reverse is clearly not true. They would have to navigate the academic commonplace that television is a medium essentially opposed to intellectual life, liable to "rot the mind." The pseudo-medical conceit should alert us that this script serves social performative rather than evaluative functions. Along with "TV is a waste of time" and "I never watch, I'm just too busy," "TV rots the mind" announces the speaker as an ideologically mature consumer of mass media, savvy about its modes of interpellation, resistant to them, and surfeited with more serious labor. To acknowledge oneself as a regular TV watcher in a community of Shakespeareans is to raise questions about one's bona fides in all these registers.

What follows is an exercise in teasing out some of the ways our critical instincts can be affected by prevailing media scripts, and an attempt to write against the grain of a scholarly stance that separates the intellectual life of Shakespeareans from the technologies we encounter on a daily basis. Media scripts might be viewed as a meta-critical corollary in Shakespeare criticism to the media allegories Peter Donaldson has identified in Shakespeare film (2002): to focus attention on them is to foreground the social performatives of Shakespeare scholarship. The first half of this essay looks back to an earlier moment of Shakespearean engagement with media transformation in this mode, tracking the modernist media scripts that bias Ball's silent film readings. Ball's account of an early French adaptation of *King Lear* captures in small the allegory of cinematic progress and theatrical belatedness that organizes his study as a whole. The starring roles are played here by specificity arguments about film and theater. The second half of the essay extrapolates some principles of self-reflection, outlining two kinds of media script that thread through current Shakespearean criticism and practice. In this way, the essay takes up Ball's invitation to begin to reckon our daily experience of media convergence into our lives as scholars.

MODERNIST MEDIA SCRIPTS: THEATRICAL/ PRIMITIVE VERSUS CINEMATIC/PROGRESSIVE

In the first and second decades of the twentieth century, filmmakers and early critics alike tended to map the idea of modernity as a radical historical break onto specific formal properties of film. A dominant strain in this analogical thinking is the privilege accorded decoupage—analytic cutting—as an emergent technique only available in film. Analytic cutting, the logic goes, is cousin to abstract, multi-perspective painting: unfolding multiple angles of view, marking sudden shifts of scale in space and time. If acceleration and discontinuity constitutes the modernist condition, film thus has aesthetic properties that make visible those essential experiences of modernity in ways that other media cannot fully capture.[4] A corollary strain of analysis relegates single-shot staging and cinematic tableaux to the status of residue, derivative of the old order of theater.

Ball's study of silent Shakespeare films is strongly slanted by this modernist media script. As he sums it up, "rapid shifts are the stock in trade of film" (1968: 301). This idea grounds the historiographic narrative that emerges as Ball surveys the different ways Shakespearean materials are handled in silent film: a narrative of progress from primitive, "theatrical" devices to modern, "cinematic" ones that privileges speed and discontinuity. Ball's discussion of an early *Lear* adaptation, Louis Feuillade's marvelous *Le Roi Lear au village / A Village King Lear* (1911, Gaumont), typifies the pattern. The film is compelling in its own right, as one of the earliest site-specific, immersive adaptations of Shakespeare on screen. But I am primarily interested here in the biases it solicits from Ball and other critics, and the ways different notions of the "modern" and the "experimental" inflect what they find in it.

Because *Le Roi Lear* is likely to be unfamiliar to many readers, some brief context and description may be helpful. As its title implies, *Le Roi Lear* transposes the *Lear* story to a provincial French village. Its settings include well-appointed farmhouse parlors, a solicitor's office, the village café, and a winter landscape of old stone walls, a working canal, and a distant churchyard. Feuillade was a prolific filmmaker, and is best known for the fantastical urban crime series he developed during the war—*Fântomas* (1913–15), *Les Vampires* (1915–16), and *Judex* (1917)—works that figured prominently in the Surrealist mythology of French modernism.[5] *Le Roi Lear* is a single-reel entry in his first experiment with the serial form, a series titled *Scènes de la vie telle qu'elle est* ("scenes from life as it is"; 1911–13). At first glance, this *scène de la vie* seems to have little to do with the fantastical stories that made Feuillade famous. The film assimilates the *Lear* story to two, not entirely congruent impulses. Emphasizing natural light and location shooting, Feuillade aims, as he puts it, to "eschew all fantasy and represent people and things as they are and not as they should be," and give "the impression of a previously unrecognized truth" (Abel 1988: 54); yet this realist aesthetic combines with a stripped-down but intimate mode of film melodrama to offer a decidedly pessimistic take on contemporary bourgeois fears of downward mobility. Release notes in a contemporary trade journal summarize the story:

> A Village King Lear—This story, taken from life, closely resembles Shakespeare's tragedy. An old blind farmer is persuaded to transfer his property to his two heartless daughters. Neglected by them, he is found wandering helplessly about, and is taken to his solicitor's office, where a meeting with his daughters is arranged. Here the eldest of his children, shamed somewhat at the position, and also touched a little by remorse, takes the poor old fellow home again, to be treated in the future with more compassion.
>
> (*Bioscope* 1911: viii)[6]

The film proceeds in ten long-take tableaux, all but one with a fixed camera. Medium shots predominate, with intra-scene cutting only to inter-titles and diegetic text (a newspaper headline, a letter). Feuillade alternates between interior sets and location shooting in a particularly interesting way and does some remarkably subtle things with deep-focus blocking. He also makes thoughtful use of the *Lear* story, not merely transposing it to the provincial setting but fruitfully combining character functions so as to clarify the inter-generational conflicts at stake. Together these effects suggest a meta-narrative of sorts, about the close relationship between theatrical looking and cinematic looking.

None of this is evident from Ball's account of the film. Although in his assessment no silent films constitute "good Shakespeare" (because all lack the essential verbal power of the playtexts), Ball is an astute formalist reader, attuned to what makes exciting visual drama and interested in a complex taxonomy of adaptation strategies. His mis-reading thus seems less a matter of clumsiness than a symptom of the exceptionalist script that governs the study. In aesthetic terms, *Le Roi Lear* plays a transitional role in Ball's story of silent Shakespeare, marking the exhaustion of "primitive," stage-based adaptations and *film d'art* projects, and pointing towards a future "which led more and more to contemporary subjects and less and less to the conventions of theater" (Ball 1968: 131). This conclusion seems not a little peculiar when Ball notes that Feuillade's interest in telling a story "from life" resonates with the realist experiments of André Antoine, whose *plein air* aesthetic first emerged in the theater. But what the experienced theater scholar registers here—complex traffic between contemporary performance media—is quickly overwritten by a story of technological progress that aligns long-take staging with the theatrical and primitive, over and against the full expression of film as a modern medium (with all the possibilities of intra-scene cutting, moving camera eye, etc.).[7]

If we suspend Ball's exceptionalist assumptions, it becomes clear that Feuillade's work substantiates a more integrative approach to the history of film aesthetics. Indeed, Le Roi Lear makes an especially good case for keeping one eye on medium specificity and the other on media convergence and recycling. And, interestingly, while Ball's "rapid shift" script echoes dominant strains of early film historiography, it is clearly less in line with contemporary developments in film theory than with contemporary developments in Shakespeare film (compare Ball's privileging of camera movements and cutting, natural lighting, and "contemporary subjects" with the aesthetics of a Franco Zeffirelli). By contrast, by 1968, when Shakespeare on Silent Film was published, a number of writers—beginning with André Bazin—had recuperated strategies such as depth of field and long-take staging as properly cinematic.[8] Since then, pre-war films such as Le Roi Lear have regularly attracted scholars with an agnostic approach to the cross-pollination between different media. Ball is working, in other words, according to a commonplace script that carries the authority of medium specificity but whose aesthetics (privileging speed, discontinuity, and a specific realist idiom) have only partly to do with the formal properties in which they seem so invested.

As Ball's example makes clear, the scripts we work with constrain our perceptions and habits of reception; specificity claims, in particular, tend to obscure the formal traffic between different media. What follows is a short account of what Le Roi Lear looks like if one takes a deliberately anti-exceptionalist approach to its experiments with location shooting, its long takes, and its depth of field staging—actively seeking the way theatrical effects can be recycled in cinema. Besides yielding a richer sense of a specific film, to read in this way is to expand our sense of the formal properties specific to a given medium—and to reconsider the importance of apparently residual theatrical conventions such as tableau to modern film mise en scène.

Le Roi Lear opens on an interior set, a well-to-do farmer's parlor whose appointments (framed keepsakes on the wall, checked cloth on the table) evoke a milieu pitched just above the impoverished settings of Zola. An old, blind man sits at the table in the foreground, in a throne-like chair at screen center, filling his pipe with tobacco. In successive scenes the rest of his family—faithful servant, two grasping and neglectful daughters, two sons-in-law—will enter from an exterior door at screen right, in the background, crossing forward into this central space or its analogues in other settings. In this central position the blind father is first attended by his servant, then solicited by his daughters and sons-in-law, then progressively displaced. In his solicitor's office, similarly seated at a desk in the center foreground, he signs away his property. Returning to his older daughter's house, he is relegated to a seat by the window (frame right, medium shot) from which he struggles unsuccessfully to regain his former privilege. He escapes to the bleak canal where, as the inter-title tells us, he intends to drown himself. And he is restored in the closing scene, not to his central position but to the chair by the window—suggesting a conclusion less sanguine about the care on offer from the younger generation than the release notice in *The Bioscope* would have it. The choreography of these tableaux underscores differences of class and status among the characters, evoking a host of anxieties about the unstable French economy shared by other realist melodramas of the period.

In theatrical terms, the film's series of tableaux are extraordinarily dynamic and evocative, coalescing around a central space in the screen foreground, blocked so as to pull figures downstage towards this point as the action intensifies.[9] Two aspects of this pull downstage center are particularly striking in *Le Roi Lear*. First, the foreground space towards which the action drives is often vacant: the empty center of a weakened domestic sphere, the focal point for divestiture of property and status.[10] The emptying out and filling in of this space is one of the film's central devices of suspense. In a particularly marvelous tableau at the solicitor's office, for example, one daughter's grasping hand remains poised just outside this area for much of the scene. She reaches towards the white paper square of her father's will from screen right, eager to snatch it away the moment he signs. The centripetal pull of such emptying gestures is reinforced by competing business in the surrounding frame: the elder daughter folding linen, greetings and leave-takings, the covetous glances and jostling shoulders of in-laws hovering around the solicitor's desk. Balance and symmetry in these movements clearly matter here, as Bordwell observes (1996: 12–14); yet Feuillade seems equally interested in the compositional possibilities of disharmony and in competition between dramatic figures.

These competing pulls on viewer attention are intensified by deep space blocking, as figures advance and grow, retreat and diminish in relation to each other. Indeed, Feuillade's work shows an extraordinarily disciplined, expansive interest in the possibilities of upstaging and downstaging afforded by a fixed camera and long take: figures and objects in the foreground of the screen "reveal" and "cover" the action, objects, and figures behind them, in a symbolic choreography (Bordwell 1996: 16). In the solicitor's office, for example, arriving daughters and in-laws loom as they move forward to cluster around the old man, gradually filling the frame; once he signs the will the group swallows him up as they exit through a door upstage right. The blocking actions literalize his social invisibility once he has been divested of property.

Feuillade's play with depth of field makes it clear that long take and tableau staging offer opportunities for experimentation in their own right. These devices testify to the complex aesthetic traffic between theater and film—not to a break—but they may still produce decidedly modernist effects. In *Le Roi Lear* such effects build slowly because Feuillade's ensemble blocking is so fluent and the domestic interiors of melodrama so familiar. The working of "reveal and cover" in this film are obviously quieter than the fiercely playful eruptions of incongruity that characterized later avant-garde experiments. Yet they gradually develop the quality of spookiness, of dream-revealed-in-the-ordinary, so valued by Surrealist filmmakers in particular. This effect is most intense in the scene at the canal. This scene breaks from shallow focus into depth along a perpendicular, in a way that suggests an explicit interest in the cinematic possibilities of the theatrical reveal. The scene begins with a cut to the canal bridge, replacing the farmhouse parlors and paneled offices of earlier tableaux with an environment that is visually and aesthetically their opposite. A foreshortened field of grainy stone cuts across the middle of the frame horizontally; winter-bare trees rise behind this blank stone wall, black against an equally blank sky. The blind man enters this foreshortened field from screen right and gropes his way left. As he moves, the camera pans left with him, leaving him isolated against the abstract lines of wall and branches and keeping always outside the vacant center of the frame.

This scene looks remarkably different than the deep-space staging that comes before. Yet it depends fundamentally on the visual and narrative structures established by the opening tableaux—and not only by way of contrast: the horizontal pan and deep blocking for a fixed camera emerge as cognate staging devices. The old man's exit to open air and natural light cannot be read without reference to the interior space, either in terms of choreography within the frame or in narrative terms. His exit is set up ironically, to underscore limitations on both the blind man's understanding and ours. After he gropes around the dark parlor to the door and opens it, moonlight streams in like revelation, but this revelation is one a blind man clearly has no access to. And if *we* have any expectations of epiphany, these are abruptly foreclosed when he enters the bleak, foreshortened winter landscape of the bridge. What the camera offers us here is an existentially empty space that cannot be penetrated. The images that linger are symbolic abstractions: the old man's bulging blind eyes, the contrasting horizontal and vertical lines of stone wall and bare branches, the isolated, inaccessible figure against a flat, patterned expanse.

The sudden shift of perspective in this scene signals that we are in the gravitational field of *King Lear* 4.6, the scene of blind Gloucester's fall from a fictional cliff at Dover. The blind father plays the combined roles of Gloucester and Lear here: an object of pathos, symbol of sudden reversal, and figure of imperfect understanding. As the scene continues to shift perspective, it does so in a way that seems to align us with the Lear/Gloucester figure. The slow pan keeps the screen center always slightly ahead of this composite character, symbolically empty until the point that he stumbles off the end of the bridge (a moment that puns, Abel suggests, on contemporary "fears of falling" down the social scale). As the blind man stumbles, the visual field opens into deep focus again and we gaze down a canal path and stream, gradually obscured by two advancing figures, the old man's servant and, a moment later, a gossip. With this return to deep focus, the pan resolves into a cinematic reveal and cover: we catch a glimpse of the flowing water and a canal boat moving inexorably towards us "like fate itself" (Abel 1984: 331), only to have that movement obscured by the arrivals. The pan makes as strong a meta-cinematic claim, in other words, as the moments in later screen *Lears* that seem to echo it: when Lear falls out of the frame in Peter Brook's film (1971), and when the character doubling Lear and Gloucester in Kristian Levring's adaptation (2000) stumbles out of a similarly unforgiving landscape.

Far from offering us unmediated access to life "as it is," this dynamic reveal suggests the profound limitations on what we can know of any "slice of life"; or to put it differently, the deeper filmic truth that seems to be offered here belongs less to the effects of social realism and more to the accidents of art or grace—something we grope towards, stumble into or out of, glimpse momentarily. The dreamlike quality of this exit into daylight blindness, the abstracted, symbolically loaded juxtapositions of the isolation shot, and the constraints on our ability visually to penetrate this slice of life make it clear why Surrealist artists might have been drawn to such an avowedly realist *mise en scène*. Yet significantly, it is the film's renovation of theatrical devices, not its break from theater, that animates its most vividly "modernist" epiphanies.

SHAKESPEAREANS AT THE MOVIES

Ball's responses to *Le Roi Lear* illustrate how easily reductive media scripts can pass under cover of specificity claims—limiting what even the most experienced viewer sees in a film. If he seems an easy setup—a critic working with dated conceptions on even more dated material—it is worth noting that much of his progressive narrative still prevails in our field and in media studies as well. Ball makes a useful illustration not because he was a naïve viewer but because he was a complex and thoroughly sophisticated one whose insights as a playgoer, filmgoer, and historian were constrained in a particularly telling, historically conditioned way.

An objection might be raised that the real obstacle to moving past the separate spheres logic in Shakespeare studies is that unlike Ball, most Shakespeareans are not in fact serious moviegoers—neither regular nor "complex viewers" of the kind called for in recent work on visual culture (Caws 2002: 149). Yet the field is increasingly divided generationally in this regard, and the market niches we inhabit are more diverse than might be expected. Returning to the case of television, for example, it is clear that academics now make up a defined and profitable audience, one actively targeted by what Dana Polan calls "savvy TV" or "quality TV" (2006). This genre targets "an audience of presumably astute intellectuality, ego-stroking its ostensibly discerning ability to tap into learned references and arcane in-jokes within the television experience" (2006: col. 1). This strategy accommodates the "TV rots your mind" script by asserting both qualitative and ontological difference: "It's not TV . . . It's HBO" (the premium US cable channel, Home Box Office). Thus we find Shakespearean allusions in *The Sopranos*, or a teaser shot of Foucault's *"Society Must Be Defended": Lectures at the College de France, 1975–6* on Jed Bartlett's bookshelf in *The West Wing* (2006: col. 1).[11]

Ultimately, individual viewing habits—Ball's and ours—are not the critical issue. All Shakespeareans operate (and have for decades) in a richly audiovisually mediated culture. The aesthetic, technical, social, industrial aspects of film and other media affect how we practice Shakespeare in the classroom and as scholars, in ways that go far beyond individual viewing experiences. Shakespeareans participate in the larger patterns of filmgoing that organize our academic and consumer surrounds. As evidence of this participation we might note the privilege long accorded to experimental and independent films (reflecting the long ties between academia and avant-garde cinema); or our increasing savvy about distribution and "box office" (reflecting a general rise in "insiderism" among film consumers).[12] Exploring such patterns, a cultural historian of Shakespeare studies at the turn of this century might ask: how do habits of audition and use nurtured in a robust visual and print culture shape academic reception and practice? What media scripts circulate between Shakespeare studies and this larger surround? Two kinds of inquiry seem essential for self-reflection: into the history of the scripts we stage, and their institutional effects in our field. Both approaches help us navigate between the reductive poles towards which academic media scripts all too easily gravitate: technophobic scripts, grounded in the notion that new media are essentially bad for us, and technophilic ones such as Ball's, grounded in equally reductive visions of cinematic progress.

Historicizing media scripts

Media historians regularly observe that every modern representational technology has evoked strong and remarkably similar anxieties. Compared to the (nostalgically idealized) forms that precede it, each new medium appears unresponsive to individual and communal needs, and often downright threatening. For Walter Benjamin, the newspaper and novel destroy the "chasteness" and embedded life of storytelling; for Fredric Jameson, photography challenges the fullness of novelistic representation. For many years television played the aesthetically impoverished and dangerous newcomer but Web-based electronic media now regularly inhabit that role.

We can find examples of such technophobic scripts at work in much of the commentary on Michael Almereyda's Hamlet (2000), a media allegory concerned with modern arts of memory, film and video (Rowe 2003). For numerous critics and reviewers, Hamlet's melancholy preoccupation with his video gadgetry and compulsive recording illustrates the dangerous alienations of "postmodern media," cutting him off from human connections. Hamlet's technologies are not periodized, however, but compose a suggestively belated and polychronic mix: Polaroids, Pixelvision camera, floppy disks, digital workstations, television, a "film/video" and payphones. And notably, the postmodern media that most urgently access contemporary fears of alienation—cellphones, email, textmessaging, iPods, chat rooms, social networking, gaming—are absent from the film, though Almereyda sets it in the year 2000 (Cartelli and Rowe 2007). And when we finally see Hamlet wired, at the end of the film, he is hooked up to the oddly fey and archaic gear of a fencing match. Almereyda clearly means to engage our fears about the alienating effects of modern technology, but in a way that discriminates between different kinds of use rather than assimilating all media to a single technological moment or script. Indeed, the film explores the overlapping roles of media consumer and media user: the one vulnerable, passive, and subject to official counter-memories; the other resistant, actively carving out a safe space for recollection and reflection.[13]

At stake in competing interpretations of the film are competing models of reception that have a long history. Technophobic readings tend to assimilate the functions of media consumption and use. At their most sophisticated, such readings call into question the differences between these two functions; at their most reductive, technophobic readings unreflectively internalize what film historians call the "hypodermic" model of reception, articulated by Frankfurt school theorists Theodore Adorno and Max Horkheimer. In that model, mass culture is understood to inject ideology into a passive audience via a complex mechanism of stimulus and response. Visual media are imagined here as delivery systems: acting directly and easy to consume, they work on the emotions rather than the intellect of an audience stereotypically figured as children and young adults.

The limitations of this model were beginning to be felt in sociological audience studies of the 1940s, and it has been gradually replaced in communications studies by the idea of active "uses and gratifications." This second model is grounded in a vision of "different audiences us[ing] the same media [and even the same content] to meet different needs, according to" varied interests and reception contexts (Brooker and Jermyn 2003: 9, 53). Combining nuanced textual analysis with careful sociological assessment, this cultural studies version of audience research has emphasized the situated and habitual components of reception: focusing on specific locations and practices, and emphasizing the heterogeneity of reception modes. One consequence of this emphasis on locations and practices has been a shift in governing terms for the subjects of reception: away from the abstract, passive, and primarily visual operations imagined of a *spectator* (in the singular), to the situated, active, and synesthetic processing of *audiences* (in the plural). In film studies, that shift is reflected in the increasing emphasis on film exhibition (work by scholars such as Miriam Hansen, Richard Abel, and Tom Gunning); in television studies, one can find it in scholarship on domestic and public spaces of television viewing (Lynn Spigel, Anna McCarthy).

In Shakespeare studies, the shift from spectator to audiences has been relatively organic and unremarked, legible in conference programs and essay titles over the past decade, driven perhaps by the expansion of interest in cultural studies.[14] Yet the underlying conceptual shift in reception theory, from hypodermic effects, to uses and gratifications, to situated habits and practices, has lagged behind. Why should this be so? It cannot be simply that many of us lack the disciplinary knowledge base in media studies; we have seen corresponding shifts in a number of more closely connected fields: in performance history, for example, where heterogeneous audiences and diverse exhibition spaces are old news; and in textual studies, with its turn to a robust cultural history of production. And the connections with cultural studies in our field are themselves long and deep. It seems likely that these competing models of reception are linked instead to our fears and fantasies about screen Shakespeare, in a way that is hard for the field to do without. Giving up an attachment to reductive versions of the hypodermic model, for example, may allow a more agnostic stance towards the strengths and weaknesses of different visual media. But it also means relinquishing the ideal of Shakespeare as a simple engine for a shared civic experience. This may explain the lag between Shakespeare and film criticism (which has pressed forward with the latter models) and guides to teaching Shakespeare on film and video, where the ante is high for civic effects and affects.[15]

Media scripts as institutional practice

Considerable affective energy seems to be invested in the disciplinary divisions that Ball describes in his preface: post-Enlightenment oppositions between pleasure and labor, entertainment and scholarship that underwrite his sense of moonlighting in film history as "great fun" (1968: 15). It would be easy to reduce this mid-career diversion function to a simple iconophobic opposition between high- and low-brow art. But the politics of interdisciplinarity in Shakespeare studies are more complex, and more dynamic, than this binarism suggests. To trace them fully is beyond the scope of this essay, but one way to begin to do so is to call attention to the institutional payoffs and constraints, at different career stages, of the ascription of a specific arena as newfangled, "alternative," or "fun." Ball's pleasure in his twenty years of labor in Shakespeare films implies liberation from intellectual discipline in both its institutional senses of restraint and punishment. In this respect, it seems symptomatic of a mode of interdisciplinarity Marjorie Garber links to transgressive play:

> Learning is always a little bit transgressive, and what we learn around the edges of orthodox courses and established disciplines often sticks more than what we learn when we're in harness. The pleasure of thinking that such associations of scholars or intellectual interest groups are voluntary [enables our] search for something that escapes the mantle of duty.
>
> (2003: B20)

The benefits and also the costs for Shakespeare studies of investing such pleasures in the divisions between media have partly to do with the politics of canon reformation; as Garber observes, "if the new interdisciplines that now occupy and preoccupy us so excitingly were to become the center of the academy, they would in turn become conventional, and the center of intellectual interest and provocation would move elsewhere" (2003: B20). But more significant costs result from the casting of whole fields in the role of new worlds, defining long-cultivated intellectual landscapes (television studies, comparative media history) as the dark and wild margins of knowledge. That formation allows Shakespeare studies as a field to avoid the difficult work of sorting through what constitutes competence and rigorous training in the increasingly multi-mediated arenas of Shakespearean practice. Finally, it reinforces a generational dynamics familiar in many humanist fields, establishing in popular culture an arena of counter-taste and counter-expertise where those in the social limbo of academe negotiate their transitional status (Sconce 1995). With so few of the senior scholars who work on adaptation housed in programs that train future Shakespeareans, screen adaptations are readily available to cathect guilty attachment to the performance-based pleasures that lead many students to Shakespeare studies—and also ambivalence about the disciplining of taste and expertise by a profession in which the prospects of advancement are so uncertain. Garber's theory of play-between-the-disciplines belongs, by contrast, to the relatively more comfortable transgressions of established, mid-career faculty, anticipating our second-book swerve into popular culture.

"At stake in every struggle over art," Pierre Bourdieu observes, "there is also the imposition of an art of living, that is, the transmutation of an arbitrary way of living into the legitimate way of life which casts every other way of living into arbitrariness" (1984: 57). The media scripts we play out in Shakespeare studies—including the construction of screen arts as an arena for counter-Shakespearean practice—offer one of the most fruitful arenas for foregrounding and imagining productive alternatives to the institutionalized arts of living in our field.

NOTES

1   See for example McGann (1997), Grigely (1995), and Roach (1996).

2   See: Brewster and Jacobs (1997) on the traffic between early cinema and theater; Stam (2005) on the *querelle de l'adaptation* in mid-century French theory; Zryd (2006) on the alignment of avant-garde and academic interests in the 1960s in America.

3   I am coining the phrase "media script" on the model of Anna Wierzbicka's notion of "emotion scripts", as a way of foregrounding the social logic of different critical stances and the performative value, in academic venues, of different lines of formalist analysis (1994: 189).

4   The modernity of film—the notion of a profound aesthetic break that reflected and epitomized the cultural upheavals of the early twentieth century—is a hallmark of early accounts of the medium. Bordwell notes the preference among early film historians for the "progressive" devices of editing (e.g. Griffith, Porter) over what they saw as residually theatrical resources of the long take (1996: 10). Elsaesser observes that this bias organizes early nationalist competition for the high ground of cinematic sophistication (1990: 11). See also Collick's arguments about the Englishness of screen Shakespeare style in relation to theater (1989), and Shaughnessy on theater-to-film historiographic plots (2006). From the early years of film criticism, the exceptionalist line of analysis developed in parallel with counter-arguments about film as a total art form, synthesizing all the capacities of all other media.

5   See Michelson (1966) and Waltz (1996) on the figure Feuillade cuts in that mythology.

6   Abel (1984) lists two extant prints, held at the Cinémathèque Française (35mm, 330 m,) and at the Library of Congress (LOC; 35mm, 399 feet; incomplete). Catalogue descriptions and summaries in early film weeklies such as *Moving Picture World* (July 8, 1911) and *The Bioscope* (1911) are mildly inconsistent with the action of the LOC fragment.

7   Ball expresses uncertainty about whether he saw this film (Ball 1968: 337), a caveat that underscores the difficulty of archival access and the spotty conservation of early works. But it also underscores the way that a scholarly reliance on the accounts of others tends to reify specific media scripts, as the same description is recycled by critic after critic.

8   Bazin recuperated *profondeur du champ* and drew genealogical connections between these early experiments in long take and tableau staging and the work of Welles and Renoir (Bazin 1951: 18–19; Bordwell 1996: 10).

9   Bordwell finds this characteristic of Feuillade's later work and typical of the period generally (1908–18): "With its effect of enlarging the characters, preparing for a confrontation, and narrowing the gap between the figures, the movement from background to foreground became the norm for initiating the scene's action or developing the drama to a higher pitch of intensity" (1996: 16).

10 Abel (1987: 12–13) finds such vacant screen-centers in Feuillade's later work; Bordwell critiques Burch's misreading of "decentered" *mise en scène* (1996: 11); and Michelson discusses spatial dislocation in *Les Vampires* (1966: 75).

11 For a more robust account of televisual Shakespeare see essays by Holderness (2002) and Pearson and Uricchio (2006). On earlier "quality TV" traditions in Shakespeare, including the BBC Shakespeare project, see Willis (1991), the collection assembled by Bulman and Coursen (1988), and essays by Willems (1994) and Taylor (1994).

12 See: Zryd (2006) on ties between academia and avant-garde cinema; Acland (2003) on the rise of insiderism as a consumer practice. Henderson (2006b) observes a recent shift among Shakespeare on screen scholars away from avant-garde to popular films—one that might be linked to Sconce's observation (in 1995) that "middlebrow" seemed likely to be the next cutting edge in screen studies. On the politics of the popular as an interpretive category in Shakespeare studies see also Lanier (2006).

13   Lanier (2003), Rowe (2003), Donaldson (2002), Cartelli and Rowe
     (2007).
14   For example, Courtney Lehmann and Lisa Starks (2002) use the term
     "spectator" in the title of their recent volume on critical theory and
     popular cinema, yet their introduction and collected essays are
     straightforwardly interested in audiences: reception communities,
     specific markets, etc.
15   Recent exceptions include the work of Annalisa Castaldo (2002),
     Gregory Semenza (2005), and interactive resources such as the *Hamlet
     on the Ramparts* website (http://shea.mit.edu/ramparts/welcome.htm
     accessed May 30, 2007).

4

SHAKESPEARE 3.0

Or Text Versus Performance, the Remix

W. B. Worthen

Shakespeare may remain our contemporary, but to recall Polish director Jan Kott's massively influential book of that title (first published in Poland in 1964 and almost immediately translated into English) is to mark a sea change in our access to and imagination of Shakespearean drama. "The Kings"; "Hamlet of the Mid-Century"; "Troilus and Cressida—Amazing and Modern"; "King Lear or Endgame"; "Titania and the Ass's Head": the chapter titles thumbnail innovative Shakespeare performance at the mid-century. They recall both the brilliant productions Kott describes and those he inspired: the endless bloody staircase of murderous royal ambition; the excitement of finding contemporary irony in one of Shakespeare's least popular, never clapperclawed plays; the discovery of *King Lear*'s Beckettian landscape of anomie; and the reality of theatrical magic deployed in Peter Brook's *A Midsummer Night's Dream* (1970), perhaps the landmark production of the period. Yet much as Shakespeare would hardly recognize the technologies we use to realize his plays today, so too Shakespeare in the third millennium measures its distance from Jan Kott along the axis of technological innovation. And much as Kott worked to bring the critical discourse of contemporary theatre to bear on the isolated "literary" critique of Shakespeare, so too the rise of digital culture marks a potentially profound shift in the identities of drama, particularly the ways in which we imagine the interface between writing and performance.

Although we understand Shakespearean drama, and Western drama more generally, across the boundary of "text and performance," it is important to understand that this interface is historically and culturally inflected by the means through which textuality—both as writing and in performance—is materialized. Here, I want to argue that the rise of digital culture has provided important ways for reimagining the book, and so for resituating what I will call an "information theory" understanding of drama, including Shakespearean drama. Without insisting on the rise of information theory as the cause (it can hardly be that), we can see an information theory paradigm of the transmission of drama unfolding in the ongoing relationship between printed plays and dramatic performance, a model of performance that the rise of digital culture enables us to engage more critically. Given the centrality of Shakespeare's plays to the digitally strengthened critique of the book, how do the contemporary disciplines of dramatic scholarship (or more accurately the disciplines increasingly disengaged from the drama—literary studies, theatre studies, performance studies) frame the relationship between writing and performance? If we take the critique of "information" to be anticipated by the critique of "print," a critique specifically epitomized by the unresolved challenges posed by dramatic performance, we might be able to seize a more compelling direction for the study of drama, now, in the digital era.

First inscribed in manuscript, and first published through stage performance, Shakespeare's plays dramatize the destabilizing cultural relationship between Western drama and the technologies that produce it: writing and performance. For Shakespeare and his fellows, the principal dramatic technology was the stage and its players: plays had a very subsidiary life as printed texts. Over the next four hundred years, Shakespearean identity slowly migrated from the stage to the page, as the dissemination of printed literature and the rise of literacy assimilated the drama—however fitfully, unevenly, and incompletely—to the canons of literature. And as our sense of the identity of drama became increasingly more literary, the stage itself came to be understood as a site of reproduction. To explore this subject is to measure how differently we seize Shakespeare—or Shakespeare 3.0—today, and the impact of contemporary technologies both on our understanding of Shakespeare's plays and on the disciplined practices we use to encounter the drama. Shakespeare 1.0 wrote plays for a theater and a culture undergoing the slow transformation from orality to literacy; neither his audiences nor all of his performers could be assumed to be fully literate. The plays were handwritten in manuscript, laboriously recopied into parts (again by hand), and this palimpsest of writing was owned by the playing company, which frequently disposed of such discardable materials after they had ceased to be of use. Despite Shakespeare's pretensions to literary status, well registered in the sonnets, the written play was largely an instrumental document, used and used up in the making of the play on the stage: it was the rare exception for companies to use printed texts for rehearsal. Granted, Shakespeare's role as "literary dramatist" was created by his appearance in print, and Lukas Erne and others have vigorously argued that the plays bear the trace of Shakespeare's possible aspiration to a literary career through the means of print publishing.[1] But whether or not there was a significant market for the quarto publication of plays, the general dearth of folio-style editions might suggest that whatever the pretensions of Jonson, Shakespeare (or Heminge and Condell), and eventually Beaumont and Fletcher to print authorship, plays were routinely regarded as having their principal identity in performance. Whether in manuscript or print, Shakespeare 1.0 was performance software, directing the operating system of early modern theater practice to configure the hardware of the material theater in certain ways.[2]

While *performance* encompassed a wide range of activities, by the sixteenth century the use of a written script or scenario had been associated with *dramatic theater* for nearly two millennia; from Greek tragedy, inseparable from the invention of writing, to the medieval craft guilds guarding the "book" of their individual Corpus Christi plays, writing enabled, preserved, and possibly instigated Western notions of drama and its performance. But plays in manuscript were nearly as vulnerable and evanescent as the theatrical performances they motivated. Rendering writing in a more robust, durable, and reproducible form, print enabled drama to gain a stable identity apart from performance—a *literary* identity.

More to the point, print culture mapped a different understanding of the identity of drama, one in which the "work" seemed to exist on the page, and its performance could be understood merely as one instance, an interpretation, a kind of "edition," of its inherent complexity. The transformation of Shakespearean dramatic writing from performance software to literary software took some time, but we can see the now-familiar outlines of Shakespeare 2.0 taking shape in the early nineteenth century. Charles Lamb's well-known essay "On the Tragedies of Shakespeare, Considered with Reference to their Fitness for Stage Representation" (published in 1811) is usually remembered for its astonishing (but increasingly commonplace) claim that the "Lear of Shakespeare cannot be acted" (Lamb and Lamb 1908: 136). Lamb naturally points to the inadequate and "contemptible machinery by which they mimic the storm," but his hesitation regarding Shakespeare on stage finally has little to do with the verisimilitude of the theater's ability to "represent the horrors of the real elements." A reader of Shakespeare, Lamb finds the essential dramatic action of Shakespeare's play taking place in Lear's mind, and in his own:

> It is his mind which is laid bare. This case of flesh and blood seems too insignificant to be thought on; even as he himself neglects it. On the stage we see nothing but corporal infirmities and weakness, the impotence of rage; while we read it, we see not Lear, but we are Lear,—we are in his mind [. . .]
>
> (Lamb and Lamb 1908: 136)

Like many of his academic inheritors, Lamb claims an affection for the stage, but cautions against taking performance as the thing itself. Recalling the impact of his own theatergoing, Lamb notes how difficult it is "for a frequent playgoer to disembarrass the idea of Hamlet from the person and voice of Mr K [John Philip Kemble]," or how often we "speak of Lady Macbeth, while we are in reality thinking of Mrs S [Mrs. Siddons]." Yet while he would never "be so ungrateful as to forget the very high degree of satisfaction which I received some years back from seeing for the first time a tragedy of Shakespeare performed, in which these two great performers sustained the principal parts," stage performance captures only an immature and singular impression of the myriad-minded poet. For the actors' performance:

> seemed to embody and realize conceptions which had hitherto assumed no distinct shape. But dearly do we pay all our life after for this juvenile pleasure, this sense of distinctness. When the novelty is past, we find to our cost that instead of realizing an idea, we have only materialized and brought down a fine vision to the standard of flesh and blood. We have let go a dream, in quest of an unattainable substance.
>
> (Lamb and Lamb 1908: 126)

Mocking flesh and blood, Lamb ignores the rich complexities of movement, gesture, intonation, acting; it might just as readily be thought that performance elaborates the inert writing on the page, materializing it into the densely ambiguous practice of social life. Instead, anticipating the values of later commentators—both Harold Bloom and Harry Berger, Jr come to mind—Lamb senses that the deepest access to the plays, our richest encounter with what Shakespearean drama *is*, takes place in reading. Shakespeare 2.0 requires a more sophisticated operating system than theatrical convention, one that indeed drives different aesthetic hardware: the solitary reader. Shakespeare 2.0 is software for reading, and running Shakespeare 2.0 on a residual platform—the stage—seems to lose a significant degree of functionality.

Resistance is futile: with the rise of print as the dominant means for the dissemination of dramatic writing, the literary identity of Shakespeare and the primacy of fundamentally literary ways of calibrating page and stage was assured, not least by the now common-sense understanding that reading guarantees the rich, ambiguous multiplicity of Shakespeare while the theater can only illustrate a single, "derivative" reading (Bristol 1996: 61).[3] Yet, nearly from the moment of print's achieved cultural dominance in the nineteenth century, its displacement of the identity of drama from the stage to the page was complicated by the rise of new technologies for making and recording performance. In its first century or so, film viewing had much in common with theater: you could see a film several times when it was first released, but were then reliant on art-theater and campus film-club "revivals" to see that production again. While the film performance remained "the same" (degradation of the film stock aside) and so seemed to participate in print's assertion of mechanical reproduction as the guarantor of the work's identity, access to film performance participated in the occasional structure of live performance.

Video, more specifically the plunging price of video players, trans-formed this occasion, making it possible to view Shakespeare films and recordings of stage plays at home. More importantly, widespread access to video performance transformed the Shakespeare film into a readily readable, re-readable and citable document, an instrument of criticism and pedagogy with a perdurable and disseminated existence, like an essay or a book. For all that film and video have renovated Shakespearean performance in the modern era, contributing at once to new theatricalities as well as enabling the teaching of Shakespeare-in-performance (what we might, with considerable reservation, call "Shakespeare Performance Studies"), in some ways the uses of recorded Shakespeare continue to echo the "derivative" relationship of per-formance to print that informs print culture. Essay topic: How do the Zeffirelli and the Luhrmann films present different interpreta-tions of *Romeo and Juliet*? Be specific and be sure to cite examples from the text.

And yet, while recorded Shakespeare enables a print-oriented pedagogical culture to treat performance like a book—most often like a critical book offering a narrow *interpretation of the play*—film and video nonetheless evade and exceed the categories of print. They encode the drama within both a technical apparatus (the evolution of cameras, improved depth of field, color, etc.) and an ideology of the visible (perspective, camera angles, editing conventions, realism) that stand markedly outside the distinctive visualities of both early modern and late modern stages, and of literature as well. With the rise of recording technologies—photography, film, television, radio, video, digital reproduction—the identity of Shakespearean drama has again undergone a cultural transformation: performance is no longer an evanescent thing, a local thing, nor even a time-bound temporal thing. Though it is possible to stop, start, and replay the performance, the typically public film showing (Shakespeare 2.1?) generally preserves the temporal continuity of live performance. The increasingly domestic video performance (Shakespeare 2.2?) facilitates rewinding and replaying, and adds the retemporalizing functions of fast forward and reverse; it also relocates performance to the privacy of the home. But digital Shakespeare, Shakespeare 3.0, is released from a single platform of production and from a single site of consumption. Shakespeare 3.0 is mobile, portable—play the DVD on your TV or computer or portable DVD player, download it to your video iPod.

At the same time, digital technology also shares a curiously familiar principle with the apparently transcended technology of the book: random access memory. Packaged in its codex-emulating slipcase, divided into "chapters" and readily "bookmarked," enabling an instantaneous shuffling between the now-discrete moments of performance, Shakespeare 3.0 articulates performance as a commodity for personal consumption, read in the private, portable, legible structure of the book. Shakespeare 3.0 is our contemporary with newly pervasive immediacy: an archive of Shakespeare performance is delivered to my desktop, not in the cumbersome form of big film reels, nor even in the more convenient VHS format, but in the bookish form of the DVD, so easy to page around, view a scene, stop it, dwell on the particulars, and compare to another scene, or another film. Indeed, despite the tired claims that performance is always opposed to writing, performance is now delivered through the same medium as writing, the computer screen, and is of course technically identical to writing, composed of bits of binary code. Shakespeare 3.0 appears as a window next to a text I am writing, sometimes with a window showing a Folio or Quarto page, perhaps even a digitized photo facsimile of an earlier release, the classic 1.0 version of 1623. Like many of the documents I read, Shakespeare 3.0 can be downloaded directly to my desktop: writing, print, performance occupy the same virtual space, and need never occupy any materiality at all. In the digital era, both writing and performance are virtual all the way down.[4]

The analogy between the computer's hardware and the theater's material structure and personnel, between the computer's operating system and the theater's basic conventions of training, production, and performance, and between the computer's software and the text, the dramatic script that directs the OS (operating system) to undertake a specific set of activities, is hardly exact. My iteration of "Shakespeare 1.0, 2.0, 3.0" more accurately captures the shifting interface between writing and performance in the identity of drama. I am laboring here to re-describe a relatively familiar history in the language of digital culture for several reasons: first, to suggest how deeply our under-standing of cultural processes (and the processes themselves) may be transformed by the metaphors we use to represent them; second, to suggest the more pervasive ways in which our conception of writing and performance might be altered by the application of new tech-nologies; and third, to ask how our contemporary disciplinary regimes engage (Shakespearean) drama. As Jerome McGann argues, the "critical possibilities of digital environments require that we revisit what we know, or what we think we know, about the formal and material properties of the codex" (McGann 2001: 19)—to which we might add, of texts and textuality, and the relation between texts and other means for the representation of writing, such as the stage. How does our understanding of drama change when drama is identified not with the material bodies of live actors (theater), nor with the material traces of printed poetry (literature), but with the technologies of digitized *information*? In moving from Shakespeare 2.0 to Shakespeare 3.0, is our use of technology both reflecting and enabling a dynamic change in the means with which we have understood Shakespeare, and Shakespearean drama, across the troubled interface of "text and performance"? Or are we merely translating the ideology of print culture into a new structure of production?

Despite the analogies between print and digital media as technologies of dramatic storage, Shakespeare's participation in a digital global monoculture is not participation in a culture of signification or *performance*, but in a culture of *information*. In Claude Shannon's classic formulation, the "semantic aspects of communication are irrelevant to the engineering problems" confronted by digital communications technologies (Shannon 1964: 27). Information is a function of choice, of our ability to choose from alternatives, but not quite in the way that laymen (that is, most of us) might think, confusing *information* with *meaning*. Remembering that while the computer descends from Charles Babbage's imagined Difference Engine (1822), in the engineering sense, information happens when an isolated event in a field of variables—a variation in the frequency of a signal, for example—has the probability of making a difference, of enabling a significant distinction to be made. Although all information systems require some degree of redundancy, the *value of information* is defined on the curve of probability: the probability of information increases as the probability of redundancy decreases.[5] Digital technologies depend on this conception of information, the probability that, as Mark C. Taylor suggests, this difference "*makes a difference*. Not all differences make a difference because some differences are indifferent and hence inconsequential. Both too little and too much difference creates chaos," or what Norbert Weiner and others recognized as "entropy," assimilating information to the fundamental principles of physics (Taylor 2001: 110).[6] "Information" is not identifiable with "meaning" in a technological sense: it is *dissociated* from the contextual field of meaning, *abstracted* from a material conveyance, and then *selected* from a field of transmission.

The "performative" consequences of this dissociation of meaning from information are everywhere visible: it is precisely the definition of "information" as a consistent encoding of data capable of being downloaded in different devices (and therefore in different contexts of signification) that enables the contemporary digital revolution, particularly the ability to represent the *same* data—a photograph—on the page of a book, a laptop screen, an iPod, a mobile phone, a T-shirt. This has crucial cultural consequences as well, for allowing "information to have a stable value as it [is] moved from one context to another" enables information, as N. Katherine Hayles argues, to be "conceptualized as if it were an entity that can flow unchanged between different material substrates"—fully identified, in other words, with the binaristic sequence that flows between, say, your laptop and your iPod. It is precisely this ability to abstract "information from context and thus from meaning" that drives the reification of "information into a free-floating, decontextualized, quantifiable entity" (Hayles 1999: 53–4, 9).

Writing is an information system of this kind, involving the repetition with variation of a standard set of elements—letters, punctuation, spacing—that we are able to isolate as coherent signals and then construe according to hierarchically nested protocols, as words, sentences, and paragraphs, which are themselves understood within larger generic structures (novel, poem, play). Digital technology has had a profound impact on our understanding of the materiality of writing: as an instrument of analysis and as a model for the transmission of information, the application of digital technologies has revolutionized our understanding of the history of writing, especially the history of the printed book. Though it is surely true that the Derridean deconstruction of language and the decentering of the Author variously associated with Roland Barthes and Michel Foucault provided the theoretical impulse behind a disseminated view of "textuality," the ease with which texts can now be digitally encoded, stored, and displayed (along with the multiplex nature of "versioning") provided the platform not only for imagining different forms of virtual representation of books, and different ways for performing/ reading performance on the screen, but also for reimagining the history of the book, particularly the different significance that alternative instantiations of the "same" text might have.[7] As McGann suggests, "We no longer have to use books to analyze and study other books or texts. That simple fact carries immense, even catastrophic, significance" (McGann 2001: 168).

The reputed advance of print over oral and manuscript culture was twofold: print enabled a much wider dissemination of textual information and appeared to assert that "information"—the "work" of literature—was a stable entity apart from its specific materialization. Four or five centuries of print culture solidified this view, that *Hamlet* is essentially *the same thing* in various editions. The fact that some of these editions embody the vehicle of the words in very different material (paper, size, binding, illustrations) and cultural terms (editorial apparatus, publishing house), let alone actually materializing different words on the page, bears witness to the extent to which mechanical reproducibility appears to guarantee the intrinsic "logic" of print (Kernan 1987: 48–55). In this narrow sense, the figuration of the "text versus performance" paradigm in the age of print anticipates the rhetoric of digitized information: *Hamlet* should remain the same in various editions, as well as when it is produced on a different platform—the stage—of representation; mechanical reproducibility should guarantee our ability to identify corrupt versions as well, those that are conveyed through corrupting channels of transmission: oral reporting, theatrical performance.

In this view, print culture treats the "drama" at once as instrumentalizing software *and* as representational information, a set of data whose significance should remain unchanged by the various platforms of its materialization. Indeed, even misprints or potentially authorized divergences between editions—sallied, solid—can be regarded as a kind of static, not differences in the authorial message but material occlusions distorting the abstract purity of the signal from author to reader. The New Bibliography of W. W. Greg, A. W. Pollard, Fredson Bowers and others, in its effort to lift the "veil of print" from the underlying, integral "work" of the author in this sense considers print as at once guaranteeing identical transmission and inserting distortion into the signal, degrading the authorial work as it passes into materiality.[8] The Hinman collator is the perfected image of print culture: a difference engine designed to purify the code.

In what ways has the structure of "information culture" had an impact on the text/performance dichotomy that has sustained the understanding of literary drama including Shakespeare since the rise and dominion of print? And how might an understanding of digital culture enable us to shift the terms of that dichotomy today? Information culture makes the material platform irrelevant to the "information" it displays. But surprisingly, one consequence of digital (or information) technology on print has been the *undoing* of the "information-logic" of print: aspects of the early printed texts of Shakespeare that had once seemed like static *corrupting* the authorial code now seem like significant differences, providing information about the writing, transmission, and historical significance of the work of art. The notion that the Quarto 1 (Q1), Quarto 2 (Q2), and Folio (F) texts of *Hamlet* are merely differently valued platforms of the same work has been to a significant degree displaced by the notion that these are distinctly materialized *works*, each inflected by the contexts of productive use. While this sense of the value of different early states of the text was emergent well before the widespread dispersion of digital technologies, it has been deepened and to some extent instrumentalized by the ways digital technologies functionalize writing and texts. The "polynomial" element of Shakespeare's plays, the multiple and confusing speech prefixes, variable spelling, punctuation and capitalization (to say nothing of variants long known to be significant) imply that the "information" actually varies with its material platform; the code is itself changed by the systems it drives, the systems it renders capable of signifying, of *meaning* something (see McLeod 1982).

Furthermore, this "information" version of print has had important consequences for the study of performance, especially of "literary" drama such as Shakespeare. For while it was clearly possible for the drama to have two distinct platforms of realization—page and stage—understood as relatively different means of production for the first century or two of print, by the nineteenth century the modern notion that the stage could and should function like another edition of the text became dominant common sense. It is not surprising that literary scholars such as Harold Bloom still understand drama this way, as the inscription of intended signals that can be "received" through different means (reading, acting), but whose signals should not be significantly altered (in his view, rendered less ambiguous) by the platform on which they are represented. What is a bit more arresting, though, is the persistence of this notion of writing and performance in performance-oriented criticism of the drama. The "stage-centered reading" of Shakespearean drama that arose in the 1970s tends to confirm rather than contest the hierarchy of page-to-stage, working to valorize performances that disclose the "theatrical" essence lodged in the text, in effect working to make theatrical knowledge appealing to literary scholarship (perhaps as a means of institutionalizing this kind of theatrical study in the densely anti-theatrical precincts of English departments). In this sense, understanding the text as "information" designed for a specifically theatrical platform of reception enables readers to filter out the static of merely literary, unstageworthy interpretations. More to the point, it enables us to ground *appropriate* theatrical activities and meanings as the felicitous operation of the determining software in the theatrical operating system (and, yes, the echo of Austin is apposite here); it identifies the excessive, outrageous departures to proper production by identifying those textual elements that should predominate in performance.

The notion that Shakespeare's "theatre was different from any we know today, but the essential act of performance was the same," and that the plays "were written for performance and reveal their true natures only in performance" can be seen as merely reciprocating a print-inflected understanding of dramatic "information" (Brown 1981: 8, 1).[9] Rather than regarding reading as the proper site for the reception and decoding of authentically Shakespearean signals, the first genera- tion of stage-oriented criticism urged "the stage" and "performance" as the privileged site of proper reception of the text's innate signals. The fact that this notion of "the stage" and "performance" is fully dematerialized (despite every "act of performance" being in material terms as historically variable as the printing of books—*what* stage? *which* performance?) reveals that this understanding of Shakespeare's code similarly participates in the abstracting of "the work" from its material register, characteristic both of print and of the "information" culture. Burbage and Branagh are both actors, but surely the differences in training, in the social and cultural role of theater, in the impact of performance technologies and dramatic genres (to say nothing of nutrition, film, Freud, and so on) render them examples of the *same* activity only in something like the way *Pac Man* and *Doom* are both video games. Predictably enough, a critical backlash against the supposed domination of "theatrical" Shakespeare in the contemporary classroom has set in as well, in which the "imaginative labor of turning words on the page of the Shakespeare text into the discourse of criticism" is set against a supposedly naive and enervating appeal to "the authority of performance" (McLuskie 2005: 249).

This paradigm also seems to sustain and mystify the most recent disciplinary conflict in the academic study of dramatic performance, surrounding the rise of "performance studies" as a field and method- ology in the 1980s and 1990s. Given its historical and conceptual predication on print, it is perhaps not surprising that literary studies has had a complex, wary, and often dismissive regard for the drama, and particularly for the study of the drama's theatrical dimension. In the US, at least, this has had clear institutional consequences: the nearly complete disappearance of non-Shakespearean drama (Restoration and eighteenth-century drama, modern drama, contemporary drama, American drama) from graduate and undergraduate teaching in English studies. At the same time, the assimilation of drama to print has had important consequences for its institutionalization in theater departments too, embodied both by the distinctively anti-literary bias of "theater history" and the relatively un-critical orientation of theater "training" on university campuses. Arising in the early 1970s through the collaboration of Richard Schechner and Victor Turner, performance studies has morphed into a diverse "post-disciplinary agenda" (Roach 1996: xii), practiced and institutionalized in different ways at diverse US universities, and indeed understood somewhat differently elsewhere. (In places such as the UK and Canada, which still have a vital, critical and dispersed theatrical culture, "performance studies" is more often taken to include the study of dramatic literature and performance, generally a peripheral element of US performance studies.) In part, the definition of performance studies in the US can be understood as the consequence of an institutional imperative to carve out a zone of theoretically eclectic and politically engaged activity; it embraced a theoretical agenda that could at once rehabilitate and enlarge the study of performance in the traditional humanities and social sciences.

As Shannon Jackson has shown, the marginalization of drama and performance in English studies had partly to do with the anxious desire to masculinize the profession of literary studies in the 1940s and 1950s, particularly at the elite Eastern private universities. In theater departments, the marginalization of a critical or theoretical engagement with drama arose from the largely technical and pedagogical agenda of the land-grant universities. Performance studies can be seen to rearticulate this dialectic in the terms of the institutional and disciplinary history of the past two decades. Jackson regards the "'cultural turns' in humanities and social sciences" as having advanced the study of performance while only "occasionally" producing "a reductive consciousness with regard to the discipline of theatre, ahistorically casting theatre studies as an 'unblurred,' canonical field that awaited dispersal from the interdisciplinary intervention of performance studies." Those instances of reductiveness, however, are hard to ignore, and have been motivated by institutional as much as critical or disciplinary principles. What Jackson calls an "infrastructural preoccupation that both required and maintained" the "epistemological separation" between literary and theatre studies enabled performance studies to refigure the gap (Jackson 2004: 173–4, 217). Performance studies has claimed to liberate the study of performance from both elements of this institutional captivity: freeing it from the perceived textual determinism of literary studies and from confinement to an increasingly residual form of aesthetic performance, theater ("the string quartet of the twenty-first century" in Schechner's memorable phrase), which rarely had much critical purchase in the humanities or social sciences to begin with (Schechner 1992: 8).

This is not to say that performance studies has not crucially shifted the terms, methods, and consequences for the analysis of performance, and even of dramatic performance: several foundational books in the field—Peggy Phelan's *Unmarked*, Joseph Roach's *Cities of the Dead*—make stunning use of dramatic theater to engage with larger questions of performance. What has resulted in the US academy is a powerful blend of theoretical engagement with a wide range of practices and behaviors, "cultural performance and its challenge of social efficacy," as Jon McKenzie puts it (McKenzie 2001: 22). Performance studies' interdisciplinary promiscuity has enabled a closer rapprochement with more traditional areas of inquiry—psychoanalysis, art history, ethnography—in large part by distinguishing between its progressive agenda and the apparently retrograde traditions of theater and drama studies. At the same time, though, this rapprochement has tended both to reiterate and reify conventional attitudes about drama and theater, largely by reproducing the print-era formation of "text versus performance."

The resistance to (especially narrative, text-based) drama in contemporary performance studies is symmetrically reciprocal with the changing technologies through which the "text versus performance" debate has been framed. To the extent that dramatic writing is conceived as an "information" structure, it is readily assimilable to the print-inflected canons that continue to animate performance studies, where plays (far from being underdetermined as they are in literary studies) are generally taken to exemplify an ideologically over-determined, even oppressive archive for the reiteration of dominant cultural values. Plays are thus opposed to a more resistant, localized repertoire of embodied strategies of performance, taken to operate outside the sphere of writing.

I take these terms from Diana Taylor's superb book *The Archive and the Repertoire*, which enables us to situate performance studies within the larger perspective of the historical succession of dramatic technologies. Examining live performance traditions in Latin/o America, Taylor argues that: "Performances function as vital acts of transfer, transmitting social knowledges, memory, a sense of identity through reiterated, or what Richard Schechner has called 'twice-behaved behaviors'" (Taylor 2003: 2–3). However, to seize these "acts of transfer" seems to demand a ground-clearing move that surprisingly reinstalls the print-culture rhetoric of "text versus performance": despite the "deep interconnections of all these systems of intelligibility and the productive frictions among them" (Taylor 2003: 6), attending to performance and embodiment requires displacing "the preponderance of writing in Western epistemologies" (2003: 16). Following the lead of Dwight Conquergood, Taylor sees the specific utility of writing in the sphere of colonial domination as representative of writing as such: literacy and its practice is identified with a coercive stabilization of oppressive "meanings," while the oral, enacted, unwritten but nonetheless significant practices of performance remain the means for the transmission of unlicensed, resistant memory and history.[10] Many indigenous performances evaded written form, and many contemporary performances—political demonstrations as well as "performance art" (though many such works are in fact scripted and published)[11]—avoid the conventional machinery of theater (particularly the notion of a predetermined script that is used to structure the performance). Taylor therefore argues that to engage history through the history of performance requires a shift both in the objects and methods of study, in which we move "the focus from written to embodied culture, from the discursive to the performatic" (2003: 16) and so develop a delicate, tactful and powerful means for analyzing performance that does not reduce it to discursive terms.

While Taylor's account of the uses of popular performance genres to subvert the colonial script is persuasive, reducing this specific historical formation to an essential opposition between the technologies of writing and the practices of performance should give us pause, not least for its ways of echoing the priorities of print culture merely by claiming to reverse them. Writing appears to fix meanings in a culturally dominant and historically unchanging form, and performance forms that use writing—such as dramatic theatre—participate in writing's inevitable reiteration of a dominant history through the mechanical reproduction of *the same*. Unscripted performance, for all its palpable conventionality, seems mobile, always changing, and resistant. If one can hear the accents of editors such as W. W. Greg here, it is no surprise: while an earlier generation of print culture had devalued performance for its transformative "corruption" of writing, a contemporary generation of performance culture values it in precisely the same terms. Indeed, "theater" emerges here as a kind of print-culture fantasy, a stage that could be fully scripted by the book. We can also see this reversal masking as revolution elsewhere along the disciplinary horizon.

This reiteration of "text versus performance" sustains Taylor's methodological distinction between the *archive* and the *repertoire*. The *archive* represents the imagined concatenation of written history, deriving from "the degree of legitimization of writing over other epistemic and mnemonic systems" (Taylor 2003: 18). "'Archival' memory exists as documents, maps, literary texts, letters, archaeological remains, bones, videos, films, CDs, all those items supposedly resistant to change" (2003: 19). Taylor notes that while the archive's documents "might remain the same," what actually "changes over time is the value, relevance, or meaning of the archive, how the items it contains get interpreted, even embodied" (2003: 19). Interpretation supports the archive's fundamental purpose: "the archive, from the beginning, sustains power." The *repertoire*, on the other hand, is not centrally located, despite its manifestation in space and time. If the image of the cultural archive is fixed, the cultural repertoire is mobile, enacting "embodied memory: performances, gestures, orality, movement, dance, singing—in short, all those acts usually thought of as ephemeral, nonreproducible knowledge" (2003: 20). Yet the instability of this opposition is hinted at both by the absence of, say, *acting* from the repertoire (acting is too closely associated with the theater, and so is understood to be plotted by writing), and by Taylor's suggestion that "As opposed to the supposedly stable objects in the archive, the actions that are the repertoire do not remain the same. The repertoire both keeps and transforms choreographies of meaning" (2003: 20). The archive is fixed, like writing, but its objects are only "supposedly stable"; the subversive practices of the repertoire nonetheless have a conventionality so akin to writing that they can be characterized as writing, *graphe*: choreography.

The tendentious artificiality of the distinction between archive and repertoire is fully captured in Taylor's sense of the drama's entombment in the archive: much as bones "might remain the same, even though their story may change," so, too, "*Antigone* might be performed in multiple ways, whereas the unchanging text assures a stable signifier" (Taylor 2003: 19). Like most critics of writing, Taylor assumes a print-culture sense of writing's conventional stability, and assents to the information theory view of drama: writing does not materialize the work as an individual, historical, local performance, nor does it provide software that is itself changed by its use. But Taylor's example points precisely to the drama's troubling place in the history of writing, its anomalous identity as "information," and so to its troubling effect on the paradigm of archive and repertoire. First, we might ask, "What *Antigone*?" The Greek text, itself the result of the critical labors of millennia of scholarship, a text that is always plural, each edition differently concatenating ancient texts and commentaries? A translation? In what language? What "unchanging text" is *Antigone*? And what is the "stable signifier" it assures?

Taylor is surely right that the study of performance requires us to "acknowledge the need to free ourselves from the dominance of the text—as the privileged or even sole object of analysis" (2003: 27), at least to the degree that we regard "the text" as the determining feature of theatrical signification. And while she suggests that the tendency to "treat all phenomena as textual" differentiates the practices of cultural studies from the emerging paradigms of performance studies, we might also think that Taylor's monolithic portrayal of writing, drama, and theater encodes her paradigm in a "literary legacy" to the degree that she regards the rhetoric of print as essentially defining dramatic writing, and so the functioning of dramatic performance. For Taylor, the dramatic theater is a bland platform for the transmission of scripted data, from the dead hand of the author through the scripted performances of the archivist actors to the deadened minds of the audience. Although some theatre certainly does work in this way, it seems fairer to say that the practices of the repertoire intervene and enact the process of transmission; embodied practices such as editing, reading, memorization, movement and gesture produce both a sense of what the text *is* and what *we want to say with and through its use, what we want to make it signify.*[12]

Taylor's notion of the fixity of the archive and the mutability of performance may seem oddly overemphatic to anyone involved in the apparently overdetermined field of Shakespeare studies. Here the archive has become radically unfixed (which text?) while the repertoire of performance is *applied* to the performance of drama with the kind of interventionist rigor Taylor reserves for non-theatrical performance. The embodied knowledges and practices of theater operate as a "process, a praxis, an episteme, a mode of transmission, an accomplishment, and a means of intervening in the world" (Taylor 2003: 15) not only on relatively rare occasions but *routinely,* as is witnessed by the long history of literary resistance to the Shakespearean stage.

The dichotomies archive/repertoire, text/body and page/stage fail to engage the impact of digital culture on the drama, which is to undo the "information" paradigm for the transmission of dramatic "data." For much as print has taken an "information theory" view of theater, the impact of digital culture has been to undo these claims with regard to print itself. The decision of the Oxford editors to use the Folio text as copy text insofar as it registers the theatrical practices closest to the moment of Shakespeare's involvement; the widespread contemporary preference for parallel texts of *King Lear* over conflated texts; and renewed attention to how a given edition materializes a specific, specifically meaningful work: all these practices resist the stability of "the work" of Shakespeare and the possibility of its merely iterative transmission, the function that Taylor assigns both to the *archive* and to performances of "archival" works. In this regard, then, performances emerge not as "new editions" but in effect as new works, not dependent for their authority on the transmission of authorized "information" but asserting a specific kind of authority through the means by which they materialize or operationalize the drama. While there is certainly an archive of printed, recorded plays, it is simply false to claim that this materialization is, in effect, a merely mechanical form of reproducibility. Although performers and performance scholars would have some reason to bridle at this remark, McGann's sense that "editing is the paradigm of performance scholarship" has force here (McGann 2001: 114). To McGann, the editor is not merely revisiting the bones in the archive and lending them a new interpretation; he or she is producing the text as a new manifestation, materialization in history, one in which its semantic and bibliographical identities are inseparable. We cannot tell the dancer from the dance.

And yet our ways of analyzing digital culture vis-à-vis drama have not quite caught up with the troubling logic always implied by viewing drama as print "information." We might expect the Shakespeare DVD to revolutionize the "text versus performance" question, but rendering the drama as information has had some surprising consequences. At just the moment that digital culture's engagement with print seems to revolutionize our understanding of print by undoing its "informational" logic, ramifying the book as a complex and mutable performance, digital media—in the case of DVD Shakespeare—represents dramatic performance in terms of the book, implying that the proper access to performance should be bookish: read the chapters, listen to the director. Indeed, placing the DVD on the computer effectively renders the performance not as a focus of attention but as a site for distraction, enabling us not only to page around in the performance but to check sources, see the costume designs, download the lesson plan, order a pizza. More to the point, the place of drama in performance studies emulates this logic, urging a more densely theorized, multiplex view of performance that nonetheless depends on maintaining the otherwise transcended logic of print.

Like all emerging technologies, digital technology is having a deeply contradictory impact on the interpretive formations with which we understand contemporary culture. On the one hand, both as instrument and as paradigm, digital technology has revolutionized our understanding of print; both the history of the book and our sense of the historicization of writing have been irreversibly altered. The critique of "information" that has accompanied the dissemination of digital technology has made an alternative line of critique possible: much as digital technology has revolutionized the history of the book, it should also enable a rethinking of the paradigms for the uses of writing, particularly of forms of writing used across multiple platforms of representation, such as drama. Indeed, the history of dramatic writing and performance itself enacts the materials for this critique, helping to ground the critique of information in a much longer and more significant epistemological problematic. But we will not be able to grasp these opportunities to reflect on an important instrument of cultural transmission—drama, and particularly drama by Shakespeare—if we miscast the terms of the question, and merely reiterate the dichotomy of text versus performance, writing versus embodiment.

We might take solace from the cautionary allegory of a recent play by Manjula Padmanabhan. In *Harvest*, the main character Om decides to provide a better life for his family by contracting with the Interplanta company to donate his organs to a wealthy American. As a result, the family apartment is upgraded to Western standards, and the family is forced to live an infection-free life, ingest plastic food, and generally be farmed for their antiseptic healthy organs, soon to be delivered to America. At one point in the play, it appears that the guards mistake Om's brother Jeetu for him, and take him away to have his eyes removed; but when he returns, they have replaced his eyes with an optical feed, one that injects his brain with the virtual sensation of embodiment: he sees the beautiful American harvester, Ginni, all the time. As the play proceeds, Jeetu finally donates his entire body to Ginni. More literally, Ginni is downloaded into his body, given an embodied existence, while he (ecstatically) uploads his mind into the computer, where the fact of his disembodiment is made irrelevant through the fact that he continues to have sensation, experiencing himself as virtually "embodied." Padmanabhan's savage farce resonates with the notorious fantasy of Hans Moravec's *Robot*, in which Moravec imagines the blissful day when he will be able to upload his mind to the computer, escaping the tattered rags and bones of the body altogether. As an allegory of drama, *Harvest* suggests that the drama itself is known through its various materialities: new book, new information; new bodies, new information. The play's bodies—the page and the stage, different books, different actors—are not exchangeable "information" platforms. Not only does the text fail to determine the performance, it is itself changed by performance, by production and reproduction, by each and every encounter with the repertoire of life.

NOTES

1 See Erne 2003; for further discussion of the impact on the modern sense of drama of a print-centered understanding of Shakespearean authorship, including both Erne's and W. W. Greg's views, see Worthen 2005: Chapter 1.

2 On the economics of play publication, see Blayney 1997, the subsequent challenge by Farmer and Lesser 2005, and Blayney's 2005 response.

3 Lamb's views persist in Harold Bloom's sense that "In the theater, much of the interpreting is done for you, and you are victimized by the politic fashions of the moment" (Bloom 1998: 720). See also Harry Berger's lively understanding of how "imaginary audition" attempts to preserve the dialogical character of dramatic writing while not limiting the reader to the material meanings of the stage (Berger 1989).

4 I explore some of these issues, particularly the relationship between information technology, theatrical technology, and the structure of the DVD in "Performing Shakespeare in digital culture" (Worthen 2007: 227–47).

5 That is, if we are choosing between two equally probable messages, then the information value of each is relatively high; since both messages are equally probable, then the choice of one over the other implies a significant differentiation. If one message is considerably more probable than the other, its information value is relatively low; in the series 2–4–6–8– . . . the probability that 10 follows so exceeds the probability of it not being 10 that there is relatively little information implied when 10 appears next (although if 11 were to appear, a new binary would arise: is the 11 surprising "information" or the result of static or interference in the system?). If there is only one message

to choose from, there is no information to communicate; much as adding 1 to the series 1–1–1–1– ... conveys little information, so, too, saying "what a storm!" during a hurricane might be a meaningful act, but not really informational. Or think about reading any English sentence. If the first word begins with the letter *J* the probability that the next letter will be *b, c, d, f, g, j, k, l, q, r, t, v, w, x,* or *z* is zero, so the number of alternatives is substantially smaller than if the first word begins with the letter *A*, which can be followed either by a space or by any letter of the alphabet. In this case, then, there is considerably greater freedom of choice after an initial *A* than after an initial *J*, so there is more information communicated by the letter after the *A* than after the initial *J*. I have taken this example from Warren Weaver (Weaver 1964: 11).

6   Norbert Weiner—the inventor of cybernetics, control-via-feedback— argues that the "transmission of information is impossible save as a transmission of alternatives. If only one contingency is to be transmitted, then it may be sent most efficiently and with the least trouble by sending no message at all. The telegraph and the telephone can perform their function only if the messages they transmit are continually varied in a manner not completely determined by their past, and can be designed effectively only if the variation of these messages conforms to some sort of statistical regularity" (Wiener 1962: 10; the first edition was published in 1948).

7   For some background, see Gary Taylor 1993 and 2000. Jerome McGann has outlined this trajectory in two landmark books, *The Textual Condition* (1997) and *Radiant Textuality: Literature After the World Wide Web* (2001).

8   The phrase "veil of print" comes from Bowers 1955: 87. See also Greg 1951. The critique of the New Bibliography is now relatively familiar, but an excellent summary can be found in Maguire 1996.

9   J. L. Styan's landmark effort to bring about a colloquy between critical and directorial practice might also be seen in these terms; see Styan 1977. I discuss this interplay in somewhat different terms in Worthen 1997, as well as the misapplication of J. L. Austin's "performative" in both literary and theatrical studies in Worthen 2003.

10   See Conquergood 1995, Conquergood 1991, and Conquergood 1992.

11   See Worthen 2005: Chapter 3.

12   I recently returned to the University of Texas Harry Ransom Humanities Research Center to work on Samuel Beckett's papers; since the last time I used this archive, both the exterior and interior

of the building have been extensively redesigned and rebuilt. The reading room is on a different floor, looks nothing like the old reading room, and access is provided in new ways. The old card catalogue has been replaced by an online catalogue so I arrived with call numbers in hand, ready to copy them onto the paging forms (which have not changed). In this respect, our sense of the archive is continually modified by the repertoire of behavior with which we encounter it.

5

SHAKESPEARE FOR READERS

Lukas Erne

In *Shakespeare as Literary Dramatist*, published in 2003, I argued for an alternative to the Shakespeare many have long believed in, so it is perhaps appropriate to invoke that argument as my starting point here.[1] *Shakespeare as Literary Dramatist* offers an alternative to the beliefs that Shakespeare was indifferent to the publication and afterlife of his plays and that the only form of publication he ever sought for his plays was the stage. It suggests instead that Shakespeare was acutely aware of and cared about his rise to prominence as print-published dramatic author, that Shakespeare and his fellow actors of the Lord Chamberlain's Men had a policy of having Shakespeare's plays published, and that Shakespeare anticipated and catered to a readership for his plays.

If Shakespeare was not simply a jobbing playwright but a self-conscious literary dramatist, then this may help us understand why many of his plays seem too long to have been performed in their entirety. They may be too long because Shakespeare wrote his plays with a double reception in mind, the page and the stage, and knew that the long, reading versions would be considerably abridged before reaching the stage. There is ample evidence for such a practice. Ben Jonson's *Every Man Out of His Humour* (1600) prints the play "*AS IT WAS FIRST COMPOSED* by the AUTHOR B. I. *Containing more than hath been Publickely Spoken or Acted*" (title page). John Webster's *The Duchess of Malfi* (1623) includes "diuerse *things Printed, that the length of the Play* would not beare in the Presentment" (title page). In the address "The Stationer to the Readers" in the 1647 "Beaumont and Fletcher" Folio, the bookseller Humphrey Moseley tells us that when the plays of Shakespeare's successors were performed, "the *Actours* omitted some *Scenes* and Passages (with the *Authour's* consent) as occasion led them". Since Shakespeare's plays are, on average, considerably longer than those in the "Beaumont and Fletcher" Folio, it seems very likely that many of Shakespeare's plays were substantially abridged too.

A correlative of the argument that many of Shakespeare's play texts were originally too long and thus would have been abridged before reaching the stage is that the texts that have come down to us do not correspond to those that were performed on stage. This ought to have serious repercussions on how scholars editorially mediate Shakespeare to today's readers. Prior to the 1980s, the dominant paradigm in the transmission of Shakespeare's plays had been to try to recover the text as the author originally conceived it.[2] With the publication of the influential Oxford *Complete Works* in 1986, however, the stated aim became to edit not so much an original, authorial but a "socialized," theatrical text (Wells *et al.* 1987: 16). The Oxford editors "have devoted [their] efforts to recovering and presenting texts of Shakespeare's plays as they were acted in the London playhouses" (Wells and Taylor 1986: xxxvii), producing an edition for "anyone who wishes to consider Shakespeare's works *as performed* in his lifetime" (Wells *et al.* 1987: 16; italics in original). In practice, this means, for instance, that the Oxford editors base their edition of *Hamlet* on the First Folio text (*c.*3,550 lines) rather than the earlier Second Quarto text (*c.*3,800 lines), which seems to be based on Shakespeare's "foul papers," because they believe that the Folio corresponds to the play as it was performed.

The editorial theory of the Oxford Shakespeare has been incisively discussed by David Scott Kastan. He writes that the edition seeks:

to present the "texts of Shakespeare's plays as they were acted in the London playhouses which stood at the center of his professional life." But how are we to know how "they were acted"? How can this information be recovered from the witness of the early printed play texts? ... an appeal to the promptbook can no more certainly be used to reconstruct a performance text than an appeal to the playwright's "foul papers" can be used to reconstruct authorial intentions, not least because the promptbook is itself no less a category of desire than foul papers are. No early promptbook of any Shakespeare play survives, and none exists for any play of the period that would suggest that it was intended as a definitive playing text.

(1999: 65)

Paul Werstine has described "the quest for a stable entity called a 'performing text'" with the word "quixotic" (1988: 169). Given the unbridgeable gap that separates the printed Shakespeare texts from what would have been performed, it seems undeniable, as Andrew Gurr has pointed out, that "the current shift of editorial target from the author's copy untouched by theatre hacks to the script as it was first staged, which is the announced aim of the collected Oxford edition of 1986 and of almost all subsequent editions and series of editions, must be acknowledged to be unattainable" (2004: 71–2). Indeed, if the Oxford editors had based their edition on the versions that bring us closest to the plays "as they were acted in the London playhouses," they would have been obliged to offer readers the theatrical abridgements that we guess—imperfectly recorded—behind the "bad quartos." Gurr makes this point about *Henry V*: "Oxford's principle required them to print not the author's foul papers but the quarto text" (2004: 76).[3] Ann Thompson and Neil Taylor, editors of the recent Arden *Hamlet*, similarly recognize that Q1, the shortest of the three substantive texts (c.2,200 lines), is "the only one of the three that could plausibly have been acted in its entirety" (2006: 8, 11).

The Oxford editors' desire to recover the play as it was performed has had profound effects not only on their and subsequent editors' choice of copy text but also on the treatment of stage directions. Since stage directions in Shakespeare's early playbooks are relatively scarce, Wells has argued that "the editor needs to identify points at which additional directions, or changes to those of the early texts, are necessary to make the staging intelligible" (1984: 68). He adds: "Needless to say . . . the editor has to think in terms of the Elizabethan stage. No serious editor, I suppose, would disagree with this" (1984: 70). Yet it has been argued that the Oxford editors' interventionist editing of staging, although supposedly undertaken "in terms of the Elizabethan stage," results not in a genuine recovery of how the staging was but of how we now think it should have been. As M. J. Kidnie has written, "it is a mistake to assume that the staging we currently lack would seem familiar or natural to us, in keeping, that is, with our own contemporary theatrical expectations." Rather than telling us how a play was performed in Shakespeare's time, the Oxford editors' added stage directions result, as Kidnie adds, in "a specifically modern and, for this reason, accessible virtual performance" (2000: 465, 466).

In the introduction to the Norton Shakespeare, Stephen Greenblatt has warned us against "the dream of the master-text," a stable, "definitive" text that grants us unproblematic access to what Shakespeare wrote (1997: 71). Greenblatt's point is well taken. Nevertheless, it seems that the greatest fallacy that has bedeviled editorial theory and practice in Shakespeare studies in the last twenty odd years is not the old-fashioned "dream of the master-text" but the seemingly appealing but in fact illusory dream of the performance text, which has found its most influential expression in the Oxford *Complete Works*.

What seems to motivate the attempted editorial recovery of the play "as it was performed" is that, independently of whether the performed play text *can* be recovered, it is what *should* be recovered, since plays were written to be performed. Yet this idea is complicated not only by the evidence that Shakespeare desired publication on stage *and* page but also by what makes Shakespeare's plays still available to us today. Early modern theatrical scripts of Shakespeare's plays have not survived, whereas printed texts have; and the very existence of these printed texts means that they were not only written to be performed but also printed to be read. While the number of spectators was no doubt superior to that of readers of Shakespeare's plays, the number of the latter is by no means negligible. Fifty-eight quarto or octavo editions of Shakespeare's plays were printed before the publication of the First Folio in 1623. If we assume an average print run of 800 copies (Blayney 1997: 405–10), that makes a total number of copies approaching 50,000, many of which are likely to have gone through the hands of several readers.

Rather than trying to recover the irretrievably lost early modern theatrical performances, I propose to pursue here the more modest aim of focusing on what can be recovered: the early modern texts printed for readers in those thousands of early quarto and octavo copies, and in hundreds of copies of the First Folio in 1623. An aim of this undertaking is to recover what is specifically *readerly* about early modern Shakespeare playbooks—not the dialogue, which is read by readers and heard by audiences alike, but that part of the dramatic text to which only a reader has access: the stage directions (which, as Anthony Hammond has rightly argued, include speech headings) (1992: 75–7). In Shakespeare studies, stage directions have been studied chiefly for evidence about, first, the nature of the manuscripts from which the printed editions were set up and, second, early modern staging practices. The first pursuit was important for the New Bibliography movement and is exemplified by W. W. Greg's "Appendix of Illustrative Stage Directions" in *The Editorial Problem in Shakespeare* (1942: 158–81). The second has been important for stage historians such as Alan Dessen and Leslie Thomson, who have been studying stage directions for the "theatrical vocabulary" they provide (1999: vii). Useful and accomplished though much of it has been, this symptomatic criticism, analyzing stage directions as signs or indications of something else that precedes or follows it, has prevented us from focusing on the stage directions themselves as part of the dramatic text.

What may have contributed to this lack of attention is the free editorial treatment of stage directions in modern editions. Now I would agree that expanded and regularized speech headings and added stage directions are often useful for students and actors. I do not advocate "unediting" Shakespeare. Yet editors' interventions can obscure the fact that "most stage directions are authorial in origin" (Dessen and Thomson 1999: viii–ix). There have been isolated voices reminding us that "one should not forget that [stage directions] form part of authorial speech" (Pavis 1988: 89), and that "stage directions remain an element of the literary dramatic text as integral as dialogue" (Kidnie 2000: 462), but the attitude that dialogue text is somehow a more important part of the dramatic text than the stage directions, that the former is the "primary text" and the latter the "secondary text," clearly lives on.

At least in one respect, however, this hierarchical order should arguably be reversed and the non-dialogue text considered the privileged part of the dramatic text. As we listen to Shakespeare's dramatic dialogue in the theater, the author disappears behind all the characters to whom he gives a voice. Indeed, this has been described as Shakespeare's "greatest quality as a dramatist": "Shakespeare is the supreme ventriloquist. He can enter into the hearts and minds of a vast range of characters, often expressing diametrically opposed opinions, leaving us with no certainty as to which of their points of view he might have agreed with" (Wells 2005: 14). Yet readers, unlike spectators, also have access to the non-dialogue text, the text, that is, in which Shakespeare does not give voice to one of his characters and where we may therefore hope to observe him speaking in his own voice.

This view is developed by Marga Munkelt, who, in a rare article devoted to the literary dimension of stage directions, has argued that they can occasionally serve as "a possible reflection of various points of view in literary and theatrical interpretations" and thus as "a key to the author's intentions" (1987: 253). Munkelt focuses on the entrances of groups of characters and shows that these entrances usually follow certain conventions, in particular, strict adherence to rank, meaning that social importance has precedence over theatrical importance. So in the opening stage direction of *The First Part of Henry IV* (Q1, 1598), Lord John of Lancaster follows after the king but precedes Westmoreland, despite the fact that Henry's son does not speak whereas Westmoreland does. But at the beginning of what corresponds to Act 3 in Q1 *Richard II* (1597) is the following stage direction: "*Enter Duke of Hereford, Yorke, Northumberland, Bushie and Greene prisoners*" (E4r).[4] As Munkelt points out, Bolingbroke (here given his official title at this point of "Duke of Hereford") is not yet king, but the extent of his power is not only dramatized in the play (the execution of Bushy and Green shows him fully in control) but is also suggested by the order of the entrance direction, which places him before York, his uncle, who "precedes him not only in age but also in his official position as the King's deputy" (1987: 256). Thus extra prominence is given to the person out of place in terms of official ranking.

Another significant stage direction occurs at the point where modern editions start Act 5 of *The First Part of Henry IV* (Q1, 1598): "*Enter the King, Prince of Wales, Lord Iohn of Lancaster, Earle of Westmerland sir Walter Blunt, Falstalffe* [*sic*]" (I1v). Falstaff is the only character who is deprived of his title—"sir Walter Blunt," but not "Sir John Falstaff." He appears at the very end of the list of characters, far removed from Prince Hal. The direction contrasts strikingly with that at the beginning of the play's second scene: "*Enter prince of Wales, and Sir Iohn Falstaffe*" (A3v). Here, names and titles are formally recorded, although Hal and Falstaff address each other very informally throughout the scene as "Hal," "lad," and "sweet wag" (A3v). In 5.1, Hal offers to fight Hotspur in single combat and decisively turns away from his former companion Falstaff, silencing him impatiently ("Peace chewet, peace", I2r), and, in a moment that looks ahead to the rejection scene in *2 Henry IV*, he tells him to "Say thy prayers" (I3r). It is thus interesting to notice that the stage direction seems to participate in Falstaff's fall from favor.

Munkelt establishes that "stage directions as non-verbal material can provide both literary and theatrical interpretations" (1987: 268), but she does not address another significant area of specifically readerly dramatic text, namely variations in the appellation of characters in stage directions and speech headings. A few instances of such variation are well known. The character now usually called "Lady Capulet" is referred to as Mother, Wife, Lady, Old Lady, or Capulet's Wife in speech headings (Q2, 1599). The Countess in *All's Well that Ends Well* is variously called Mother, Countess, Old Countess, Lady, and Old Lady (F, 1623). Puck is sometimes Robin (Goodfellow). A common variation is that between name and title: Theseus is sometimes Duke, Hippolyta Duchess, and Titania Queen. Claudius in *Hamlet*, Lear, John in *King John*, the Richards and the Henrys are also simply called King. Several characters are variously referred to by their name or as clown, including Costard in *Love's Labour's Lost* and Launcelot in *The Merchant of Venice*. Others fluctuate between name and racial label: Shylock is sometimes Jew; Aaron is sometimes Moor.

In an influential article about variation in non-dialogue naming, R. B. McKerrow explained in 1935 that the designation of a character in early Shakespeare playbooks often changes "according to the particular aspect of his personality which is at the moment prominent" (1935: 459–60). However, writing in the heyday of the New Bibliography, McKerrow did not raise the question of what the designation changes might tell us about Shakespeare's perception of a character at various points of the action. Rather, he was interested in how non-dialogue naming "may throw a light on the genesis of the MS [manuscript] used by the printer as copy," and went on to argue that "a play in which the names are irregular was printed from the author's original MS" but that "a copy intended for use in the theatre would surely, of necessity, be accurate and unambiguous in the matter of the character-names" (1935: 460, 464). McKerrow's theory remained long unchallenged but has received two serious blows in the last twenty years. First, it has been established that non-dialogue naming in early modern theatrical manuscripts can be just as irregular as in authorial ones (Werstine 1988; Long 1997). Second, Richard F. Kennedy (1998) has argued that naming variation in a number of early Shakespeare quartos originates not with the author but with the printers at the press. Speech headings are printed in italics, and a compositor had a lower provision for italic than for regular roman type. If many of the same speech headings (or many speech headings starting with the same initial) appeared on the same page or sheet, they could create type shortage (especially for capitals); if so, Kennedy argues, compositors felt free to adopt a different speech heading.

Recent scholarship thus confirms that naming variation was fairly common in theatrical manuscripts but also warns us that not all fluctuations in a printed Shakespeare playbook need have originated with the author. It remains true that "Each time he summoned a character, Shakespeare was free to rename her, and he was just the author to exploit that freedom" (Cloud 1991: 92). However, before we build an argument on a specific naming variation, we would do well, following Kennedy's article, to test whether the speech prefix in the printed book is likely to be identical with that written by Shakespeare. For instance, the alternation of "*Iew*" and "*Shylock*" in Q1 and F *Merchant of Venice* has attracted attention (Drakakis 2000), so it seems important to know that Kennedy, at the end of more than ten pages of dense bibliographical analysis, writes that the "inescapable

conclusion . . . is that Shakespeare put '*Iew*' as [speech prefix] throughout his manuscript to designate the character modern editors have
changed to '*Shylock*'" (1998: 202).

What is true independently of the origins of specific variation is
that extra-dialogical naming variation exposes a reader to an experience
not shared by a spectator, an experience that deserves to be analyzed.
What this experience would seem to suggest is that dramatic character,
in an early Shakespearean playbook, is not as stable a concept as
modern editorial regularization implies. It further suggests, in keeping
with "the inherently social nature of drama and theater," that "the
identity of dramatic character need not be an internal affair; it can
be relational and interactive" (Cloud 1991: 93). Lady Capulet's speech
heading is "*Wife*" when she enters with her husband in the first scene
(A4r), but it is "*Mo*[*ther*]" at the end of her encounter with Juliet in
the third scene (C1r). Similarly, a speech by the Countess in *All's Well
that Ends Well* is ascribed to her by two speech headings: before Helen
enters, she is simply the "*Cou*[*ntess*]" (TLN 443); following Helen's
entrance, she is the "*Old.Cou*[*ntess*]" (TLN 451).[5] As Randall McLeod
points out, "the new speech tag . . . states, in the author's voice, that
the speaker of the dialogue to follow is *Old.*," an example that nicely
illustrates McLeod's more general points that Shakespeare's "specific
choices of tag do interpret dialogue through selective emphasis" and
that the "variant speech tags . . . remain behind in Shakespeare's
'voice'" (Cloud 1991: 90–2). While Shakespeare usually disappears
behind his characters, "invisible, refined out of existence, indifferent,
paring his fingernails" (Joyce 1956: 219), speech prefixes occasionally
allow a rare glimpse of him, though one which is reserved for his
readers.

Several of Shakespeare's history plays offer fertile ground for analysis
of speech headings as "a response of the writer (or of the observer)
to the hero moment by moment" (McLeod 1986: 137–8). This is
particularly true for plays in which the crown changes heads. Although
the plays usually make clear at what point a character is or is not
king, Shakespeare's speech headings at times reflect not a clear-cut,
political but a more dynamic, psychological identity. In Q1 *Richard III*
(1597), for instance, once he has ascended the throne, Richard is
consistently called king in stage directions and speech headings, until,

in the last act, after the ghosts of his victims have cursed him in his sleep and he wakes up from his dream, fearful and despairing, he is simply "Richard" (L4v). The next stage direction momentarily restores him to "King Richard" (sic, M2r) when he assembles and addresses his troops before the battle, but once in battle, deprived of his horse, he enters simply as "Richard" (M3r). A few lines later occurs the last stage direction mentioning him: "*Alarum, Enter Richard and Richmond, they fight, Richard is slain* . . ." (M3r). By carefully participating in the disintegration of Richard's power, the speech headings confirm what Peter Stallybrass has written: "in the Renaissance the personal name is often the name of deprivation, the name of a person when stripped of social function" (2000: 108).

Richard II offers another instructive example. Up to the scene at Flint Castle, all stage directions and speech headings in Q1 (1597) refer to the monarch as "King." But in this scene—the play's turning point—the king is simply "Richard" when he enters (F4v). Theatrically, Richard's deposition is anticipated by his descent to the "base court"— "Downe, downe I come" (G2r); typographically, it is anticipated by his appellation in this stage direction. Speech headings in the deposition scene, not added until 1608, similarly constitute a subjective response to Richard: although he still enters as "king" (H1v), speech headings reflect the loss of regal power we are about to witness by consistently calling him "Rich." (H1v–H3v). When Richard, in Q1, first appears after his abdication, on his way to the Tower, the stage direction reads "*Enter Ric.*" (H2v) and is placed off-center, to the right of the dialogue text, fully enacting Richard's removal from the center of power. In his conversation with the Queen, the first speech heading similarly calls him "Rich[ard]" (H2v), though the appellation reverts to "King" for the rest of the scene. Interestingly, the dialogue shows the same hesitation—the Queen refers to him both as "not King Richard" (H2v) and "the King" (H3v). By the penultimate scene, however, after Bolingbroke has appeared on stage as the new monarch (now called "King" or "King H[enry]"), he is "Rich[ard]" (I3v–K1r) throughout in stage direction and speech prefixes (McLeod 1986: 139–44).

Speech headings in *The Third Part of Henry VI* (First Folio) similarly seem to constitute a subjective response to the character of the king. They also fully participate in the instability of the English crown as dramatized in that play. Henry, the feeble king, recognizes in the opening scene that "my Titles [i.e. title's] weak" (TLN 152), a statement the speech headings seem to reinforce by variously calling him "*Henry*" (or "*Hen.*") and "*King*" (or "*K.*") up to 3.1 in modern editions, the moment when he is captured (TLN 56–1497). Once he has been crowned, the power-hungry Edward, by contrast, is consistently called "*King.*," "*K.Edw.*," or "*K.Ed.*," and this even in the scene (4.3 in modern editions) in which Warwick uncrowns him and has him sent to the Archbishop of York under arrest (TLN 1500–2376). Henry is momentarily restored to royalty in the speech prefixes ("*K. Hen.*," "*King.*") of the scene in which he is released from the Tower and appoints Warwick and Clarence protectors (TLN 2379–2452). Yet by the play's close, in the scene in which Richard kills him, he is again simply "*Hen[ry]*" in the speech headings (TLN 3076–134).

It seems important to add that not in all cases where a character wins or loses a royal title is the shift in power accompanied by unstable, shifting appellation in speech headings or stage directions. For instance, *Henry VIII* offers a clear-cut case: Katherine is "Queen" throughout 2.4 and 3.1, but when she reappears in 4.2 after Anne Boleyn has been crowned, she is "*Katherine Dowager*" (TLN 2548) in the stage direction and "*Kath[erine].*" (TLN 2552–753) in the speech headings. Yet on other occasions, as we have seen, naming variation in speech headings and stage directions fail to conform to what the dramatized changes in rank and title would lead us to expect and thus may be of particular significance in giving the reader access to a more subjective response to the characters.

Variation in non-dialogue naming thus constitutes one source of readerly meaning; naming absent from the dialogue is another. Characters' names in stage directions and speech headings offer privileged access to meaning arguably intended by the author but made available only to readers, not spectators. The king in *Hamlet* is a case in point. He is called "*Claudius*" in Q2 and F in the opening stage direction to the second scene and "*Claud.*" in his first speech prefix in Q2, but never in the dialogue. Claudius, as Harold Jenkins pointed out, "is an unexpected name for a Danish king," which may suggest that it was the result of a deliberate, careful choice, suggested by "the Roman emperor who married Agrippina, his niece and mother of Nero, referred to at [3.2.384]" (1982: 432, 163). Emrys Jones argued that Shakespeare may well have consulted "Suetonius' Life of the Emperor Claudius . . . for some traits of his own Claudius in *Hamlet*" (1977: 27). Suetonius was among the classical authors edited by Erasmus, and it seems likely that Shakespeare also drew on him in *Macbeth* (Jones 1977: 27–8). With the name "Claudius" in *Hamlet*, Shakespeare may thus alert readers to significant textual and intertextual meaning, meaning to which he provides no access for spectators, who never hear the name in the theater. The performance critic J. L. Styan has argued that "the stage expanding before an audience is the source of all valid discovery" (1977: 235), a view with which I disagree and which Styan himself arguably contradicts by repeatedly referring to the king in *Hamlet* as "Claudius" (e.g. 1971: 23).

Henry V offers another interesting instance of readerly meaning in the disguised king's famous encounter with three of his soldiers in the night before the battle of Agincourt. Shakespeare provides full names for the soldiers when directing their entrance: "*Enter three Souldiers, Iohn Bates, Alexander Court, / and Michael Williams.*" (TLN 1934–5). John Bates is also mentioned in the dialogue, but the other two are not, though their names, or abbreviated names, reappear in speech headings. Williams and the king famously engage in an argument over the question of the English monarch's responsibility. The king may have the better of the argument, yet without fully dispelling the doubts voiced by his soldier about the legitimacy of his military enterprise. Interestingly, the soldier, nameless for a theater audience, is called "*Will.*" in most of the speech headings (twenty-one times; plus five times "*Williams.*," and twice "*Wil.*"). Indeed, as the argument between the king and his soldier comes to a head, there are sixteen successive alternating mentions of "*King.*" and "*Will.*" on the same page (indeed the same column) of the First Folio (TLN 2038–70). "Will," as a reader of the 1623 Folio may well have remembered, is of course Shakespeare's name for the poet-speaker in his 1609 *Sonnets*, a thin disguise for Shakespearean self-referentiality. It therefore seems significant, as Annabel Patterson has pointed out, that "*Will.*" does in Folio *Henry V* what the play does in general, namely to question the heroic view of the king (1989: 88–91). Patterson calls Shakespeare's use of "*Will.*" "the most private gesture of independence that a playwright writing for the stage could conceive," but it seems more accurate to call the gesture *readerly* rather than purely private (1989: 89).

Other names may be passed over more quickly: the two Capulet servants in the opening scene of *Romeo and Juliet* are called "Sampson" and "Gregorie," names that seem as unusual for servants as "Claudius" is for a Danish king. Sampson recalls the great Hebrew hero whose superhuman accomplishments are recorded in the Book of Judges (Chapters 13–16), while Gregory is a Papal name, in particular the name of the warrior Pope Gregory VII (Levenson 2000: 143). The mock-heroic names of Shakespeare's servants may well serve to stress their self-aggrandizing postures, but again it is important to realize that "Sampson" is a name available only to readers. The king in *Love's Labour's Lost* is called "*Ferdinand K*[ing] *of Nauar*" (i.e. Navarre) in the opening stage direction of Q1, but the only name an audience hears is "Navarre," which is why an audience may have been led to think about Henri of Navarre and recent French politics (Harbage 1962). As there never was a king of Navarre called "Ferdinand," a reader, however, may have been led to speculate about the name's topical significance, and Ferdinando Stanley, Earl of Derby, who died in April 1594 (around the time when London's theatres reopened) clearly provided a possible clue (Yates 1936; Bradbrook 1936).

Several features of *Macbeth* require specifically readerly attention. The play is extant in a single substantive text, printed in the First Folio in 1623. The speech heading for the protagonist is usually "*Macb.*" in F, and stage directions refer to him as "*Macbeth*" throughout. This deserves two comments. First, even though Macbeth is called "King" (TLN 1154) and "his Maiesty" (TLN 1401) in the dialogue, the speech headings and stage directions refuse him the title of king. By contrast, the speech heading for King Duncan is "*King.*" (e.g. TLN 18), though it is "Duncan" in most modern editions. Crowned monarchs in Shakespeare usually have "King" as their speech heading. Lear is an exception in that he is usually referred to as "*Lear*" in speech headings and stage directions, but even he is occasionally called "*King*" in both Q1 (E3r and I4v) and F (TLN 37). Not so Macbeth. When Macbeth first enters after being crowned, the stage direction provides an entrance for "*Macbeth as King*" (TLN 992), not for "King Macbeth," as if distinguishing between seeming and being, the clothes and the man. Throughout the Folio, the non-dialogue text refuses to recognize Macbeth's legitimacy as a monarch. This point is obscured in Nicholas Brooke's edition in the Oxford Shakespeare series (1994), where the opening stage direction of the banquet scene reads: "*Banquet prepared. Enter King Macbeth, Lady Macbeth as Queen, Ross, Lennox, Lords, and Attendants*" (3.4.0). F reads simply "*Enter Macbeth, Lady, . . .*" (TLN 1254).

Second, the speech heading "*Macb.*" is noticeable for its similarity to that of Macbeth's opponent Macduff: "*Macd.*" This is particularly conspicuous when the two are in dialogue: nine speech headings reading "*Macb.*" or "*Macd.*" appear within just over forty lines (TLN 2436–78). This similarity is further emphasized by the fact that occasionally the speech headings of both characters are further shortened to "*Mac.*" and thus become identical (TLN 147, 505, 507, 592, 675, 687, 1274, 1369, 1623, and 1930). It seems interesting, in this context, that even though regicide makes Macbeth the play's chief traitor, Macduff is also styled a traitor by his wife and her murderer (TLN 1764–69, 1806). Malcolm lengthily tests whether Macduff is an adherent or an enemy to Macbeth, and the outcome of the test arguably proves nothing either way (Braunmuller 1997: 88–93). A reading experience of Folio *Macbeth* can thus strengthen the sense that the play moves towards the crucial opposition between Macbeth and Macduff, who, though ostensibly opposed to each other as good is to evil, occasionally appear to be oddly alike.

Another feature of the non-dialogue text might be seen as reinforcing such a reading: two minor characters, Seyton and Seyward, both enter the play in the last act, the one loyal to Macbeth, the other to Macduff. These characters, like Macbeth and Macduff, have speech headings which are identical: "*Sey.*" (TLN 2312, 2388, 2427, 2434, 2481, 2489, 2493, 2495, and 2501 for Seyward; TLN 2248, 2250, 2329, and 2337 for Seyton).

The play further stresses the antagonism between Macbeth and Macduff by providing each of them with a wife: "Lady Macbeth" and "Lady Macduff." Neither of these labels is present in F (they go back to Rowe), nor, in conformity with her husband, is "Lady

Macbeth" ever called "queen" in speech prefixes or stage directions (though she is so referred to in the dialogue—"The Queene (my Lord) is dead" [TLN 2337]). Stage directions call her "*Macbeths Wife*" (TLN 348), "*Macbeths Lady*" (TLN 1151) or simply "*Lady*" (TLN 647, 725, 836, 2111, 2160), and "*Lady.*," "*Lad.*," or "*La.*" serve as her speech headings. "Lady Macduff" is "*Macduffes Wife*" in the stage direction (TLN 1711) and "*Wife*" in the speech headings. In fact, she is never referred to as "Lady" in the text, neither in stage directions and speech headings nor in the dialogue (contrary to "Lady Macbeth" whom Macduff and Banquo call "Lady" at TLN 840, 885, and 894). Clearly, the label "Lady Macduff" became established by analogy to "Lady Macbeth." Yet it may be significant, considering Macduff's unexplained desertion of his wife, that her speech headings keep reminding us that she is his wife. A passage such as "*Wife*. Sirra, your Fathers dead" (TLN 1746) can be seen as profoundly ironic in that it simultaneously spells out that she is Macduff's wife and that she is acutely aware that he does not behave like her spouse, an irony to which the Folio speech headings decisively contribute.

With regards to the witches, recent work has centered on the question of whether they are called "weird sisters" or "wayward sisters" in the dialogue. Holinshed, Shakespeare's source, has "weird," but the First Folio does not, spelling instead "weyward" (compositor A: TLN 130, 355, and 596) and "weyard" (compositor B: TLN 983, 1416, 1686). The only authority the *Oxford English Dictionary* (OED) adduces for believing that "weyward" and "weyard" are seventeenth-century spellings of "weird" is *Macbeth* itself. On the other hand, spelling was in its pre-regulative phase, and an early reader may have inferred both, where we think either/or (De Grazia and Stallybrass 1993: 263–4).

The issue of the sisters' correct epithet may have deflected attention from the question of how present the word "witch" is in the text. In F, several stage directions call them "*Witches*" (e.g. TLN 179) or the "*three Witches*" (e.g. TLN 2), though the speech headings do not and call them "1.," "2.," and "3." instead. In the dialogue, the word "Witch" occurs only once (TLN 104), in the words of "A sailor's wife," as reported by "the first witch":

1. A Saylors Wife had Chestnuts in her Lappe,
And mouncht, & mouncht, and mouncht:
Giue me, quoth I.
Aroynt thee, Witch, the rumpe-fed Ronyon cryes.

Considering "Witch" not only designated a "female magician, sorceress" but was also "a contemptuous appellation" for a malevolent or repulsive-looking woman (OED), an audience, in the given context, might have understood the word as emotive rather than referential.

Whereas "witch" thus only occurs once in the dialogue, the word is omnipresent in modern editions owing to expansion of the speech headings to "FIRST WITCH," "SECOND WITCH," and "THIRD WITCH." Ironically, even the Oxford *Complete Works*, whose editors' stated aim it is to recover the play "as it was performed," thus exposes the reader to a potentially quite different experience from that undergone by a spectator: in this edition, the opening scene consists of a stage direction and eleven lines of dialogue, in the course of which the reader comes across the word "witch" no fewer than ten times. By contrast, an audience does not hear the word a single time in the course of this scene, and only once in the course of the entire play, and thus might have been led to think differently of the "witches" from the way modern readers do.

I have argued that we need to take seriously the editorial and critical repercussions of a Shakespeare who is becoming an increasingly plausible alternative to the one we have long believed in, a Shakespeare whose plays led a double existence, and were intended by their author to lead a double existence, not only on stage but also on the page. One repercussion is that we need to recognize that the plays that have come down do not give us access to the plays as they were performed, only to how they were printed. Instead of chasing a play's unattainable early modern performance, we may therefore want to focus our attention on the readerly specificity of Shakespeare's early modern play texts. I have tried to show that one area of these play texts that still awaits a full examination is precisely the part that no audience ever gets to hear: stage directions and speech prefixes. The relatively free modern editorial treatment of stage directions and speech prefixes makes it particularly important to try to recover how this part of the dramatic text signifies in the early modern printed play texts. Since it is the only part of the dramatic text in which the author does not disappear behind his characters, it seems legitimate to ask whether it occasionally shows us Shakespeare responding to and interpreting features of his own plays. I hope the present analysis has indicated one direction in which the return of the author in Shakespeare studies might profitably lead.

NOTES

1   Erne 2003. I wish to thank Patrick Cheney and Neil Forsyth for their incisive comments on an earlier version of this article.
2   For an influential formulation of this editorial ideal, see Greg 1942.
3   See also Erne 2007: 5–25.
4   References to early printed books are cited using the pagination markers then in use, namely the alphabetically ordered gathering of pages (E, for example), the page within the ordering (4), and the front or back of the page (recto=r, verso=v). Sometimes "sig." is used before such entries. [Ed.]
5   I refer to the through-line numbering (TLN) adopted in Hinman (1996).

6

CUTTING BOTH WAYS

Bloodletting, Castration/ Circumcision, and the "Lancelet" of *The Merchant of Venice*

Patricia Parker

Scalpellus . . . A pen knife: a fine instrument to let bloude with. A lancelet.
Cooper, *Thesaurus* (1578)

The lancelet used by surgeons . . .
Rabelais

A little crooked Lancet . . . the acuitye or poyncte (of) which cutteth on both sydes.
Guillemeau, *French Chirurgerye* (1598)

If you prick us, do we not bleed?
Shylock

The Merchant of Venice—where the knife of the Trial Scene evokes the threat of forcible circumcision or castration by a "Jew," and Morocco, from another circumcised nation, challenges "Let us make incision for your love,/To prove whose blood is reddest" (2.1.6–7)—is pervaded by cuts and incisions of multiple kinds, from Shylock's preparing to cut a "pound of flesh" to the gelding of both "person" and "purse" (Shell 1982: 55), Antonio as a castrated ram or "tainted wether"(4.1.114) and the Jew deprived of both "daughter" and "ducats" (2.8.15). At the same time, it is traversed by the sense of writing (or *graphein*) as a grafting or cutting—making words on "paper" issue "life-blood" (3.2.265–6)—and by reminders of the movement from Old Testament to New, from "carnal" cutting to the spiritual "circumcision of the heart."[1]

Earlier criticism of the play based on such figural progression characterized its trajectory as moving from the "justice" demanded by the Jew to Christian "mercy," foregrounding not only Portia's "quality of mercy" speech and the conversion of Jessica, Shylock's daughter, but the more marginal figure of the "Clown"—called in most editions Lancelot (or Launcelot) Gobbo—who leaves behind the house of the Jew for the punning new "liveries" (2.2.109) of a Christian.[2] What I want to do here, however, is to approach the play's multiple inscriptions of incision or cutting (including castration and circumcision) through the Clown himself—whose very name imports a cultural semantics crucial to both cutting and bloodletting, though this has been obscured by the editorial tradition. I then examine the ways in which his presence within this play of Christian, Muslim, and Jew both evokes the traditional logic of providential progression and undoes it, enabling (in ways appropriate for a knife that famously cut both ways) a double-edged or contrary reading of the trajectory itself.

Ever since Rowe's eighteenth-century printing of "Launcelot" (which appears in none of the early texts of the play), editors have reproduced a name that has generated the critical distraction of a connection with Arthurian legend. But the Clown who appears in the Quartos and Folios as "Lancelet" or "Launcelet" (with the surname "Iobbe") introduces into the play the well-known name for this two-edged knife. The slowness of editors and critics to recognize a meaning that was commonplace in the period underscores not only the imperative to historicize the language of the plays but the need to return to the early texts themselves.[3] At the same time, the figural networks of which this familiar item of material culture was a part provide a signal instance of the importance of going beyond a more narrow focus on the "object" in order to register its overdetermined status.[4]

Contemporary polyglot dictionaries make clear that the uses of this "lancelet" or "launcelet" were crucially related to the central issues of The Merchant of Venice. Palsgrave's Lesclarcissement de la langue francoyse (1530: 237/1) has for English "Lancet" the French counterpart "lancette" for which "lancelet" was the familiar variant, as in Rabelais' reference to "le lancelet qu'utilisent les chirurgiens" (1994: 501). John Baret's Alvearie or Triple Dictionarie (1573) informs its readers that the surgeon's scalpel or cutting knife is "a Lancelette or like instrument," while Thomas Cooper's Thesaurus (1578) provides not only its frequent comparison to a "pen knife" but the definition of Latin Scalper as "A launcelet, cissours, or other yron toole wherewith incision is made." John Rider's Bibliotheca (1589) has "A Launce, launcelot, or surgeons knife, wherewith they use to let blood" and "a Launcelot to cut wounds," making clear that "lancelet" and "launcelot" were simply variable spellings for this incising knife, while Minsheu's Guide unto the Tongues (1617) defines "Launcelot" or "Lancelot" as "a fleame, or Chirurgians instrument" used in "letting blood . . . launcing, cutting, or scarifying," underscoring its use not only for "bleeding" but for cuts in the flesh as well.[5]

Contemporary descriptions likewise underscore not only that "lancing" had the sense of cutting with a lancelet (or its variants lancet, lancer, and lance) but that pricking with its sharp point—as in Shylock's "If you prick us, do we not bleed?" (3.1.64)—was part of its well-known function. Lodge's translation of Seneca on bloodletting advises "Thou needest not to open thy breast with a deepe and vast wound; a lancet will giue way to that great libertie, and in a pricke consisteth securitie" (1614: 288), while Johann Wecker's Compendious Chyrurgerie (1585) advises that the surgeon make "incision" in a fleshly swelling by "pricking it with a lancet point, or quill" (1585: 153).

Launcing is done with a Lancelot . . .
> Gyer, *The English Phlebotomy* (1592)

the Surgeon . . . whetting his lancet to cut the throte of the disease.
> John Boys, *Exposition* (1610)

Have by some surgeon, Shylock, on your charge,
To stop his wounds, lest he do bleed to death.
> Portia in *The Merchant of Venice*

The knife inscribed in the name of "Launcelet" or "Lancelet" was repeatedly featured in surgical and bloodletting texts—from early references to "rasours & lancettes" to the choice of "The Lancet" as the name of one of the oldest medical journals.[6] "Lancelet" (or "lancelot") was used interchangeably with "lancet" throughout the sixteenth century. Ambroise Paré—who provides an illustration (see Figure 6.1)—describes how to make "the lancet enter more easily," so that the "incision" will "open a veine, and draw bloud," warning of the danger that the patient might bleed to death ("you must stop the blood as speedily as you can . . . lest hee poure forth his life together with his blood," Paré 1634: 358), in ways that resonate with Portia's warning to Shylock to have some "surgeon" by. In England, prominent descriptions of this material instrument and its dangers, along with the benefits of bloodletting, abound in the decades leading up to the play. In 1542, the translation of Guy de Chauliac's *The questyonary of cyrurgyens* mentions a lancelet or lancet as an essential part of any surgeon's chest (sig. Aiiir).[7] In 1543, the influential treatise of Giovanni Vigo records under "Incision" the use of a lancelet or "lancet" for cutting an "apostume" (tumor or boil) and underscores the danger of a fatal bleeding in its advice on the veins from which blood might be taken—including in the breast or chest (1543: 116–18, 360–2, 385–8).[8] In 1563, Thomas Gale's *Certaine workes of chirurgerie* cites this knife among the "instruments . . . which are in most use and ought to be had in redynes of the Chirurgian" (sig. 13v), for "phlebotomie or lettynge of blode" (sig. 5v) as well as for fleshly incisions, and warns of the "great flux of blood to folowe" if "it

The figure of a Lancet to let bloud withall.

Figure 6.1 "The figure of a Lancet to let bloud withall"
Source: Ambroise Paré (1634) *The Workes of That Famous Chirurgion Ambrose Parey*, by permission of the Henry E. Huntington Library

happeneth the greate vaynes, and arteries to be cut" (sig. 13v). In 1564, the "newly corrected" edition of William Bullein's *Goodly Regiment against Fever Pestilence* (1564) instructs on how to use the lancelet or "launce" in the "openyng of a vein" to "let the pacient bleede," along with the direction to "launce not verie depe"(1564: 36) lest the incision prove mortal.

The danger is foregrounded yet again in 1566, in John Securis's *A Detection and Querimonie of the Daily Enormities and Abuses Committed in Physick*, which inveighs against abuses by "letters out of bloud" (sig. Diii), warning that "they will cutte" and "they will launce," as they "rashely go to worke in all thynges." The year before it, the English publication of the works of Lanfranco of Milan advises on "howe incisyon shoulde be done in the brest" so that there be no "errore committed" (1565: 71). And in 1585, John Banister's translation of Wecker's *Compendious Chyrurgerie*—which repeatedly refers to the "scarrifying lancet" used for "pricking" the flesh as well as for bleeding (1585: 153, 187)—advises of the swelling called the King's Evil that the surgeon work with his "lancet, by little and little," since "in making incision" there may follow great "profusion of blood" (1585: 88). In ways equally suggestive for *The Merchant of Venice*, where gelding figures almost as prominently as bleeding and blood, he goes on to describe the use of this knife for incisions in the scrotum and testicles, advising the surgeon on how to divide the membrane "with your lancet" (1585: 210).

Closer to the time of the play, even more detailed descriptions of bleeding, "pricking" or cutting the flesh with a lancet or lancelet appeared. William Clowes' *A Proved Practice for All Young Chirurgians* (1588)—whose illustration of a "surgeons's chest" includes a man being bled with this instrument—details its uses for "bleeding," including "a bodie full of euill humors" (1588: 166), and treats of its hazards in an exchange with a "shifting fellow" who refuses to believe that "a prick with a small poynted thing, as is a launcet" can be as "daungerous, as that which is cut asunder by a razour, knife, or other sharpe weapons," when a mere "prick" with one can be deadly (sig. pir). Nicholas Gyer's *The English Phlebotomy* (1592) provides detailed instructions on how to use a lancelet or "Lancelot" that include:

> Launcing is done with a Lancelot or some instrument called in Greeke *Epidermes*; and in Latine *Scalpellum*. The member is cut by little and little with this Chyrurginall instrument, sometime it striketh but the very skinne: sometime it goeth in deeper... and the deeper the Instrument goeth in, the more aboundant is the effusion of blood.
>
> (1592: 288)

Throughout *The English Phlebotomy*, Gyer returns again and again to the dangers of such incisions, contrasting "ignorant Barbers" with the skilled surgeon, who uses "a fine Launcet" with care, so that the incision is not mortal (1592: 201). Most strikingly for *The Merchant of Venice* and its so-called "bloody creditor" (3.3.34), in a period where a bloodletter could be described as "whetting his lancet to cut the throat of the disease" (Boys 1610: 72), Gyer also condemns mercenary "bloodsuckers," "Arabians, barbarous phisitions" (1592: 230), and counterfeit "Iews or Egiptians" who "kill thousands" of "faythful Christians" (sig. A4ii) by bleeding.

In the same decade as the play, two other major discussions of bloodletting and incision make clear the contemporary associations of the two-edged knife evoked by Lancelet's name. Peter Lowe's *The Whole Course of Chirurgerie* (1597) repeatedly refers to the importance of the "lancet" as well as the potential dangers of bloodletting, adding that even if used in a different part of the body, it might effect a castrating or gelding. Commenting on treating of the "veines in the head" that if certain "veines be cutte, they cause a man to be sterile," Lowe claims that such cutting of veins was "practised amongst the *Schites*" (or Shi'a Muslims) to "effeminate them" for use "like women" and cautions that the surgeon's lancet "goe not too deepe" (sig. Cc3r-v). In another passage noting that a surgeon "must haue diuers lancets," some "large, some round pointed" and others "long sharp pointed," he advises on the extreme care that must be taken to "pricke" the "veine softly" rather than "suddenly" (sig. Ddv).

The most detailed illustration of common lancets or lancelets is provided in the translated *French Chirurgerye* (1598) of Jacques Guillemeau, whose title page prominently features a bloodletting and the piercing of a man's naked breast with what is likely this same knife, since so much of his text gives instructions for incisions with it in the breast, scrotum, and other "incarnate & fleshlye" parts. Prominent among his illustrations of the "Instrumentes of Chirurgerye" is an entire page filled with lancets or lancelets of various kinds (see Figure 6.2). According to Guillemeau's key, the smallest ones at the top left corner—the sharp point marked "B" and the rings ("C") with lancelets ("D") hidden within them—are for secretly pricking the fearful but unsuspecting patient without his "perceavinge." The larger lancets depicted on the entire left side—with a razor ("G") for comparison—include ("F") a straight-blade or "rectifyede Lancette, wherwith we open an Apostemation, wherin we make incisiones, & scarifications," called by the "Latinistes" a "Scalprum Chirurgicum" (with "H" to mark the "poyncte" that "cutteth on both sydes"); "The Lancet to phlebotomize called in Latine Scalpellus" ("L"); a "little croockede Lancet"(marked "N," its "acuitye or poyncte which cutteth on both sydes" surrounded by "O's"); and at the lower left corner, "The crooked lancet which is occluded in her case" ("P") and an opened case just barely showing "The blade of the Lancette" ("M") it encloses.[9] The most complicated of all—apart from the secretly pricking rings—is at the top right corner, its blade curving downwards hooked into a privet or surgical probe, described as "A propre Instrumente to launce the fistles [or fistulas] . . . & make a greate inscisione," a cut for which "the foresayede croockede lancet [must] be but reasonable sharpe."

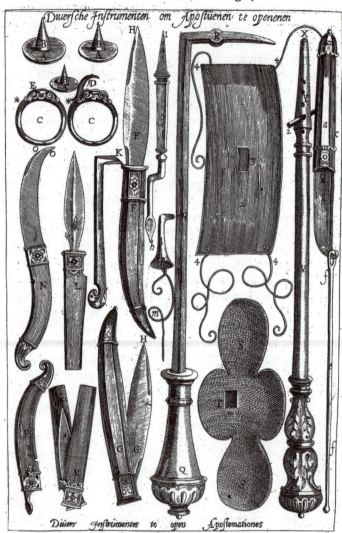

Figure 6.2 "Divers Instruments to open Apostemationes"
Source: Jacques Guillemeau (1598) *The French Chirurgerye*, by
permission of the Henry E. Huntington Library

The text that follows describes the uses of these lancets or lancelets for bloodletting and for "Apostemations" or boils (fol. 17v)—including "Broade & narrow lancets" needed for ample cuts or when the "vaynes lye profoundly occulted in the fleshe" (fol. 28v)—and, as always, the care to be taken lest the patient bleed to death, emphasizing the importance in making certain incisions of not spilling any blood at all but cutting only the "incarnate or fleshye" part (fol. 20v). An entire section is devoted to incisions "with the lancet" in the breast in particular, with care not to "cut in anye vayne, arterye, or synnue, which lyeth occult and buriede" (fol. 19v); while other sections are devoted to incisions in "the Scrotum" or "bagg wherein the testicles are contained," where the surgeon preparing to cut into "the privityes" must "pricke" with "a stronge crooked lancet" (fol. 21r–v), working "gentlye" because of the "daunger of hurtinge of the testicles above" (fol. 22r). A lengthy section devoted to "phlebotomye" or bloodletting similarly advises that "the place, where we will pricke" be chosen carefully and "the poyncte, and acuitye" of the lancet be inserted "not abruptly, and rudely, with a hastye thrust" (fol. 28r) but "gently," taking care that there is no "arterye touched & opened . . . whereby the patient bleedeth to death" and "with great torment endeth his life" (fol. 27v).

The sense that the knife invoked by the name of "Lancelet" was potentially fatal was thus a commonplace part of its repeated description in early modern England. John Woodall's *The Surgeons Mate* (1617)—which typically cites it as a staple of the "Surgeons Chest"—devotes an entire chapter "Of the Launcet" not only to its uses but to the danger it can pose to life itself. Advising the "Surgeons Mate" to carry at "least six of the best sort of launcets" (1617: 18), Woodall warns the barber-surgeon "that his launcets be not too spear pointed" and that the incision be not "overlarge" or "too deep" (1617: 19). Throughout the century following the play—which included the invention of a "Lancet, for the more safe bleeding" that was purposely more "blunt" because of the "harm" in "Blood-letting" when "a Vein be prick'd through" (Fabricius Hildanus 1674: 3–4)—the lancelet, launcelot, launce or lancet continued to be the name for this well-known material instrument. One text, Scultetus's *The Chyrurgeons Store-house* (1674)—in describing "A Lancet" able to "perforate any place" as well as "let blood"—includes for this knife capable of "cutting with both edges" its use for incisions in the "preputium," prepuce, or foreskin through which the "yard not perforated is opened" (1674: 48), once again recording the multiple bodily uses to which it was put in ways suggestive for the choice of the name of "Launcelet" or "Lancelet" for the servant of the "Jew," who fears he will be a "Jew" (2.2.112) unless he leaves his service.

> They cryed aloude, and cut themselves as their maner was, with knives and lancets, til the blood gushed out.
>
> 1 Kings 18: 28 (Geneva Bible)

The lancing or cutting conveyed by the name of "Launcelet" or "Lancelet" for the bond-servant of the Jew who leaves him for the new "livery" of a Christian was thus prominently identified with bloodletting and incisions in the period of The Merchant of Venice. His name—which is repeated incessantly (no fewer than 27 times) within the play—is sounded most frequently in the scene that enacts his decision to leave behind his Jewish "master" (2.2), a change that also enables him to facilitate the elopement of the Jew's "daughter" and the gelding of Shylock's "two sealed bags" and "stones" (2.8.18–20). It is therefore telling that the lancelet or lancet itself was identified as an instrument of castration, through an influential biblical text that was simultaneously combined with the cut of "carnal" circumcision in contrast to the "spiritual" circumcision of the heart: the self-castration or mutilation of the idolatrous Priests of Baal, which the Geneva Bible and other contemporary translations described as performed with "knives and lancets," or the very instrument used for bloodletting and other cuts (1 Kings 18:28, Geneva 1560). Contemporary texts routinely identified this familiar Old Testament instance of a gelding or bodily cutting with the lancet or lancelet. To cite just one example, George Abbot—future Archbishop of Canterbury—refers not only to the lancing or cutting of an apostume or swelling but to the "Baals Priests" who "cut and launce themselues" with this same knife (1600: 437, 524).

1 Kings does not expressly indicate whether Baal's priests castrated themselves or simply used their knives and "lancets" to cut their bodies. But multiple English writings repeatedly aligned these "Priestes of Baal" who "launce themselves" with the classical "Priests of Cybele" who (like the gelded Attis) transformed themselves from "he" to "she." One early modern polemic against the Judaizing of a return to the "Hebrew" testament assimilated priestly "shavelings" or the tonsure described as a circumcising (or literally "cutting around") of the head to the "Priests of Baal" who did "launce themselves," comparing the latter to Cybele's castrated followers (Gataker 1624: 29). The lancing of Baal's priests with knives and "lancets" was at the same time aligned with the carnal cutting of both circumcised nations—an elision important for *The Merchant of Venice*, where the cultural fantasy of forcible circumcision or castration by the Jew is joined by the "incision" explicitly invited by Morocco, whose invocation of his "scimitar" and service to the Sultan "Solyman" (2.1.24–6) simultaneously evokes the other bodily cuts identified with Moors or Muslims and Turks. Billerbeg's *Amurath* (1584)—describing the circumcision of the son of the Great Turk—compares his "Monkes" to the castrated "Priests of Cybele" (sig. Ciir), the familiar counterpart to the Priests of Baal who "launce" themselves, an Old Testament cutting repeatedly conflated with "Mahometans" in the period. Marlowe's *Tamburlaine* (Pt. 1: 4.2.1–3) has the Sultan Baiazet describe the "priests" of "Mahomet" in terms that directly recall the priests of Baal ("Ye holy priests of heavenly Mahomet/That sacrificing slice and cut your flesh,/Staining his altars with your purple blood"). Even more strikingly, a sixteenth-century history of "the Turckes" (Cambini 1562: 5) writes of places that have "bowed the knee before the idol Baale, which is Mahomethe," directly assimilating Turkish or Muslim forms of bodily incision to the familiar biblical instance of cutting with "lancets" and knives.

Perversely—given that the priests of Baal are described in the Hebrew Scriptures as an idolatrous *contrast* to Israel—this biblical instance of cutting or lancing with the very "lancets" evoked by Lancelet's name was applied not only to Moors or Turks but to the other circumcised nation, the Jews, represented as idolatrous practicers of an outward or carnal cutting rather than Christian or spiritual circumcision of the heart. John King directly compared the "Priest of Baal" who would "cut and launce his owne flesh" for his "idoll" to the "idolatrous Iewe" who "will freely bestowe his iewelles and earinges to make a golden calfe" (1599: 212, 389), while William Cowper conflated the "idolatrie" of the "Israelites" who "made a Baal to themselues" (Hosea 2.8) with the Priests of Baal from the familiar passage, referring to "The Baalites of Idolatrous Israell launcing themselues with kniues" (1616: 286). Still another early modern text observed that "Baal's priests," like the "Corybantes, Galli, & c," were "instructed to cut and slash themselues," in a passage on the difference between "true Religion and Idolatry" that begins with the "Idolatrous practises" of the "Israelites" (Littleton 1662: 283). Even Gyer's *English Phlebotomy*—already cited for the prominence it gives to the lancelet or lancet used for bloodletting—not only condemned the dangerous bleeding practiced by "Arabians, barbarous phisitions," and counterfeit "Iews or Egiptians" but contrasted Christian baptism to "The Priests of Baal cutting and launsing their owne bodies" (sig. A3r), or the kind of carnal cutting the New Testament had superseded.

In the period of *The Merchant of Venice*, this Old Testament instance of a lancet or lancelet used for such bodily cutting or castration was repeatedly cited as an example of the outward and idolatrous in contrast to the inward or spiritual. The connection between this lancing and circumcision was further enabled by an influential Pauline passage that contrasted the spiritual "circumcision of the heart" to Jewish circumcision re-cast as "concision" (Philippians 3:2), or itself a bodily mutilation, from *concidere* ("to cut up"). At the same time, this influential passage presented the Judaizing champions of such "fleshly" circumcision as "dogs" (Lupton 2005a: 95)—a combination reflected in the early modern description of both Jews and Muslims as "circumcised dogs."

> Whereas the wicked Jew too often tyrannically abused ... Circumcision ... [we must make] such Incisions into our souls, with the lancers [ie lancelets] of true repentance.
>
> Thomas Fuller, *The Infants Advocate* (1653)

Identification of "lancets" or lancelets as the instruments used by the Priests of Baal therefore suggests another way in which "Lancelet" or "Launcelet" in its multiple early modern resonances matters to *The Merchant of Venice*. The "lancelet" or "launce," however, figured not only the knife used for "bleeding" and the fleshly cut of castration but in addition the redemptive lancing or bloodletting of Christ in the crucifixion that enabled the very movement from "flesh" to "Spirit." Early modern texts repeatedly recalled the "brest" of Christ "pearc'd" with a "Launce" on the cross, whose bloodshed, ascribed to the Jews (Matthew 27:25), has been aligned by critics with the baring of Antonio's "breast" to the "knife" of the Jew. At the same time, contemporary texts figurally connected this "bloodletting" (identified with the "lancet" of a "Surgeon") both backward to the Circumcision of Christ and forward to the drama of conversion itself. The lance that caused the outflowing of the blood and water of redemption and baptism on the cross (John 19:34; 1 John 5:6) was depicted as wielded by a blind Jew who was converted and cured of his blindness as a result of this lancing.[10] But it was also conflated with the knife of the Circumcision (as "the first time Christ's blood was shed and as a foreshadowing of the blood Christ shed on the cross—both ascribed to Jews"), a ritual depicted with the mohel or circumciser wielding a menacing knife and "the representatives of the Old Covenant—namely the priest and the surgeon"—performing their task "at times even with a cruel delight."[11]

While we know from the text of the priests of Baal that their carnal cutting was identified with the "lancet" used by the bloodletting barber or surgeon, it may prove impossible—for a time that maintained the fiction that there were no Jews in England—to find the precise English equivalent for the izmel or knife used for circumcision. But in the figural substitutions that were part of the familiar habits of biblical reading in the period, text after text conflated both the bloodletting lancet or lancelet of the "Surgeon" and the "launce" of the crucifixion with the knife that first shed "blood" at the Circumcision, or what one early modern text called an "earnest" or down payment on the ultimate "Redemption" by Christ the Surgeon or Physician, "who by his spirituall knife, first cutteth off the foreskinne of our hearts, and makes them bleede" (Anon. 1611: sig. F24). Robert Southwell's "His

Circumcision"(1595) conflates the lancing of Christ on the cross with the "knife that cut his flesh" at the Circumcision, casting both as a phlebotomy or bloodletting in which "the head is launst to work the bodies cure" (1595: 6), in lines where "head" is both "prepuce" or foreskin and Head of the Church. Another early modern text subsumes both Christ's being made to bleed through the "Circumcisers knife" and the lancing on the Cross with the "Blood-letting" of the "Physitian" or "Surgeon" who worked the redemptive "cure" (Anon. 1638: 51).[12]

The figural trajectory that extended from the circumciser's shedding of Christ's blood to the final lancing of the crucifixion—and conflated both with the lancet or lancelet of the bloodletting "Surgeon" or "Physitian"—thus provides an even more overdetermined contemporary context for the name choice and trajectory of "Lancelet" or "Launcelet" in The Merchant of Venice. The very name (repeated yet another four times in the scene with Jessica on "converting Jews to Christians" [3.5.35]) would have suggested, in other words, not only the bloodletter's or surgeon's knife evoked by Morocco's "let us make incision in our bloods," Portia's counsel to have some "surgeon" by, and Shylock's "If you prick us, do we not bleed" or the biblical instrument of gelding or castration but also the bloodletting on the cross that enabled conversion itself, and the replacement of Jewish or "carnal" incisions with the circumcision of the heart.

The lancelet or lancet used for lancing apostumations or boils was at the same time the material instrument identified with the lancing of the boils of Job, a pivotal figure (as a Gentile from the Hebrew scriptures) for the movement from Old Testament to New—one of the reasons that Lancelet himself bears the surname "Iobbe" or Job (Drakakis 2000: 116).[13] I would add that the alternate surname "Gobbo," applied to his bent and blind father, simultaneously recalls the description of the Jews as both bent and blind from the central conversional text of Romans 11, where the grafting of Gentiles onto the Jewish root suggests yet another meaning of lancing and "launce" in the period.[14] The crucial passage for this redemptive lancing was Job 5:18 ("he maketh a wounde and he healeth"), a text glossed with "he is both a Father and a physitian, he lanceth us not unlesse need be" (Trapp 1657: 56) and he "woundeth not as an Enemy, but as a Chirurgion; not with a Sword, but a Lancet" (Manton 1685: 203).

The lancelet or lancet was in this regard not only a figure for the progression from Old Testament to New but for the movement from justice to mercy, from "Sin" as "an incision of the Soule, a Lancination, a Phlebotomy" (Donne 1640: 132) to the cure worked by "that Chyrurgion whose Lancet threatens none but the imposthumated" (Allestree 1667: 159). This spiritual cutting and healing by what one writer called "the Lancet or incision Knife of Truth" (Saavedra 1700: 345) was so frequently invoked as to become (like the material object itself) a cultural commonplace in the period—from "cutte me, burne me, launce me, that fynally thou mayst haue mercy on me" (Bonde 1526: 278) or the "conscience must be troubled by launcing" before the "soule can be cured" (Udall 1588: sig. Dv) to the counsel that "Surgeones of soules, in all their launcing and cutting" ought "to aime at the cure, that is the conuersion of their patients," a "spirituall" lancing ultimately more "gentle," as one contemporary text put it, than the "iewish Iudiciall lawe" that cut off and "condemned to death" (Taylor 1612: 261, 714). The very circumcision of the heart that was to replace Jewish or "carnal" circumcision was figured as an incision into the soul (rather than the body) by a lancelet or lancet. A text that treats first of the bodily cutting of the Old Testament—the "Priests of Baal, who with knives and lances cut themselves till the blood gushed out" and the "signe" of circumcision, which "the wicked Jew too often tyrannically abused"—goes on to describe "soul-Circumcision" (on the analogy of the "Surgeon") as making "Incisions into our souls with the lancers [or lancelets] of true repentance" (Fuller 1653: 2, 43, 58). Even the sense of writing itself as engraving or cutting so important to *The Merchant of Venice*—which was already assimilated to the lancelet routinely paired with the "pen-knife" in the bloodletting treatises, in a period when "lance" could likewise mean "To make a dash or stroke with a pen" (OED verb 5)—was appropriated for the law written not in stone but in the heart, figuring the transition from the "letter that kills" to the law so cut or "engraven in our hearts, as it may never be wiped out again" (Calvin 1583: 473).

The lancelet or lancet was thus not only a commonplace material object but part of the figural movement from Old Testament "letter" and "flesh" to New Testament "Spirit," a progression that was at the same time cast in the familiar racialized metaphorics of washing the

"Ethiope" or "Black-moor" white. One text that turns on the double
sense of "Launce," as the spear that pierced the "side" of "IESVS"
(in a crucifixion where his "bloud" was shed by "impious Jews")
and as the lancet that simultaneously effected a cure, compares the
issuing of blood and the water of baptism through this lancing to
the redemption enabled by the Surgeon who not only heals but
blanches or whitens the "Black-more borne, where Phoebus too much
warmes" (Abbot 1623: 7), the traditional figure of blackness evoked
not only by Morocco ("Mislike me not for my complexion, / The
shadowed livery of the burnish'd sun," 2.1.1–2) but by Jessica's
recall of the Black Bride of the Song of Songs on the threshold of her
own conversion (Hall 1992: 103), in a play where "Chus" (yet another
biblical figure of blackness) is described as the Jew's countryman
(3.2.285) and the converted Jessica's "blood" is described as "Rhenish"
or "white" in lines that contrast her "flesh" as "ivory" to Shylock's
"jet" black (3.1.39–42).[15]

> Hagar's offspring . . .
> the Moor is with child by you . . .
> *Merchant of Venice*

As the lancing or incising instrument that could prove fatal but could
also deliver the body from excessive or obstructive humors—a figure
commonly extended to the body politic as well—both the material
or surgical and the figurative or spiritual implications released into
the larger play by its insistent sounding of Lancelet's name resonate
far beyond the scenes in which he actually appears. Lancelet directly
himself invokes the bodily "humors" (3.5.63) for which this surgical
instrument was used. But in the Trial Scene from which he is absent,
Shylock likewise defends his choice of "a weight of carrion flesh"
over the apparently more rational economic calculus of "three thousand
ducats" with "say it is my humor" (4.1.40–4); and the humoral
economy to which this bloodletting and impostume- or tumor-lancing
instrument was central is further foregrounded by Bassanio's condemnation of the "current" of the Jew's "cruelty" (4.1.63; Paster 2004:
207), in lines that combine bodily humor and blood.

In this most pivotal of scenes—where the potentially fatal bleeding of Antonio as a sacrifice both echoes the bloodshed and lancing on the cross and evokes the blood libel identified with the knife-wielding Jew—Portia's counsel to have some "surgeon" by "lest he do bleed to death" not only recalls the warnings surrounding the lancelet in the bloodletting treatises (underscored by Antonio's "For if the Jew do cut but deep enough,/I'll pay it instantly with all my heart," [4.1.280–1]) but casts the "Jew" himself (the "cut-throat dog" of Venetian description) as the barbarous "Barber" of Gyer's and other contemporary descriptions, the alien within the body politic killing "Christians" by such fatal bleeding, as well as symbolically by the extortionate material "bleeding" that was its double.[16]

Portia—disguised as Balthasar (both a "second Daniel" and the Moor among the Wise Men of the East who in an "Epiphany" acknowledged Christ as the prefigured Messiah)—enters into a dispute with Shylock that includes the mastery of humoral discourse itself and urges the "gentle (and here Gentile)" softening of his "hard heart" by the "gentle rain" of "mercy" (Paster 2004: 209). But she also, in ways that recall her ambiguous "I stand for sacrifice" in the Casket Scene (3.2.57), simultaneously *effects* a sacrifice (Enterline 1995: 240), laying the foundation for the Duke's condition of Shylock's conversion, within the oppositional binaries of "letter" and spirit, blindness and sight on which "Epiphany" depends. And she symbolically gelds or castrates Shylock—the "stony adversary" of the Duke's opening description (4.1.4)—just as the condition imposed for the casket choice of Morocco had earlier gelded him of the possibility of heirs. If she becomes effectively the "surgeon" who works the cure for both Antonio and the Venetian body politic (invoking the "mercy" of the ultimate Surgeon or Physician), in a successful and Lancelet-like verbal quibbling (Newman 1987: 30–1) that bests Shylock as the adversary in this contest, she also cuts the Gordian knot of a legal impasse not just by the application of the letter of the law to which Shylock had appealed but by the revelation of a new law applying to an "alien," not earlier revealed but there from the beginning.

Fulfilling what in this sense came with the figurative implications of the lancelet in the period, Portia thus delivers not only Antonio but Bassanio from the bondage of a "bond" and threatened loss of

"Christian blood," for which the consummation of her marriage to Bassanio—the joining of their bloodlines and sacrifice of her own virgin blood—had been postponed (Paster 1993: 92). From one perspective, what is achieved is the relieving of Antonio's own "patient" or Job-like suffering (from a story in which lost prosperity is ultimately not only regained but increased); the rehearsal of the lancing in Job that both wounds and heals; and the Christian "comedy" of the conversion of the Jew whose grafting in is described in the Romans 11 adumbration of that comic plot. But, from another perspective, what she completes in this scene is not only the symbolic gelding of Shylock for which Lancelet's enabling of Jessica's defection had been the initial instrument but also the "bleeding" of Shylock of everything he holds most "dear," and a forced conversion that is not a decision but a cultural incision, deracination or cutting off (Berry 2006: 246).[17]

As the knife that lances the boils of Job and a familiar figure for the movement from judgment to mercy, the resonances of the "Lancelet" who abandons the Jew and facilitates Jessica's conversion and abandonment of her father might be argued (from a figural vantage point) as confirming the critical paradigm of the play's movement from flesh to spirit, Old Testament to New (Drakakis 2000: 116), or the redemptive curing of the "blind Jew" whose lancing led to his own conversion. But in ways that undermine the binaries of such straightforward or teleological progression and a play where conversion itself is so uncertain and open to question, Lancelet functions as a much more promiscuous transactor of exchanges that are at once "economic, sexual, and religious" (Mentz 2003: 183) and as a character whose own identity is uncertain, in a plot that includes not only Christians and Jews but Muslims and Moors. Shylock calls him "Hagar's offspring" (2.5.42), a term that might identify him as a Gentile but could also situate him among its Muslims (Shell 1982: 52), understood as descendants of Hagar (Abraham's bondswoman) and their son Ishmael, in contrast to Christians as Abraham and Sarah's legitimate line.[18] As "the play's nonpareil of indeterminate hybridity" (Harris 2004: 207), Lancelet is also its principal boundary-crosser (Hall 1992: 105), reversing Portia's rejection of Morocco and Aragon (from Spain, that most "mingled" of nations) for a Christian of her own "kind" through the miscegenation (3.5.37) of his impregnating a "Negro" or "Moor" (Shapiro 1996: 173; Spiller 2000: 155), who remains unseen and outside the plot's conversional telos, in a scene whose punning "more" (rather than less) evokes divergent contrasting economies (Hall 1992: 92; Desai 2002: 314) and calls into question the more exclusive "cornucopia" of the play's own end (Mentz 2003: 184).[19] This mingling or boundary-crossing simultaneously suggests a reversal of the racialized metaphorics of conversion itself, moving not "forward" but "backward" (as the Geneva gloss to Galatians pronounced of the mixture of Christian and Hebrew), complicating the progression from "Ethiope" or "Black-more" to a baptismal whitening by what Janet Adelman calls the "muddying of bloodlines" (2003: 22) in the case of Jessica and Lorenzo as well.

The "Lancelet" that cuts both ways in relation to bloodletting and castration—suggesting not only the Trial Scene's threat to Antonio and "Christian" blood (4.1.310) but also the bleeding or gelding of both Shylock and Morocco—further complicates the sense of progression from "flesh" to "spirit" in his complaint that converting Jews raises the price of pork (3.5.36), an emphasis on the "economics of conversion" (Shapiro 1996: 132) that privileges the "flesh," just as his prodigious appetites do.[20] At the same time, his insistence that the converted Jessica remains a daughter to Shylock's "blood" (2.3.18) recalls—by looking back to her bloodline and the "sins of the father" (3.5.1; Exodus 20: 5)—the pure blood laws that sought to distinguish between Old and New Christians (Friedman 1987: 3–29), exposing the racial-religious contradictions at the heart of conversion in the period (Halpern 1997: 213; Metzger 1998: 52; Loomba 2002: 138–58).

Even the scene in Act 2 that has been used by critics to argue that the movement of this "Clown" from Jewish to Christian master parallels the progression from Old Testament to New cuts both ways, suggesting not a pious rehearsal but a subversive parody of the Genesis story in which the wrong son is given the blessing through a trick played on a father, in ways that comment not only on Jacob or "Israel" (or on Jessica's treatment of her father) but on the Christian "New Israel" in relation to its own appropriation of the Hebrew Testament.[21] It begins with an equivocating psychomachia that defies simple binary opposition—since the "devil" is on both sides at once—and yields a movement in which Lancelet, in deciding finally to leave his Jewish master for a Christian, follows not his "conscience" but the "fiend" (2.2.31). His cutting of this Gordian knot is motivated not by spiritual but by much more worldly prospects, both the attractions of mobility in itself (Mentz 2003: 181) and upward mobility to the status of "Master" identified with the gentry, to "rare new liveries" (2.2.109) not as spiritual deliverance but as "the distinctive garb worn by a gentleman's servants" (Riverside: 261), in ways that provide an ironic comment on the upward mobility and "blatant materialism" (Orgel 2003: 158) of the Christian characters within the play. Far from suggesting a clear movement "forward" in the "right" or providential direction, the scene repeatedly harps on turning backward rather than forward, from its strangely "backward" blessing (2.2.97) to its repeated verbal reversals (including "impertinent" instead of "pertinent"), a verbal "quibbling" that in very different ways from Portia's manages to "undercut the serious religious issues" and provide an "alternative perspective" on "Christian orthodoxy and social hierarchy" (Cohen 1985: 210–11), as well as "quibble against the utopian progress of the main plot" (Mentz 2003: 184).[22] Even the sense of conversion (literally "turning") that is so central to the supposed unidirectional progression of the play is subject to "confusions" (2.2.37) in this scene, as Old Gobbo (or "Iobbe") is turned around and around ("Turn up on your right hand at the next turning, but at the next turning of all, on your left; marry, at the very next turning, turn of no hand, but turn down indirectly to the Jew's house," 2.2.41–4) and may finally come dizzyingly full circle (Mowat and Werstine 1992: 48).

In a play that is preoccupied not only with conversion but with "blood" in all of its contemporary senses (including as a contested marker of religious, racial, and other distinctions), this "Clown" who has been traditionally marginalized in its criticism and frequently cut from productions bears a name that connects him with cutting or lancing of multiple kinds, both as a material object and as part of the figural contrast of justice and mercy, "flesh" and "spirit." But the Lancelet who rewards Shylock for his "preferment" (2.2.146) to his new master by effectively helping to "bleed" as well as castrate him, who tries "confusions" on his own father by cruelly pretending that his son is dead (2.2.65), and who wields the incising words of the

Clown that traditionally cut in more than one direction—crucially introduces into the play a heterogeneity of exchanges that cannot be incorporated into a single trajectory or figural frame, not only providing a complicating perspective on the play's larger issues but occupying contrary, and contradictory, positions at once.

NOTES

1 See Shapiro 1996: 113–30; Penuel 2004: 255–75. On its multiple cuts, including grafting, writing, engraving, insculpting, and "cutler's poetry/Upon a knife" (5.1.149–50), see Berry 2006. On its allusion to the prepuce or "hood," see Fienberg 1998: 452. The combination or conflation of circumcision and castration was common in the period, including in plays such as Kyd's *Solyman and Perseda*, Heywood's *Fair Maid of the West*, Mason's *The Turk*, Fletcher's *The Knight of Malta*, and Massinger's *The Renegado*. All quotations from Shakespeare are from the Riverside edition. I am grateful to the readers who commented on earlier drafts and to Jean Howard, Katherine Goodland, Lowell Gallagher, Arthur Little and members of the Columbia University Shakespeare Seminar and UCLA Department of English Early Modern/Renaissance Reading Group for lively discussion that enabled its revision.

2 On such figural readings, see Freinkel 2002: 237–91; on "liveries," see Engle 1986: 32.

3 Although Schäfer 1970: 14–15 cited "Launce" in *Two Gentlemen of Verona* (also played by Will Kempe) as a "surgical instrument" and called the post-Rowe Arthurian reference a "questionable allusion," most editors have continued the latter tradition. Even Mahood 1987, who cites Schäfer's "little knife," restricts its sense to "the Clown's cutting witticisms" and prints Lancelot because it is "more conformable to the editorial tradition" (1987: 82). Although Mowat 1994: 317 and 1998: 141 and Mowat and Werstine 1992 argue for "Lancelet" instead, they give its meaning as "lancet" or "'small lance' (a small weapon or man-at-arms)." Andrews 1991 prints "Launcelet" but, as in Andrews 2002: 166, limits its meaning to a phallic "little lance." John Drakakis, who is editing a new Arden 3 edition, is the only editor to see the importance of its surgical sense, though he restricts it to Lancelet's relation to his father "Iobbe" or Job (2000: 116, 121 n. 2) rather than examining it in relation to the bloodletting, circumcision, and castration central to the play. No mention is made

of the meaning of "Lancelet" in the discussion of bloodletting or humors in *The Merchant of Venice* in Paster 1993 or 2004.

4 For critiques of narrowly object-focused studies of material culture, see Harris 2000 and 2001; and Bruster 2003: 191–205.

5 See Baret 1573, "Lancelette"; Cooper 1578 under "Scalper," "Scalprum chirurgicum," and "Scalpellus"; Rider 1589 under "Scalpellus" and "Smilium"; Minsheu 1617 under "Launcelot"; with Thomas 1587, "Scalpellum" as "a penknife, or little fine instrument that Surgeons use to let blood with, a lancelot."

6 See Beck 1974: 105–8; Rubin 1974: 145.

7 For an explanation of the reference system here see Chapter 5 note 4. [Ed.]

8 See also Lemnius 1576: 83, where"veynes," if large, "swel out and plainlye appeare to the eye, offering themselves to the Lance, by incision hansomly to be cut."

9 In addition to this 1598 translation into English of Guillemeau, dedicated to Queen Elizabeth, illustrations of lancets appear in English texts, including Helkiah Crooke's *Mikrokosmographia. A Description of the Body of Man* (London, 1631), which contains *An Explanation of the Fashion and Use of Three and Fifty Instruments of Chirurgery. Gathered out of Ambrosius Pareus, the famous French Chirurgian, and done into English, for the behoofe of yong Practitioners in Chirurgery*, illustrating (in Chapter 1) a "phlegme or lancet" and the rings and their secretly pricking points shown, respectively, in Guillemeau (as "D," "C," and "B"). *An Explanation* is also bound with the 1634 edition of Crooke's *Somatographia anthropine*. I am grateful to June Schlueter for these references to Crooke.

10 See Mellinkoff 1993: I: 69, 98; Kolve 1996: 218–21.

11 See respectively Mellinkoff 1993: I.43, 106 and II: Figure II: 23 and O'Neill and Schultz 1986: 154–5.

12 See also Steinberg 1983: 50–64 on such figural connections in Patristic and early modern writing, including in Milton's "Upon the Circumcision."

13 On Job as a Gentile (in Uz, identified as "the country of Idumea . . . or bordering thervpon"), see the Geneva Bible on the first verse of the book of "Iob" (fol. 195v): "For asmuche as he was a Gentle and not a Iewe, and yet is pronounced vpryght . . . it declareth that among the heathen God hathe his." The Bishops Bible has "This Job was a gentile, declaring hereby that God hath his, euen among the heathen." For Job as a Gentile in the Hebrew Bible and most rabbinic sources, see Ginzberg 2.225 ("Job, the most pious Gentile that ever lived") and *Encyclopedia Judaica* 1971/73, 10: 124.

14 See Romans 11:10 ("Let their eyes be darkened that they see not, and bow downe their backe alwayes": Geneva 1560) in relation to Old Gobbo (Italian for "hunchback") and *OED* "lance" (noun 1.5) as "A branch of a tree, a shoot" (citing "graffes of the fayrest lanses") and "lance" (noun 2) as a "cut, incision, slit" in a "tree."

15 Though there is not space to unpack it fully here, the compounded senses of "livery" and the familiar Shakespearean homophone of "sun" and "son" in Morocco's "shadowed livery of the burnish'd sun" raises not only the issue of color and (blood) line, but also (as with the double-meaning "livery" for which Lancelet leaves a Jewish master for a Christian) religious overtones here, with regard to a Moroccan Muslim connected with the Great Turk. On the frequent descriptions of Islam as "Hebraizing" in relation to the shadowy types of the Old Testament (including circumcision), see Parker 2002: 2–6.

16 Gyer's text (1592) has on its title page the familiar "horse-leech" verses from Proverbs, applied in the period not only to extortionate bloodletters but to moneylenders or usurers "bleeding" debtors.

17 For the contemporary conflation of "barbers" and "barbarous" (variant: "barberous") others, including Jews and Muslims identified with "carnal" cutting, see Parker 2004: 201–44, which discusses the "barbers of Barbary" in Thomas Heywood's *Fair Maid of the West*, the "base barbarous barbers" and "Barbaria" of Dekker's *Gull's Hornbook*, the "Barbarossa," Barbary "gelding," "and "Nick" the "Barbor" of *The Knight of the Burning Pestle*, the "barberous Moore" of *Titus Andronicus*, Antony "barber'd ten times o'er" by Cleopatra, and Marlowe's *The Jew of Malta*, where either Ithamore its "Turk" or an anonymous Moorish "slave" announces that he can "cut and shave," euphemisms not only for thievery (or usury understood as "fleecing") but for the cutting (or barbering) identified with both circumcised nations (represented by Ithamore the Muslim and Barabas the Jew, precursor of Shylock). Mark Johnson has suggested to me that Portia's urging of Shylock to have some "surgeon" by also recalls the barber-surgeons' company regulations that members were to have an experienced surgeon present when performing potentially complex incisions.

18 To complicate "Hagar's offspring" still further, the well-known Pauline "allegory" of Galatians 4 identified Hagar (and her "bondage") with the Jews, so that what is designated by the phrase would depend on the perspective of the speaker. See also Spiller 2000: 161. In a period where Muslims were called "Hagarenes" or "Agarenes," the collocation of Muslims and Jews as "Hagar's offspring" (both subject to the

"bonds" of the "bondservant" rather than Abraham and Sarah's legitimate heirs) was frequently cited in early modern writing and reflected soon after *The Merchant of Venice* in the name "Agar" (or Hagar) for the Muslim wife of the renegade Jew of Daborne's *A Christian Turned Turk* (Parker 2002: 3–4, 15). The modernized "turquoise" ring of Shylock's wife Leah (named after Laban's older daughter) is "Turkies" in Q.

19 Sokol 1998: 168–9 notes the "bestiality" in this exchange on the female Moor and what Lancelet "took" her for (3.5.42), while Engle 1993: 101–2 speculates that this unnamed female figure may be a slave, or purchased servant, of Portia, suggesting yet another potential ironic commentary on Christians who pass judgment on Shylock's "pound of flesh" that is "dearly bought" (4.1.89) while insisting on keeping "many a purchas'd slave,/Which like your asses, and your dogs and mules,/You use in abject and in slavish parts" (4.1.90–2).

20 Shylock calls him a "huge feeder" (2.5.46); and Lancelet anticipates a polygamous abundance of at least "fifteen wives" (2.2.161). Mark Johnson has suggested to me the possible additional overtones (in Gobbo) of "gobbets," a term invoked elsewhere in Shakespeare (*Henry VI Pt 2*) in its sense of slicing or cutting. Minsheu derives English "Gobbet" or "mouthful" from French "Gober" (to "feed greedily"), giving its counterparts as Gobbo's homophone "Gobeau" (Cotgrave's "gobbet, or morsel") and "Gobequinaut" (a "greedie feeder"). At least one early modern text cited in *OED* for the "gob" that designated the mouth, a mouthful, and the gift of language ("gob" or "gab") puns on "Gob" and "a Man called Job, Dwelt in the land of Uz" (gob, noun 3).

21 Jessica's "in such a night/Medea gathered the enchanted herbs/That did renew old Aeson" (5.1.12–14) foregrounds the moment in Ovid's story when "Medea unsheathed her knife and cut the old man's throat; then, letting the old blood run out, she filled his veins with her brew" (Ovid, *Metamorphoses* VII.285–7; Berry 2006: 252), a part of the story that casts the daughter figure as the "cut-throat." As critics have noted, the Medea figure in the play extends to Portia as well, since Bassanio explicitly casts his venture for her as a mercenary seeking of the Golden Fleece (and himself by implication as the Jason or fleecer).

22 See Weimann 1978: 48–9, 120–50 on the subversive role of the Clown, including inversion and wordplay. The same actor (Will Kempe) may have played the Clown roles of both Lancelet and "Launce" in *Two Gentlemen of Verona*.

7

CYMBELINE, THE FONT OF HISTORY, AND THE MATTER OF BRITAIN

From Times New Roman to Italic Type

Willy Maley

LITTLE BRITAIN

In an episode of the hit UK comedy series *Little Britain*, two characters in search of a play raid the offices of the Royal Shakespeare Company, a break-in that shadows the break-up of Britain in the shape of Scottish and Welsh devolution.[1] Rewind 400 years to a passage in Drayton's *Polyolbion* (1612) that marks the make-up of Britain:

> A branch sprung out of *Brute*, th'imperiall top shall get,
> Which grafted in the stock of Great *Plantaginet*,
> The Stem shall strongly wax, as still the Trunk doth wither:
> That power which bare it thence, againe shall bringe it thither
> By *Tudor*, with faure windes from little *Britaine* driven;
> To whom the goodlie Bay of Milford shall be given.
>
> (Cited Jones 1961: 94)

Drayton's "little Britaine" was of course Brittany—Great Britain was the new entity perplexing the English, Welsh, Scots, and Irish at the turn of the seventeenth century. A sampling of recent readings reveals the extent to which Cymbeline is haunted by the present as much as the past, by the forging of a Great Britain belittled by devolution, bedeviled by the ends of Empire.

Historicism and topicality have governed criticism since 1945 (Knight 1947; Rossi 1978; Jones 1961; Harris 1966). Cymbeline is now viewed variously as Shakespeare's last Roman play (Bergeron 1980; Miola 1984; James 1997), an Italian play (Olsen 1999; Parolin 2002), a British play (Curran 1997; Griffiths 2004; King 2005; Kerrigan 2006), a Welsh play (Sullivan 1998; Hopkins 1999a, 1999b; Boling 2000), a Scottish play (Floyd-Wilson 2002), and an Irish play (Edwards 1998), a play about engendering an empire-state (Mikalachki 1995), a play as preoccupied with the "New World" as The Tempest (Feerick 2003), a play that plays with time, confounding conventional historicist readings (Marcus 1988; Parker 1989), a Jacobean masque— hence its failure (Jones 1961: 96), and even a play that repays postcolonial readings (Maley 1999). With its dramatic depiction of a crucial transition of power, one empire eclipsing another, and two colonial powers combining, Cymbeline is clearly preoccupied with the implications of empire and its aftermath. England, former Roman colony, is—in Shakespeare's time—part of an emerging British empire, its own colonies consisting of the very Celtic nations that comprised ancient Britain. Cymbeline is thus a touchstone text for critics concerned with how Britain is written. In this anachronistic drama, Roman Britain, ancient Wales, and Renaissance Italy share centre-stage (Marcus 1988; Parker 1989; Parolin 2002; Kerrigan 2006). How does this augur for Britain's reincarnation under James I? In addressing its own colonial legacy, Britain, cross-dressing as Rome, confronts its Italian inheritance (Parolin 2002: 195).

In 1947, the year of Indian independence, G. Wilson Knight argued for Cymbeline as a "history play," a nationalist celebration of the British monarchy (Knight 1947). Although his own interpretation was caught up in postwar politics, Knight resisted topicality, privileging timeless patriotism and royal celebration. In 1961 Emrys Jones observed that "topical elements of Cymbeline have received no scholarly attention," insisting that the play "centres on the character and foreign policy of James I" (Jones 1961: 89). Produced after the Union of Crowns between Scotland and England, *Cymbeline* is, like *King Lear* and *Macbeth*, one of Shakespeare's "British histories." Circling around questions of sovereignty, succession and settlement, it ruminates upon the nature of Britishness, its boundaries and modes of being. If the Roman plays are histories at a safe remove from Shakespeare's England then ancient Britain offers another avenue for oblique engagement with politics. Declaring *Cymbeline* a history, rather than a tragedy, comedy, or tragi-comedy, or pronouncing it a Roman play rather than a romance, does not solve the problems the play poses. Critics taking up Wilson Knight's historicizing remain torn as to its political message. Does it sound a cautionary note for a nation bent on becoming a second Rome, or present a ringing endorsement of the future British Empire?

ALL ROADS LEAD TO ROME

Cymbeline is Shakespeare's last Roman play—"Roman in the gloaming." Ancient Rome was looked to as an example of empire, Italy eyed ambivalently as a site of vice and advice. Yet the play's political vision remains cloudy, its attitude to Rome rheumy. While one critic sees the play's motto as "when in Britain, do as the Romans do" (Bergeron 1980: 35), one character resists doing as the Romans would have her do:

> The Queen states that [. . .] Rome never actually conquered Britain [. . .] This protest is based on what most audiences would have recognised as a patent lie; the story of Roman Britain in some form or another was widely disseminated. The Queen's misrepresentation of what was held to be fact is comparable to a tyrant's silencing of the subject [. . .] Cymbeline denies tribute on subtler grounds. He bases his position on the prior and fundamental freedom of the British people.
>
> (Jordan 1997: 84)

Here are two denials. The King denies tribute because Britain boasts ancient liberties, the Queen because she was never conquered. But does the Queen, both "the play's most Italianate character in her political machinations" and its "most outspoken British nationalist" (Olsen 1999: 289), get her facts wrong, or is her "patent lie" a partial truth? She does not deny Caesar's conquest, conceding that he made a "kind of conquest here," but "made not here his brag/Of 'Came, and saw, and overcame.'" That brag—"Veni, vidi, vici"—was made elsewhere (Redmond 1999: 304–5). The bad queen is a good historian. Moreover, her own English translation of Caesar's famous phrase is a telling one, making no mention of conquest (Crumley 2001: 302). Clinton Crumley's argument that Shakespeare gave the play's devils the best lines to heighten dramatic tension has some merit (Crumley 2001: 304).

Yet the Queen remains a conundrum. First to raise the spectre of slander, one of the play's principal plotlines, she self-identifies as wicked in her opening speech, alluding to the misogynist stereotyping of stepmothers in a self-fulfilling prophecy:

> No, be assur'd you shall not find me, daughter,
> After the slander of most stepmothers,
> Evil-ey'd unto you.
>
> (2.2.1–3)

Later Cymbeline calls her "our wicked queen" (5.5.464). But is the Queen's approach to the "fact" of conquest tantamount to "a tyrant's silencing of the subject"? And does it differ dramatically from the King's appeal to "the prior and fundamental freedom of the British people"? John Milton, who invoked ancient liberty as a cure for present tyranny, alluded to Cymbeline's withholding of tribute in his *History of Britain* (1670), a parallel prose version of *Paradise Lost*, where a series of falls—invasions, conquests—prompt fresh attempts at civility:

> But as for Tribute, the *Britans* paid none to *Augustus*, except what easie Customes were levied on the slight Commodities wherewith they traded into *Gallia* [. . .] *Kymbeline* or *Cunobeline* succeeding, was brought up, as is said, in the Court of *Augustus*, and with him held freindly correspondencies to the end.
>
> (Parry 1991: 61–2)

Milton stands between Shakespeare's queen and Cymbeline, envisaging the Roman conquest as a necessary civilizing process, but finding merit in the ancient Britons. Mary Floyd-Wilson assures us "the historical Cymbeline paid peaceful tribute to the Romans," but Holinshed, noting Augustus Caesar excused Cymbeline from tribute, is vague about whether it was he or another British monarch who refused to pay after subsequent demands (Jones 1961: 87; Crumley 2001: 300; Floyd-Wilson 2002: 101). If critics and chroniclers cannot agree, why should characters in a play? Holinshed's English section is pro-Rome, the Scottish section resistant. Shakespeare negotiates: "He thereby echoes both of the attitudes towards Rome expressed in the *Chronicles*: the paternal guiding influence in the *History of England* is attributed to classical Rome, the crafty manipulation in the *History of Scotland* to Renaissance Italy" (Rossi 1978: 111). Michael Redmond reminds us that in 1610 Ben Jonson praised "*Britayne*, the only name, made CAESAR flie" (Redmond 1999: 303). Since British identity was bound up with resistance to Rome, the Queen looks less isolated (Floyd-Wilson 2002: 103).

THE MATTER OF (GREAT) BRITAIN

Most occurrences of "Britain" or "British" in Shakespeare's works are in *Cymbeline*, making it the most British play in the canon (Thompson 1991: 87, n. 10). The play's earliest commentator, the diarist Simon Forman, translated "Britain" into "England" (Crumley 2001: 300; Griffiths 2004: 345). That critics persist in speaking of "early modern England" as the play's context suggests old habits die hard (Crumley 2001: 312). Is England the "brain of Britain" (5.5.14), or its trunk? If its head, then England's absence is the play's most violent act of decapitation:

> By omitting the word England, a choice that is usually read as concern for historical accuracy, Shakespeare confronts his audience with a national terminology that inspired wide unease in early modern England [. . .] It was not a politically astute idea [. . .] to demean the precedence of England at a time of mounting local xenophobia.
>
> (Redmond 1999: 297, 301)

"Britain" had a Roman reality before Jacobean union, but Shakespeare understood the power of the proper name to conjure a state into being (again). Cloten's unworldly utterance, "Britain's a world by itself" (3.1.13), is undercut by Imogen asking:

> Hath Britain all the sun that shines? Day, night,
> Are they not but in Britain? I' th' world's volume
> Our Britain seems as of it, but not in't;
> In a great pool a swan's nest. Prithee think
> There's livers out of Britain.

> (3.4.137–41)

The incantation of "Britain" both expresses astonishment that such a thing exists and reinforces its reality through repetition. Reinventing an ancient political entity, rebranding Roman Britain as Jacobean Britain, required prime time exposure. The Tudors emphasized their Welsh/British origins. The Stuart dynasty acquired different bases for its Britishness (Scotland/Ulster). Imogen's island imagery effectively neutralizes Britain's internal borders, forging a single geographical entity from a set of warring countries. While Imogen appears perplexed, the Queen, assured of British memory and merits, reminds her husband—and Shakespeare's audience—that "Britain" was once a name to conjure with. Echoing John of Gaunt's famous "sceptred isle" speech from *Richard II*, the Queen commends their country to the King:

> Remember sir, my liege,
> The kings your ancestors, together with
> The natural bravery of your isle, which stands
> As Neptune's park, ribb'd and pal'd in
> With rocks unscaleable and roaring waters,
> With sands that will not bear your enemies' boats,
> But suck them up to th' topmast.

> (3.1.17–23)

This rousing speech, sufficient to make "Britons strut with courage" (3.1.34), would on other lips be unequivocally positive, but this is the "wicked stepmother," not the good—if slightly confused—King, making it a "stumbling block in interpretations" (Mikalachki 1995:

303). The sceptred isle was a spectred isle, haunted by visions of colonies. In Shakespeare's day a Little Englander—or Little Briton—mentality clashed with a Great British outlook. *Cymbeline* reveals tensions not just between Little English and Great British visions, but Greater English and Little British alternatives.

James worried that the name "Britain" might not catch on. Justifying its use in his proclamation on Anglo-Scottish Union on 20 October 1604, he declared:

> Nor that We covet any new affected Name devised at Our pleasure, but out of undoubted knowledge doe use the true and ancient Name, which God and Time have imposed on this Isle, extant, and received in Histories, in all Mappes and Cartes, wherein this Isle is described, and in ordinary Letters to Our selfe from divers Forraine Princes, warranted also by Authenticall Charters, Exemplifications under Seales, and other Records of great Antiquitie.
>
> (Cited in Redmond 1999: 301)

Again, the emphasis is on Britain as isle, more geographically correct than the English "sceptr'd isle" of John of Gaunt, which erased Scotland and Wales.

In 1534 England retired as Roman Catholic, wedded to the Holy Roman Empire, and awoke as an empire in its own right. Seventy years later England went to bed an empire and awoke in a British Union, beside strange bedfellows cradling competing claims to the monarchal mantle. *Cymbeline*—like *Henry VIII*—ruminates on this process. When England broke with "Rome"—the Catholic Church—it declared itself, in the Act of Restraint of Appeals of 1533, an "empire," a term that "designated a sovereign territorial state [. . .] completely independent of the pope and all foreign princes" (Levack 1987: 2). This act "formally signaled the rebirth and the appropriation of late Roman governmental principles in a contemporary, native guise" (Ullmann 1979: 203). England's earliest imperial measures were Union with Wales (1536–43) and the act of kingly title in Ireland (1541), whereby Henry VIII ceased to hold Ireland as a "lordship," a gift from the pope, instead establishing his own imperial monarchy. Thus the accession of James and reinvention of Britain accelerated a process begun under Henry.

"This England" that became an empire to secure its independence from Rome experienced anxiety when incorporated into an enlarged polity with distinct Roman connotations. A play marking this new entity engendered unease. English nationalists were wary of being subsumed within a reprised British state. The Reformation was a struggle for national self-determination against empire. Any change to the nature of the nation threw up challenges. Critics reconcile the fact the two villains on the British side—the Queen and Cloten—are the loudest proponents of Britain by arguing that theirs is a "narrow nationalism" (Parker 1989: *passim*). Is there any other kind? Paradoxically, "narrowness" in the play is presented positively, as grounds for the British victory: "A narrow lane, an old man, and two boys" (5.3.52). The travels of Posthumus and magnanimity of Cymbeline are allegedly more inclusive expressions of Britishness. Thus the play, if not anti-nationalist, is critical of a stringently conceived nationhood that ruled out Celtic and Roman influences, and opposed union. The Queen's isolationism refuses an alternative empire, another Rome rising in the West.

Britain's birth by Caesarian section resembled vivisection, the Beast of Rome disemboweled to free a lion's whelp. "Nothing is inconceivable," runs the tagline for *Junior* (director, Ivan Reitman, 1994), starring a pregnant Arnold Schwarzenegger. The fantasy of male birth arises at the end of Cymbeline when the King becomes "mother to the birth of three" (5.5.370). *Cymbeline* bears the birthmarks of Britain in two senses, as a key moment in Roman Britain maps on to an equally vital juncture in Renaissance Britain, when the double vision of England as insulated island and embryonic empire is complicated by conceding the keystone status of Celtic countries who might prove barriers against intruders, or conduits of invasion, or both—as Cambria does in *Cymbeline*.

"LITTLE ENGLAND BEYOND WALES": MILFORD HAVEN AND THE HAVE-NOTS

If *Macbeth* is the Scottish play and *The Tempest* the Irish play, then *Cymbeline* is the Welsh play. Wales was margin and microcosm: font of Britishness, through King Arthur and the Tudors, but Celtic fringe player alongside Ireland and Scotland. Ronald Boling reminds us that "Milford Haven is situated in the south of Pembrokeshire, which was well known to Elizabethans as an English colony that called itself 'Little England beyond Wales'" (Boling 2000: 34). Henry VII, James's great-grandfather, landed there in 1485 to end the Wars of the Roses and inaugurate a dynasty: "The heart of Little England [. . .] is a militarized Milford Haven" (Boling 2000: 48), challenging the assertion that the Welsh setting "dramatizes the anxiety of being excluded from history" (Mikalachki 1995: 172, n. 29). Milford was both "happy port" and Achilles' heel, "evoking both Great British expansionism and Little England anxiety" (Boling 2000: 49). The Tudors emerged at Milford, so fittingly a play inaugurating a new Stuart dynasty returned there. *Cymbeline*'s treatment of the Welsh dimension is as deft as its depiction of Roman Britain, making of a rebellious nation a key internal colony and crucial ally against Rome. The Essex Rebellion confirmed Wales as an alternative powerbase, and it became a key comparative context for Anglo-Scottish union (Dodd 1944; 1938). James enquired of his parliament: "Do you not gain from the union with Wales and is not Scotland greater than Wales?" (Cited in Sullivan 1998: 16; Hopkins 1999a: 1.4).

Wales doubles as pastoral retreat and site of resistance, where the natives defy London's courtly disdain and Rome's imperial might. Cloten's soft civility contrasts with the hardiness of his brothers-in-law. When he is headed off at the pass, this victory for plain dealing over courtly intrigue marks a Cambrian correction for an English condition. There is no Fluellen to offer this "Welsh correction," but critics lamenting the lack of local characters forget how inclusive Fluellen's notion of Welshness was. When John Kerrigan comments that "with the possible exception of the beggars who give Imogen directions, or misdirections, towards Milford, and who do not appear on stage, the play has no *bona fide* Cambrians," he sets a citizenship test few would pass (Kerrigan 2006: 132). What was bona fide in ancient Britain, or early modern Britain? Belarius identifies himself and the royal sons he abducted and adopted as Welsh: "Sir,/in Cambria are we born, and gentlemen" (5.5.17).

Kerrigan sees the play being about "Anglo-Welsh Britain turning Scottish at a decisive moment" (Kerrigan 2006: 133). It is thus a

Tudor-into-Stuart as well as a Roman-into-British play. More than symbolic significance resides in Shakespeare's use of Wales. The Scottish-cum-British King woos an English audience by reference to a former Union, enacted on the heels of an earlier breach with Rome. Ronald Boling takes James's argument further: "Rome is to Britain what in Shakespeare's time England was to Wales. *Cymbeline*'s Britain plays a double role, empire to Wales but colony to Rome: as *Cymbeline*'s Wales is anglicized, so *Cymbeline*'s Britain is Romanized" (Boling 2000: 35). One place in particular serves as the sliding door between Romano-British and Anglo-Celtic worlds: Milford Haven, home of the have-nots. The Welsh angle is made more acute by the fact that in June 1610— as Terry Hawkes reminds us—"the year of *Cymbeline*'s composition, James's elder son Henry was invested as Prince of Wales. Among the court entertainments marking the occasion was Samuel Daniel's masque *Tethys' Festival*, which explicitly refers to Milford Haven in this capacity as 'the happy port of union'" (Hawkes 2002: 57). This haven harbored a hell. Caught between Anglo-Welsh and Anglo-Scottish alliances, England felt the pressure of its Celtic pincers, forceps for the (re)birth of Britain. Wales, like Prospero's island, proves a staging post for a homecoming rather than a final destination for metropolitan elite figures, colonial pretext rather than permanent settlement. If the play's motto is Bergeron's "when in Britain, do as the Romans do," then its postscript might be "when in Wales, do as the British do."

ENSIGNS OF THE TIMES: UNFURLING THE PROTOTYPE OF THE UNION JACK

If Wales flies the flag for Britain, it does so thanks to a Scottish king. The build-up to the 2006 World Cup soccer tournament in Germany witnessed an unprecedented debate in Britain about the flag of St George, an English emblem emerging, in the wake of Scottish and Welsh devolution, as a viable alternative to the red, white, and blue of the British Union Jack, notoriously a rallying point for racists and right-wing political organizations, from the National Front to the British National Party. *Cymbeline* participates in such debates. Its complex weave of Celtic connections has a pronounced Scottish context. The play's most remarkable scene, when the banished Belarius repels the

Romans with Cymbeline's two stolen sons, is lifted from the Scottish section of Holinshed, where a Scottish farmer and his boys beat back the Danes (Floyd-Wilson 2002). But the Scottishness of *Cymbeline* passes beyond this peculiar piece of patriotic plagiarism. *Cymbeline* ends with two flags united: "A Roman and a British ensign wave/Friendly together" (5.5.480–1). This alliance of ensigns has been read against the backdrop of the new—and in 1610 controversial—British flag, conflating the crosses of St George and St Andrew, uniting a kingdom stretching from Dover to Dunsinane:

> In "A Proclamation declaring what Flaggs South and North Britaines shall beare at Sea" of 12 April 1606, omitting, as in *Cymbeline*, any reference to the traditional names of England and Scotland, James decreed ". . . that from hencefoorth all our Subjects of this Isle and Kingdome of great Britaine and the members thereof, shall beare in their Mainetoppe the Red Crosse, commonly called St. Georges Crosse, and the White Crosse commonly called S Andrewes Crosse, joyned together." The new composite flag, imposed without parliamentary consultation, formed part of a strategy to replace local symbols, including coins and official seals, with ones that represented a single united nation.
>
> (Redmond 1999: 307)

James invoked a Roman model for the enlarged state over which he reigned, promoted the name "Britain," and introduced a multi-national flag. What finer compliment could there be to the new king? Except that in Shakespeare, this is not the Anglo-Scottish Union of Crowns but a Romano-British alliance being brokered. Moreover, as Michael Redmond reminds us, the play's most odious villain bears a name akin to the king's: "With all the allusions to Jacobean issues in *Cymbeline*, it is strange that Shakespeare assigns his villain the name Giacomo, the Italian word for James" (Redmond 1999: 312). "Some jay of Italy" (3.4.48) is the enemy of Britain.

There is another Jack-in-the-box. The impotent Cloten bemoans the immunity to attack conferred by royal status: "every Jack-slave hath his bellyful of fighting and I/must go up and down like a cock, that nobody can match" (2.1.20–1). It will be another 130 years before a Scot, James Thomson, composes "Rule Britannia" (1740), with its memorable refrain: "Rule, Britannia! Britannia, rule the waves!/ Britons never, never, never shall be slaves!" A 1798 production of Shakespeare's play included a performance of Thomson's patriotic song (Wayne 2003: 391–4). In *Cymbeline*, an anti-Jack/James reading vies with a pro-Union reading that sees virtue in the King's compromise solution. Paying tribute to Rome means paying tribute to empire, an act of self-aggrandizement. The beleaguered isle came to rule the waves through the passage from postcolonial England to British Empire. James I was both peacemaker and planter of new nations, particularly in Ireland, where a postwar settlement enabled a new British colony.

THE WHOLE NINE YEARS: HUGH O'NEILL, THE FLIGHT OF THE EARLS, AND THE ULSTER PLANTATION

There are fleeting signs of Irishness in *Cymbeline*. Arviragus, wrapped in a "mantle" at birth (5.5.362), wears "clouted brogues" (4.2.213). It was an Irishman, Edward Dowden, who christened *Cymbeline* a Romance, and another, D. Plunket Barton, who found there a "Celtic note" with a particular Irish emphasis (Barton 1919: 235–6). But by and large Ireland remains a great thing of us forgot. We overlook the Nine Years War (1594–1603), followed by another nine years in which the end of Gaelic Ulster paved the way for a British project on a par with Anglo-Scottish Union—the Ulster Plantation—and underestimate the extent to which Roman models of colonization directly influenced English activity in Ireland (Quinn 1945). When *Cymbeline* was written, Ireland was the most vexed constituency in the emerging British state, yet Irish readings remain thin on the ground, though there are signs of a sea change. Focusing on the settlement of Virginia in her insightful interpretation of environment and ethnicity in *Cymbeline*, Jean Feerick shows how Shakespeare takes "an intimate look at colonial processes," acknowledging the limits of this Atlantic venture: "In the years between 1607 and 1611, the settling of Virginia was an enterprise that few Englishmen were eager or willing to pursue" (Feerick 2003: 31, 62). Feerick's findings apply to Ireland, site of the greatest act of colonization in the period. The rebirth of Britain, harking back to—and harping on—an ancient past as a colony of Rome, coincided with the settlement of Ulster, as an upward displacement of the English Pale around Dublin produced a new locus of Britishness around Belfast, cornerstone of a unique conjunction of union and empire. Philip Edwards comes closest to claiming *Cymbeline* as an Irish play through a tantalizing treatment of its colonial politics:

> What would happen if we were to translate the ending of *Cymbeline* into Irish terms? Cymbeline defeats the Romans and immediately submits himself to the benevolence of Roman rule. So—after his staggering victory over Sir Henry Bagenal and the destruction of the English army at the battle of the Yellow Ford in August 1598, Hugh O'Neill, the Earl of Tyrone, would have to submit himself to Queen Elizabeth, acknowledge her lordship but secure his independence, and by that means England and Ireland would live in contented peace ever afterwards.
>
> (Edwards 1998: 237)

Ultimately, O'Neill could not be accommodated within the new dispensation, and *Cymbeline* was written in a charged colonial atmosphere in the wake of war and the exodus of Ireland's Gaelic elite— "contented peace" was not in prospect. O'Neill exemplifies the failure of the policy of "surrender and regrant," whereby Irish lords converted their titles into English earldoms, surrendering native status to be regranted colonial authority. In declaring himself "The O'Neill," the erstwhile Earl of Tyrone abandoned his anglicized appellation and became an enemy of England. But O'Neill had already roused the anger of the court, where he was raised. His elopement with Mabel Bagenal in 1591—a topic treated in Brian Friel's *Making History* (1989)— triggered one of the most provocative partnerships of the 1590s. Richard Bagwell called Mabel "the Helen of the Elizabethan wars" (Bagwell 1890: 223). Whether that makes O'Neill its Paris, or its Posthumus, is debatable. O'Neill's marriage to Mabel may have offered a model for Hotspur's Welsh wife, or Othello's elopement with Desdemona. Warriors, weddings, and women are at the heart of imperial romance.

LITTLE ROMAN AND LESS BRITAIN

Effeminate Italy is no proper successor to imperial Rome—masculine Britain, where mountaineers roam free, is rightful heir. Before the battle, the soothsayer predicts a Roman victory:

> I saw Jove's bird, the Roman eagle, wing'd
> From the spongy south to this part of the west,
> There vanish'd in the sunbeams, which portends
> (Unless my sins abuse my divination)
> Success to th' Roman host.

(4.2.348–52)

The allusion to the "spongy south" is gendered. It is grim up north, but gritty too, so "the heritage of ancient Rome falls on Britain" (Knight 1947: 165–6). The allusion to "th' Roman host," often overlooked, its clotted ambiguity unappreciated by editors, encompasses Roman forces, Catholicism, and Britain itself. When Britain triumphs, the soothsayer—who will say anything forsooth—foresees a new Rome rising in the west:

> . . . the Roman eagle,
> From south to west on wing soaring aloft,
> Lessened herself and in the beams o' the sun
> So vanish'd; which foreshadow'd our princely eagle,
> Th'imperial Caesar, should again unite
> His favour with the radiant Cymbeline,
> Which shines here in the west.

(5.5.471–7)

In *Cymbeline*, misogyny is repressed, then revived, effeminate Cloten and his strident mother supplanted by chaste Imogen and her manly mountaineers. She is a stepmother out of step, he a clot on the landscape. Alive, Cloten can pass as nobody but himself. Disguised as Posthumus—already a dead man—he is decapitated. Successful "passing" is the passport to new nationhood. As Parker says of Posthumus: "Unlike Cloten, he is British and Roman, Roman and

British by turn, in a series of chiastic exchanges that finally make him the play's primary combination of both" (Parker 1989: 200). This composite character typifies New Britain.

Cymbeline does more than contrast effete Italy with two-fold ballsy Britain. Attitudes to sexuality are crucial to the kind of state Britain might become—a gaunt and jealous one, its loins girded with a "salt-water girdle" (3.1.80–1), as Cloten puts it, a corset concealing unsightly bulges such as Wales, or one open to others, including the banished and beaten. Posthumus acquires psychological sophistication through awareness of sexual difference, becoming a Briton in touch with his feminine side, but to claim that "the 'woman's part' allows Posthumus to gain in interiority what he loses in imperial promise" (James 1997: 187) ignores the intertwining of self and nation whereby he proves an effective servant of empire (Oz 1998). Patriarchy prevails in a play that parodies patriotism in the insular form advocated by Cloten and the Queen. Narrow nationalists are neutralized, expansionist pro-Romans triumph. According to John Kerrigan, "conflict between Rome and Britain is articulated through sexual violence in situations shaped by the politics of Jacobean union" (Kerrigan 2006: 122). In *Cymbeline*, battles are waged, bets wagered to the ultimate enslavement of the female principle.

The character of the king notwithstanding, the patriarchal structures of monarchy and empire are upheld. In *Cymbeline*, the trap set by the cunning Italian to render Posthumus paralyzed by paranoia is offset by the battle between Britain and Rome, where a masculine victory precedes a peace acceptable to all parties. Accommodating outsiders is the key, but only to the men's room, the Union Jock's locker. According to Jodi Mikalachki: "In contrast to the ancient queen's savage refusal of empire, the masculine embrace of Roman Britain became the truly generative interaction, producing a civil masculine foundation for early modern English nationalism" (Mikalachki 1995: 322). Here, the Queen is not villain, but victim. She resists the Roman Empire, and by extension its British successor. The lost boys are raised not just by Belarius, but by a nurse named "Euriphile" (3.3.103–5). This surrogate mother bears a name associated with a pro-European position, counter to the queen's exclusive ideology, "more 'Europhile' than 'Eurosceptic'" as Kerrigan quips (Kerrigan

2006: 127). Patricia Parker detects turbulence "just behind the surface of the play's historically conservative close" (Parker 1989: 190), but the disturbance is on the surface too, as the play's conclusion throws up more matter than it can comfortably contain.

Cymbeline sets up a series of oppositions: empire versus colony; court versus country; metropolis versus margins. It is as though the BBC (British Broadcasting Corporation) and CNN (Caesar's Narrative News) were vying for ascendancy on the airwaves, broadcasting conflicting versions of events. A fable of the forging of Britain caught between Papal Bull and John Bull, colonial inheritance and imperial aspiration, the play stages competing national narratives. In its attitude to "Rome" —ecclesiastical and imperial—it appears caught between a yoke and a yardstick. James Joyce famously represented Ireland as a country crucified between two thieves—the Roman and British Empires: "I do not see what good it does to fulminate against the English tyranny while the Roman tyranny occupies the palace of the soul" (Ellmann and Mason 1959: 173). Like Cymbeline's Queen, Joyce refused two empires, but without clinging to the rock of "narrow nationalism."

In Britain too, Christ and Caesar go hand in hand. Cymbeline reigns at the birth of Christ, but by Shakespeare's time Rome meant not just empire but the Holy Roman Empire, the power of the Catholic Church (Parker 1989: 206). Yet few readings ponder the implications of a drama that ultimately affirms a Romano-British accommodation. Invoking such an alliance in a context where, having broken with Rome, England was now being incorporated into a cosmetically enhanced body politic nursing its own imperial pretensions raises questions about breaching and bridging. Heads you lose, but tails turn up trumps in the end.

No clear conclusion can be drawn from the play's final acceptance of a Roman contribution to Britain, or a British tribute to Rome. Is it a matter of an imperial and masculine model of government, or is the granting of some room to Rome in the emerging Britain a matter of faith? Despite claims for his Catholicism, Shakespeare's allegiances remain elusive. James, eager to accommodate Rome in his vision of Britain, struggled to separate religion and empire (Jones 1961: 92–3). Michael Redmond warns against looking for clarity amidst creative confusion (Redmond 1999: 310–11). His contention that Shakespeare took the patronage and complicated the patriotism is one way of explaining *Cymbeline*'s "ideological incoherence" and "interpretive confusion" (Redmond 1999: 311, 313). But is the play doing more than "muttering critical asides" (James 1997: 188)? It may celebrate Britain as a new Rome, or foretell the ruin that follows the rise, prophetic both in envisioning a new empire and in rehearsing that empire's woes: "the crises of Rome in *Cymbeline* may also be a problem for the incipient British Empire" (Hirota 2004: 290). Heather James sees it flagging up the conflict between crown and parliament that culminated in the beheading of James's son (James 1997: 155). Every reading is, as the King concedes, a "fierce abridgement" (5.5.383). An "abridgement," like a bridge, is a strategic position from which one can fight off armies. It is also, according to the OED, a "curtailment (of rights)." With the insular queen eliminated, the "Europhile" surrogate mother mourned, and Roman and British ensigns hoisted in harmony, can we not see a clear message? As England breathes out into the girdle of Britain, it risks imperial amnesia, assuming the Emperor's new clothes while kitted out in mantle and brogues. Bridges are our links with the past. We burn or blow them at our peril.

The time is out of joint, but *Cymbeline* remains timely and topical. Penned in the narrow isthmus between postcolonial, post-Reformation England and nascent British Empire, the play stages the conflict between occupation and resistance even as it anticipates a reversal that is also a renewal. Scottish courtier William Alexander urged James and Prince Henry to exceed other empires: "Make the Lyon to be fear'd farre more,/Then ever was the Eagle of before" (Cited in Williamson 2005: 243). At the turn of the twenty-first century, as one empire eclipses another, relations between the two vital to the future shape of the globe, Shakespeare's convoluted clash of cultures appears all the more pertinent. John Pocock characterized British history as "the plural history of a group of cultures situated along an Anglo-Celtic frontier and marked by an increasing English political and cultural domination" (Pocock 1975: 605–6). *Cymbeline* is played out along that Anglo-Celtic frontier, also a Romano-British frontier.

"The conflict over tribute engages questions of empire" (Jordan 1997: 69), making Imogen's aside on the nature of "tribute" a key statement:

Our courtiers say all's savage but at court;
Experience, O, thou disprov'st report!
Th'emperious seas breed monsters; for the dish
Poor tributary rivers as sweet fish.

(4.2.33–5)

This arguably undercuts her father's blithe declaration: "Although the victor, we submit to Caesar,/And to the Roman empire" (5.5.461–2). Posthumus had earlier demurred: "Statist [. . .] I am none, nor like to be" (2.4.16). Relations between nation, state and empire are as fraught today as in the time of the play's setting and staging. According to Ronald Boling:

> Cymbeline seeks peace with Rome partly because of the serviceable account of their relation now available. A historical account to which both nations are willing to subscribe makes possible the play's political peace. The English discursive construct "Britain" likewise aimed to provide a history accommodating both England and Wales.
>
> (Boling 2000: 66)

But is "Britain" an English construct, Scottish aspiration, Welsh invention, or Roman imposition? *Cymbeline* tackles a time of transition for the nations making up the burgeoning British state, a time of fragile union, flight of a political elite, and the beginnings of a new colony. Kerrigan claims "that any more-or-less postcolonial impulse to represent ancient Britain as the victim of empire was compromised by the materials they inherited from the colonizing power" (Kerrigan 2006: 130), but every victim bears the mark of their aggressor. We should think in terms of neocolonial Britain. The power of the Queen's speech means that Cymbeline's contribution to the rhetoric of resistance, in which he repeats the resonant word "yoke" (3.1.52; 3.5.5), gets overlooked. The King's claim that "Till the injurious Romans did extort/This tribute from us, we were free" (3.1.48–9), and his accompanying explanation of the overweening ambition that triggered the original demand for tribute, sees him side with the anti-imperialists. The final capitulation, in the midst of so much recapitulation, seems all the more puzzling. One solution is to see in the denouement a choice between "two imperialisms," one in thrall to Rome, tarred with tyranny, and a homegrown version, outcome of anti-imperialist struggle, bound up with liberty (Jordan 1997: 86).

This "Romish stew" of a drama is rich repast. Compliments to the chef, that broth of a bard, on his "neat cookery," recalling Guiderius's comment on Imogen/Fidele's culinary skills: "he cut our roots in characters/And sauced our broths, as Juno had been sick/And he her dieter" (4.2.49–51). An alphabet soup that spells the end of empire even as it lists its ingredients as a recipe for disaster is one way of characterizing a play that still turns heads as it stirs the pot of history.

NOTE

1 This happens in episode 6, screened 21 October 2003, BBC 3: www.bbc.co.uk/comedy/littlebritain/episodes/s1_ep6.shtml, accessed 12 June 2006.

8

PLAYING WITH CUPID

Gender, Sexuality and Adolescence

Kate Chedgzoy

I

When women's voices are brought to bear on literary and cultural concerns, what do we learn that we could not otherwise have known? In what ways do our visions of the literary and political landscapes change when we read accounts by previously unknown witnesses?

(Hageman and Steen 1996: vi–vii)

These still-valid questions were posed by Elizabeth Hageman and Sarah Jayne Steen in the introduction to a special issue of *Shakespeare Quarterly* on Shakespeare's female contemporaries that took its title, "Teaching Judith Shakespeare", from Virginia Woolf's powerful myth of women's exclusion from the literary canon in *A Room of One's Own*. Woolf's counter-factual history of Shakespeare's imagined sister Judith has been repeatedly revised and extended in the body of feminist criticism that has had a transforming effect on the study of Shakespeare, Renaissance women's writing and early modern culture more generally. But the historical figure of the real Judith Shakespeare—William

Shakespeare's daughter, not his sibling—has been obscured rather than revealed in this work. The potential for equality encoded in the sibling metaphor has displaced the inequality intrinsic to relationships between adults and children. This essay starts from the desire to take seriously the historical Judith's status as daughter, and to ask what factors shape the possibilities for agency open to such a girl. How do Shakespeare's portrayals of daughters making the journey to adulthood re-inflect the generative feminist myth of Judith Shakespeare, by introducing into the critical debate the issues of subordination by age as well as gender, and of change over time in a female life?

Feminist scholars have also played formative roles in the emergence of childhood studies as an area of politically engaged interdisciplinary critique comparable to women's studies (Clark 2003: 5). Just as the critical study of women and gender has a dual project, so childhood studies likewise aspires to render visible, interpret and contextualize the overlooked agency and subjectivity of children, and also to analyse the cultural work done by the category "child", and attendant fantasies and ideologies of childhood. What difference can this convergence of sexual politics with attention to the critical politics of childhood make to Shakespeare studies? If we allow children's voices to be "brought to bear on literary and cultural concerns", and begin to take children as "unknown witnesses" as seriously as we have learned to treat women, how will our "visions of the literary and political landscapes" be further transformed? If, in particular, we focus on female children as they pass through adolescence into adult femininity, what can we learn of the complex interrelations of the politics of gender, sexuality and age in Shakespeare's texts and in the culture from which they emerged?

For early modern girls, the transition from childhood to adulthood was profoundly implicated with sexuality and the social institutions that regulate it, because marriage constituted the crucial liminal rite marking that journey across age boundaries (Garber 1981). This journey and its vicissitudes form the subject matter of Shakespeare's romantic comedies, and have been much discussed in feminist criticism of that genre. In this essay, I am particularly concerned with the volatile, unresolved and problematic aspects of the way that female adolescence is shaped by the social regulation of the erotic. I approach this topic by exploring the interactions and juxtapositions of Shakespeare's adolescent girls with that curious boy Cupid, examining his playful, ambivalent role in young girls' transitions from childhood to adulthood. The figure of Cupid serves as the embodiment of the complex sexual dynamics that shaped the powerfully gendered transition to adulthood for young early moderns. In order to see both how Shakespeare used Cupid to stage and investigate those dynamics, and how Cupid might have enabled one of Shakespeare's hypothetical literary daughters to make sense of them, I juxtapose Shakespearean representations with a remarkable depiction of Cupid in a dramatic text written by an adolescent girl, Lady Rachel Fane, at a time when she occupied, like Cupid himself, the liminal zone between childhood and adulthood.[1]

II

Cupid is an infrequent corporeal presence on the Shakespearean stage. He makes his sole appearance as a character when he presents the masque at the banquet in *Timon of Athens* 1.2—a role that, in its playful metatheatricality and association with unregulated sexuality, displays many of the qualities attributed to him by Shakespeare and his contemporaries.[2] He is invoked in thirteen further plays and in the final two Sonnets, where he figures as the personification of and stimulus to erotic passion—"the general of hot desire" (Sonnet 154). Perhaps the most striking thing about Cupid in the Shakespearean canon is his absence from *Venus and Adonis*, the narrative of his mother's desire for a beautiful young boy who notably—perhaps riskily—resembles Cupid himself.[3] The absence of Cupid from the Shakespearean stage is not typical of Renaissance drama as a whole. Cupid featured as a character in more than seventy early modern plays, many of them masques (Berger *et al.* 1998). Sometimes alone, more often he is paired with Venus in a complexly eroticized mother–son dynamic. In Renaissance visual culture, Cupid has an alternative companion, Psyche, and with her he is a youth or young man. Venus makes a boy of him: both chronologically youthful—placed somewhere between the *putti* of European baroque painting and a sexually mature adolescent—and subordinated to maternal power in the hierarchies of age and family.

As mother and son, and as love-gods, Venus and Cupid highlight the dependency of the family on particular socially regulated cathexes of sexuality and the erotic. And as representations of child figures taking up playful relationships to desire between adult men and women, Cupids prompt us both to think about the specific cultural relations between children and the erotic, and to recognize the queerness that often haunts normative heterosexual and familial arrangements. The stage image (found in plays by several of Shakespeare's contemporaries) of Cupid snuggled on the lap of a quasi-maternal, quasi-sexual female companion evokes polymorphous erotic possibilities. Eroticizing the mother–son dyad, "the arresting image of one boy-actor holding a smaller boy-actor in his arms," must also have generated "a distinctly homoerotic *frisson*" (Pincombe 2000: 51). Though Cupid's actions are generally designed to stimulate heterosexual lust, the lovely boy as object of homoerotic desire haunts his portrayal in the Renaissance. Marlowe's Cupid in *Dido, Queen of Carthage* (published 1594) is perhaps the single most vivid embodiment in Renaissance drama of this queerly shape-shifting, disorderly child-figure. He appears in "a carnival world in which the norms of gender behaviour, sexuality, and political responsibility are turned topsy-turvy" (Deats 2004: 195), and as is often the case with early modern Cupids, he plays an active role in generating this carnivalesque atmosphere. In this, he anticipates the characteristic Shakespearean depiction of Cupid—for if, as Panofsky argued in his influential study of the Renaissance iconography of Cupid, the literature and art of the period represented two versions of Cupid, signifying illicit and divine love, Shakespeare seems to have been interested only in the first of these (Panofsky 1939: 95–128).

Cupid is often cited in scenarios where the power of love over humans—and particularly over women—is tested, and its disruptive potential registered. Though the narrative structures of comedy seek to reassert the desirability of socially orderly forms of love and courtship, the wished-for closure does not overwrite the significance of the subversive play we have witnessed. Cupid makes only one appearance in his own person on Shakespeare's stage, but a larger population of figures who share many of the boy-god's attributes and do some of his cultural and erotic work move through the plays. Youthful boy-girl-boy figures such as Rosalind and Viola serve as Cupid's Shakespearean surrogates. As objects of desire to male and female subjects and playful stage-managers of their own and other people's romantic scenarios, they foreground the mobility of gender across the sites of desiring subjects and longed-for objects in a heteropatriarchal context. Boys and women share with Cupid an inherent tendency to shape-shifting changeability, as Rosalind/ Ganymede demonstrates when s/he manipulates an imagined male suitor's love for the transgendered object s/he performs, being by turns "effeminate, changeable, longing and liking, proud, fantastical, apish, shallow, inconstant" (*As You Like It* 3.2.368–79)—all adding up to a fair description of Cupid, and recalling Marlowe's queer alignment of Ganymede with Cupid.

In her own persona, Rosalind asks "that same wicked bastard of Venus that was begot of thought, conceived of spleen and born of madness, that blind rascally boy that abuses every one's eyes because his own are out" to judge how far she is in love with Orlando (4.1.181–4). This version of Cupid both invokes illegitimacy, a transgressive consequence of pre-marital heterosexual activity that was a source of great anxiety in the early modern period, and calls up the period's frequent association of young boys with socially disorderly behaviour. Rosalind's alignment with Cupid is sustained to the end of the play, for her negotiation with the audience when she delivers the epilogue here is a highly Cupid-like performance, recalling the return of another of Shakespeare's most striking Cupid-surrogates, Puck, to end *A Midsummer Night's Dream* after another set of multiple wedding festivities. Cupid's subversive influence is thus evident in *As You Like It*—as often in Shakespeare's plays—not merely in terms of the election of inappropriate objects of desire but also in relation to the volatility of desiring positions and normative gender arrangements.

The typical Renaissance Cupid is a paradox and a shape-shifter, then, "both male and female, blind and sighted, child and adult, playful and sinister, angelic and demonic" (Tinkle 1996: 5). Though popular iconography since the Renaissance has marked him as male, the earlier volatility of his gender identity is illustrated in Middleton's *The Nice Valour*, where Cupid is "personated by a Lady" and greeted as "sweet Caelestiall boy" when she enters 'like a Cupid' (Middleton 1989: 438, 451). Cupid thus foregrounds precisely the complexities of establishing and then transgressing the boundaries between gendered and sexually marked categories of age and status that I am concerned with in this essay. His relationship to age categories was always paradoxical: poised in his representation as an adolescent between childhood and adulthood, his conventionally youthful status also contradicted his position among the oldest of the gods. Cupid's mobile identities and manipulation of erotic play blur the boundaries between child and adult subjectivity, and thereby expose the uncertain foundations of the normative power structures underpinning the family and upholding the distinction between adults and children.

Love's Labour's Lost is the Shakespeare play in which Cupid is most frequently evoked and associated with desire that transgresses social norms (Kingsley-Smith 2006). This is a play very much concerned with the transition from adolescence to adulthood, as it is inflected by both gender and sexuality. Cupid's surrogate here is not a cross-dressed girl, however, but a young boy entered upon the career in service that will lead him towards elite adult masculinity. The pageboy Moth can be seen as an incarnation of the carnivalesque Cupid when he offers his master courtship advice unlikely to promote dignity and self-possession:

> jig off a tune at the tongue's end, canary to it with your feet, humour it with turning up your eyelids, sigh a note and sing a note, sometime through the throat as if you swallowed love with singing love, sometime through the nose as if you snuffed up love by smelling love.
>
> *(Love's Labour's Lost* 3.1.8–13)

Playing with gender in the service of the erotic by suggesting that winning female favour requires the performance of the heterosexually desiring male body as carnivalesque, Moth's counsel anticipates Biron's invective against Cupid's disruptive and inversive powers, later in the same scene:

> This whimpled, whining, purblind, wayward boy,
> This Signor Junior, giant dwarf, Dan Cupid,
> Regent of love-rhymes, lord of folded arms,
> Th' anointed sovereign of sighs and groans,
> Liege of all loiterers and malcontents,
> Dread prince of plackets, king of codpieces,
> Sole imperator and great general
> Of trotting paritors
>
> (3.1.164–71)

Calling attention to Cupid's paradoxical status as a childlike embodiment of one of the oldest gods, the phrase "Signor Junior . . . Dan Cupid"—in some versions written "senior-junior"—destabilizes the hierarchies of age by short-circuiting the normal line of development from childhood to adulthood, making them co-exist in a single moment rather than inhabit positions in a hierarchical sequence. As well as causing disarray among age hierarchies, this Cupid, as "prince of plackets" and "king of codpieces", holds erotic power over both men and women, embodying, in his shape-shifting fashion, a range of possible objects of desire. Indeed, the syntax here trades a clear distinction between desiring subject and eroticized object for a diffuse sense of Cupid's power over the body's erotic zones.

Iconographically prominent as a child figure, at the same time Cupid lays bare the difficulty of determining the boundaries between childhood and the next life stage, whether that be conceptualized as youth or adulthood—a point on which there was no consensus among contemporaries (Lamb 2005). As a boy—that is, as Shakespeare and his contemporaries used the term, a male youth aged between ten and eighteen—the Renaissance Cupid inhabited a transitional phase of life in which the latter years of childhood blurred into the first phase of youth, understood as a time of apprenticeship to adulthood (Griffiths 1996: 24). Boys were of their nature shape-shifters, then, and boyhood was also a time of gender liminality. The bodily signs of youthfulness and femininity combined in Cesario's appearance and voice do not make Orsino suspect that his new page is in fact a woman, but rather provide ample confirmation that he is not yet a man:

For they shall yet belie thy happy years
That say thou art a man. Diana's lip
Is not more smooth and rubious; thy small pipe
Is as the maiden's organ, shrill and sound,
And all is semblative a woman's part.

(Twelfth Night 1.4.29–33)

As boys made their journey away from the female-dominated realm of early childhood to adult masculinity, they could be seen as still closely associated with the feminine, as Rosalind/Ganymede's remark that "boys and women are for the most part cattle of this colour" (*As You Like It* 3.2.371) highlights. Women and children of both sexes shared a space of disempowerment compared to adult men in early modern society, and the category "boy" is marked by status as well as gender, denoting subordination to adult male authority and a lack of autonomy. Unlike women and girls, however, boys could at least hope that their progress through the masculine life cycle would enable them in time to accede to a position of masculine independence and authority. This conflation of age with gender thus occludes girlhood as a distinct condition. Like the transformation of Judith Shakespeare into an adult sister rather than a growing daughter, it leaves girls out of the story of how early modern sexuality and gender were formed in relation to each other.

The prospect of change over time in an individual life—of growth to manhood—is thus of formative significance in shaping the meanings and experience of boyhood as qualitatively different from girlhood. While boys experienced youth as a temporary destabilization of the structures of dependence and autonomy that regulated the other stages of life, girls moved between a series of dependent, submissive positions as daughters, servants and wives, in a sequence of patriarchal households. As a result, adolescent girlhood was contradictory and multi-faceted, at once "a time of danger and exposure, and, consequently, of potential freedom and resistance" and, conversely, "a time when ideological forces work to inculcate femininity and produce mature women" (Higginbotham 2003). Jennifer Higginbotham highlights the uneven and potentially contradictory implications for young women of the transitions and fault lines that could provide points of

possible disruption in their movements through the circuits of heterosexual patriarchy. For elite women, service and courtship were the
key vectors of these movements, and both could be the site of girls'
first recognition of how romance and the erotic would inflect their
relationship to the structures of their social world. All these elements
are complexly intertwined in Twelfth Night, a play full of young people
making their way into adulthood via courtship and marriage in the
anomalous absence of a parental generation. Viola in her incarnation
as Cesario is an ambiguously Cupid-like figure, finding that service
in an aristocratic household both requires her to do the work of
Cupid by courting Olivia on behalf of her master in the role of
Cesario and also makes her vulnerable to his erotic influence as she
falls in love with that same master:

> I'll do my best
> To woo your lady—[aside] yet a barful strife—
> Whoe'er I woo, myself would be his wife.
> (Twelfth Night 1.4.39–41)

In a different emotional key, Maria also does the work of Cupid and
finds herself caught up in his trammels; and though nowadays she
is usually played by a relatively mature actress, the original performances of the role by a boy actor might have situated this character
at much the same life-stage as Viola/Cesario.

Boys' transition to adulthood differed ideologically and practically
from that of girls, in that it was understood to be regulated primarily
by structures of paid labour (though as we have seen in the case of
Moth, this might also take the form of service) and education. Yet
the fact that Viola takes up her Cupidesque responsibilities in her
guise as Cesario reveals that male adolescence was not devoid of
erotic or romantic elements that could be just as problematic. This
is confirmed when Jaques casts the frustrated lover as the schoolboy's
successor in his account of the stages of male life (As You Like It
2.7.146–8). In this narrative, the lover must be a temporary phase
of adult masculinity, giving way to the soldier (2.7.148–52), a
progression endorsed when Patroclus invokes Cupid to reject the
dangerously effeminizing impact of Achilles' love for him in Troilus

and Cressida. Cupid's power in this play lies in his ability to employ the erotic to turn masculine strength into weakness. His "amorous fold", though intrinsically insubstantial as a dewdrop, is at the same time an embrace powerful enough to keep a renowned soldier from the battlefield. Turning Achilles' mind—like that of Jaques' imagined soldier—to "the bubble reputation" (*As You Like It* 2.7.151), Patroclus's speech begins the process that incites him to take up arms again. Cupid's power is revealed as transient and precarious when he is identified by Patroclus with that which must be repudiated in order to achieve a desirably martial masculine identity.

Cupid's relation to adult masculinity is complex, then, and when young men on the verge of adulthood refer to Cupid in Shakespeare's plays, their comments contain a volatile mixture of identification, emulation, rivalry, defensive scorn and anxiety. Mercutio invokes "gossip Venus" and "her purblind son and heir,/Young Adam Cupid" to satirize and trivialize Romeo's sub-Petrarchan idealization of Rosaline (*Romeo and Juliet* 2.1.11–13). Emphasizing the familial relationship on the one hand serves to domesticate and thus de-eroticize Romeo's passion, and on the other suggests a queer destabilization of the patriarchal household and its dynastic marriages that Juliet's father is so concerned to sustain. Mercutio mocks and diminishes Cupid at a moment when he and Benvolio are concerned to reassert the claims on Romeo of homosocial bonds among young men against the heterosexual desires drawing their friend away from them. The disorderly, transgressive behaviour of the young men who gatecrash the Capulet feast is thus set against that event's purpose, which is to foster a patriarchally endorsed romance between Juliet and Paris. Disguising themselves as masquers in order to enter the party secretly, they reject as outworn and outdated the presentation of Cupid associated with masquing (and employed in that context, as this essay later shows, to far from conventional effect both in *Timon of Athens* and by Rachel Fane). "We'll have no Cupid hoodwinked with a scarf," insists Benvolio (1.4.4). Yet these anti-romantic masquers, affecting bawdy cynicism about love and desire, find themselves serving inadvertently as Cupid's shape-shifting agents. Unrecognizable behind their masks, and representing a youthful masculine pleasure nostalgically endorsed by Capulet (1.5.19–22), their actions ensure the meeting of Romeo and Juliet. In a comedy, this misalliance might be read as merely one of Cupid's tricks. In *A Midsummer Night's Dream*, for instance, Cupid is summoned to the aid of the erotic and romantic passions of the young, in opposition to patriarchally imposed marital arrangements, when Oberon calls on the alliance of Venus and Cupid to assist his intervention in the affairs of the human lovers (3.2.102–9). But Cupid, though stereotypically youthful himself, is no partisan of the young, and in *Romeo and Juliet* his agents mess up the smooth working of heteropatriarchal couplings with tragically damaging consequences.

In *The Merchant of Venice*, disguise, night-time revelry and masquing likewise provide the context for Cupid's role in inciting eroticized gender transgression and contravention of patriarchal authority. Here, though, the homosocial male group welcomes and supports the advent of heterosexual romance, and the female presence of Venus too is invoked when Jessica "obscure[s]" herself "in the lovely garnish of a boy" (*Merchant of Venice* 2.6.43, 45) in order to elope with Lorenzo. Jessica comments:

> love is blind, and lovers cannot see
> The pretty follies that themselves commit;
> For if they could, Cupid himself would blush
> To see me thus transformed to a boy.
>
> (2.6.36–9)

This foregrounds the erotic desirability of her androgynous appearance more strongly than it condemns its disorderly implications. In a play profoundly concerned with the relationships between daughters' heterosexual choices and the reproductive needs of the patriarchal family, Jessica's citation of Cupid as she undertakes an unauthorized marriage that sets the daughter's desire in conflict with paternal authority and social order indexes the disruptive potential of her desire for Lorenzo.

Shakespeare's Cupid is an anti-marital force, then, too disruptive of normative social hierarchies to facilitate the reintegration of erotic desire with patriarchal imperatives through the institution of marriage. Admitted to Shakespeare's dramas at moments when the course of true love is not running smooth, or the carnivalesque elements of the erotic are foregrounded, he is banished from the marriage masques in *As You Like It* and *The Tempest*—though in other dramas of the period, his energies are appropriated in such performances. The spirit of Cupid surely informs the mock-wedding Rosalind/Ganymede orchestrates with Orlando in *As You Like It* 4.1; yet in the final masque-like celebration of the social recuperation of all these wayward desires, he is displaced by Hymen, god of weddings, as the presiding deity. Cupid's non-appearance in *The Tempest*'s wedding masque is equally significant. Staging Juno and Ceres as representatives of marriage and fertility, but explicitly excluding desire as embodied by "Mars's hot minion" (Venus) and "Her waspish-headed son" (Cupid) (*Tempest*, 4.1.98–9), the masque both serves "as an antidote to premarital sexuality" (Johnson 1997: 691) and defers the union of Miranda and Ferdinand by occupying the dramatic space in which their wedding might have occurred. An alternative reading is that Prospero's masque stages a belated patriarchal attempt to wrest back control of marriage and the erotic from his teenage daughter: for according to early modern custom, the exchange of vows initiated by Miranda at 3.1.83 could have constituted a valid wedding ceremony. Miranda finds her own way of reconciling the wayward pull of desire with the social institutions that shaped an aristocratic girl's life.

Jessica's and Miranda's negotiations with the power of Venus and Cupid in relation to their social context show something of what is at stake for girls whose experience of adolescence is marked by the implication of sexuality within powerful heteropatriarchal structures, as well as by gender. Positioned at the boundaries of childhood as a chronological stage, these daughters' efforts to subvert their continuing dependence on and socially exacted submission to their familial superiors make plain that childhood is also a relational condition that does not end with accession to adulthood.

III

Shakespeare's representation in *The Tempest* of a girl whose departure from childhood is marked by a wedding masque resonates with Rachel Fane's May masque. This performance text, authored by a real-life peer of Jessica and Miranda, offers an alternative glimpse of a young woman thinking about how Cupid might impinge on the choices she makes as she approaches adulthood.

Performed, probably in May 1627, by a dozen children (ranging in age from four to twelve years) of the Fane household at Apthorpe Hall in Northamptonshire, fourteen-year-old Rachel Fane's masque constitutes a rare site where the voices of early modern child subjects are articulated. Addressing an adult audience, revealing a sophisticated knowledge of adult literary and dramatic culture, employing a dramatic mode in which the dividing lines between performers and audience, adults and children are frequently and insouciantly crossed, the masque does not disclose an unmediated child subjectivity. Rather, it shows how porous and easily crossed the boundaries between the cultures of children and adults are.

Fane's masque features many evocatively Shakespearean elements: the use of a clown figure (the jester) who mediates between perform- ance and audience; a pastoral/woodland setting; seasonal festive performance; liminal begging of the audience's favour and apprecia- tion; Virgilian allusion; metatheatrical elements; and dance and music. Shakespeare's poems were popular reading material for women of Fane's background (Roberts 2002), but we have no way of knowing whether she was familiar with his plays. Whether her masque is deliberately intertextual, or whether she and Shakespeare were drawing on the same cultural storehouse, what is significant here is the complex interplay of similarities and differences in the ways that this adult professional male playwright and youthful female amateur employ Cupid, Venus and everything they symbolize to explore the role of sexuality and marriage in the transition from girlhood to adulthood.

Fane's dramatic script begins with a pastoral anti-masque, reminis- cent in its mixing of dialogue with dancing and music, and in its concern with reproduction and new life, of the sheep-shearing festivities in Shakespeare's *Winter's Tale*, likewise presided over by an adolescent girl. The members of this rustic carnivalesque company are then replaced by "a nimpth sent from venus", come to purify the venue with frankincense in preparation for the goddess's entry. This signals the beginning of the main masque in which the stage is taken by allegorical personages of classical pastoral, including Venus and a traditionally armed and clad Cupid:

> a god of Loue w^it
> bowe aro^es & outher things
> fiting his atire
>   (O'Connor 2006: 110)

The complex relationship between performance conventions, age, status and gender makes it worth pausing to speculate about the casting of the role of Cupid in this instance. Normally in a masque, "a speaking Cupid would be a role for a professional boy actor, not an aristocratic lady" (Jowett 2006: 80). But on this occasion, only aristocratic children and other members of the household were available, so the casting could not have followed this convention. In the absence of any information about how roles were assigned, it is tempting both to speculate on how the interactions between Cupid and the predominantly female characters of the classical masque may have played upon the dynamics between audience and performers, and also to recall the precedent for a female Cupid in Middleton's *Nice Valour*.

Meanwhile Venus takes up a liminal position, "*half w^itin & half w^itout*" (O'Connor 2006: 111), and Cupid summons her to follow him, leading her by the hand. This courteous, deferential Cupid enacts maternal respect and submission within the familial performance environment, contradicting many of the disorderly, subversive qualities attributed to him by Shakespeare. He gives way to his mother Venus, staged here as a notably dignified figure, who declaims a litany of feminine divinity as she presides over a celebration of feminine chastity and virtue that could serve to counterbalance condemnation elsewhere of Cupid for tormenting women in particular: in *A Midsummer Night's Dream* for instance, Puck—who himself has something of the Cupid about him—remarks "Cupid is a knavish lad/Thus to make poor females mad" (3.3.28–9). Where Shakespeare's play shows the young women who have fallen under Cupid's "knavish" influence abandoning their former mutual friendship in order to compete over men, Rachel Fane's Venus invokes female solidarity to enable women to resist Cupid's tricks:

> The Godes Juno unto y^o giu^es welth
> Pales like wiss wisdom & strength,

> Sares corne & wine most plentyfuly can giue y°
> Diane Chaste to be whats this w^{it}out me
> When as this world was first begone
> Loue twas created tis yeet not don
>
> (O'Connor 2006: 111)

In a moment that echoes the marriage masque of Shakespeare's *The Tempest* while sidestepping its endorsement of matrimony, Venus unites the empowering influences of Juno, Ceres, Pallas and Diana, in order to reassure her audience that she will protect them from Cupid's subversive and disorderly interventions. She continues:

> But frends be all content,
> My mynde is fuly bent
> Y° shale goe free,
> From my sons inury
> Al days y^t y° doe life
> & when y° dye y^r Posterity
> Soe long as mortels Life.
>
> (O'Connor 2006: 111)

Extending this protective blessing to her audience's descendants, Venus decouples reproductive sexual activity from the effects of Cupid's arrows.

Fane's text here reads like a rehearsal for a wedding masque, a celebratory performance marking one of the key rituals of transition for early modern women; yet, like the Shakespearean wedding masques discussed above, it stops just short of matrimony. Playing with Cupid, and with the rituals of female adolescence, Rachel Fane's masque explores some of the implications of both Cupid's enjoyably disruptive energies and the ways in which they may be tamed, excluded or appropriated by the structures that shape adult femininity. In the context of this child-centred performance, the swerve away from marriage may also be simply about resisting the transition to adulthood marked by it, expressing a wish to continue to dwell in childhood. In her study of liminal passages in Shakespearean life-courses, Marjorie Garber describes the transition from youth to adulthood as one shaped through processes of individuation and differentiation, followed by accommodation within the new adult world of marriage or political power (Garber 1981: 48–9). Marriage involved "rites of separation as well as incorporation" (1981: 12); in dramatically eschewing the separation from the family of origin that was enforced on young women when they married, Rachel Fane's subverted wedding masque offers a celebration of the complex webs of relationship among all the members of a household, rather than merely of the marital dyad.

This is illustrated by the fact that Venus's assertion that her son will henceforth co-operate with her is followed by a dance in which Venus, Urania and three nymphs circle together in a feminine homosocial performance that allows no scope for either marriage or reproduction. As the dance ends, "venus speaks to ye company", relenting to reinstall Cupid-inspired passion as a possibility for the future lives of her audience, in terms that, while drawing the entire company into the conclusion of the masque in traditional courtly fashion, recuperate it for a more harmonious version of love and friendship within the feminocentric, maternally dominated and familial world celebrated by Fane's performance:

> I doe recant ye wordes I spoke of love
> For y^o shall constant all ways prove
> To me, my son, & thes my frinds
> Who will in dure y^{rs} to y^o end,
> *She goes to her place & takes urania*
> *by ye hand ye rest coopeling y^m*
> selfes together
> (O'Connor 2006: 112–13)

Venus thus shows herself willing to broker a collaboration between the often opposed interests of Cupid and Diana, and her son responds as a virtuous child submitting to his mother's authority and superior understanding:

> I am com for to accord
> To what my mother has done
> For y^t I know
> Her wisdom is soe

Y^t she cane more good
Y^n I unto ye shew
(O'Connor 2006: 113)

Though Cupid is neither banished nor punished by Fane, as he was in some earlier appearances on Renaissance stages, he is conscious of defeat. Love of a mature, female-led, somewhat domestic kind wins out over the playful erotic interventions of the subversive boy. Fane disempowers Cupid in order to place heterosexuality and marriage under the benevolent sign of female collectivity. But she also reinscribes this children's performance in a domestic context, using Cupid as a surrogate to enact a graceful compliment and acknowledgment of the importance of children's submission to parents before an audience in which the parents of several of the youthful performers were undoubtedly present.

Writing as an adolescent daughter moving towards adulthood, knowing that socially appropriate and parentally approved marriages must surely await many of her fellow performers in the masque in due course, Fane dramatized a scenario in which the complex ramifications of gender, sexuality and age for the young aristocratic woman can be explored under the sign of Cupid. Dramatic performance enabled her to carve out a small, temporary space within her father's household where she could reflect playfully on the likely course of her life, perhaps analogous in little to the construction of adolescence for boys as a time of temporary licence. Expressing in part the perspective of a young girl approaching marriageable age, the masque employs Venus and Cupid to present a strikingly affectionate, gynocentric and domestic vision of heterosexual marriage and courtship in the context of the aristocratic family. Fane's text reveals a remarkably acute awareness of the complex relations among love, kinship, marriage, desire and reproduction that shaped the adult life course awaiting an aristocratic young woman like herself.

IV

If staged Cupids are particularly prominent in masques and similar dramatic entertainments, this is partly because of the close association of Venus and Cupid with pastoral, a mode often employed in masques. More saliently, masques were often staged to celebrate marriage, domesticating and turning to socially acceptable use the potentially disruptive erotic energies embodied by Cupid. Yet Cupid's unique Shakespearean appearance as a character comes in the masque in *Timon of Athens*, a metadramatic occasion that runs counter in several ways to these attributes of the masque as a dramatic form.

The masque in *Timon* is a grotesquely distorted reflection of the Jacobean court masque as a social and aesthetic event. Instead of celebrating shared values, it provides a bitter commentary on a world in which it is a matter for "wonder [that] men dare trust themselves with men" (1.2.42). Elsewhere in Shakespeare, as we have seen, Cupid embodies a principle of erotic subversiveness or disorder, which is often recuperated but sometimes allowed to stand as a reminder of the energies that cannot always be tamely accommodated in the well-regulated adult social world. Here, though, there is no such order for Cupid to disrupt, and as a result it is Cupid's own customary role that is subverted. Cupid's task is to announce the entrance of a group of Amazon masquers, the first women to appear in the play, who body forth the pleasures of "[t]he five best senses" (1.2.116). They dance first as a company of women and then with the men, subsequently exiting again to a separate banquet, leaving the male homosocial realm of Timon's household unaltered. In the near-total absence of women from the world of this "play about men with men" (Jowett 2004: 42), the comedies of heterosexual desire Cupid is most often associated with have no scope, while the intimacies among men witnessed here are devoid of the playfulness and subversiveness characteristically associated with homoerotic Cupids. Timon's Cupid eludes the possibilities of change and multiplicity associated with his name and presence elsewhere in Shakespeare's plays, ushering onto the stage instead the representatives of sensuality, bypassing the social institutions such as marriage that harness bodily desires in the service of the social order. Since women in this play appear only as the Amazons of the masque and the prostitutes of 4.3 (who, as they enter with Alcibiades' army, share with the masquers a distinctly Amazonian quality) they are intrinsically non-nubile, and the significance of marriage in the female life-course is entirely written out. The Cupid of *Timon of Athens* is thus the *reductio ad absurdum* of all Shakespearean Cupids, a profoundly asocial and subversive figure associated with a version of the erotic that, though sensually pleasurable, goes nowhere, serves its own ends, and is entirely asocial.

The contrast between the undomesticated, unfamilial, all-male household of *Timon of Athens* and Rachel Fane's staging of a quasi-familial site of considerable female solidarity and empowerment is striking, even though in both cases Cupid appears in the context of a masque performance in an elite private household. Where participation in a domestic masque, for the young aristocrats of the Fane household, represented a pedagogically and socially approved episode in their formation as elite subjects, Timon's Cupid is a professional boy actor occupying a very different position in relation to the institutions that shaped the transition from childhood to adulthood for young people from diverse backgrounds. The masque's staging of Cupid thus briefly places the adolescent body centre-stage, but refuses the narratives of erotic and social development that in Shakespearean comedy seek to guide that embodied youthful self towards adulthood.

Just as Shakespearean Cupids problematize and transgress identity categories grounded in age and life-stage, so the performance of Rachel Fane's masque reveals that the boundaries of age and normatively age-appropriate behaviour may be porous and easily crossed. Historians of childhood pursuing the path laid down by Philippe Ariès argue that early moderns effectively considered children as miniature adults (Ariès 1962). In contrast, child performers and the roles they played— whether in aristocratic domestic settings, as discussed here, or on the commercial stage (Munro, 2007)—suggest that in fact Shakespeare and his contemporaries were both aware of the significant differences between children and adults, and had a sense that those differences could be labile and malleable.

One goal of childhood studies has been to locate the child subject in culture. The Cupids of Renaissance drama, Shakespearean and otherwise, have nothing to offer this project. Rather than representing the child's subjectivity or gaze, they inscribe adult fantasies about the erotic, drawing on literary and visual traditions in which the figure of Cupid invoked a range of qualities. Comparing Shakespeare's Cupids with that of Rachel Fane enables us to explore both how gender and sexuality are at stake in the experience and construction of adolescence, and how the complex variables of age and gender shape representation. Contextualizing Shakespeare's Cupids with reference to one staged by one of his cultural "daughters" highlights the need to continue and extend our critical attention to "other witnesses". And it enables us to glimpse the complex interplay of difference and interaction that shaped the distinct yet permeable cultural worlds of early modern children and adults.

NOTES

1 The masque forms part of MS Kent Archives Office U269/F38/3, a collection of dramatic and poetic texts composed for entertainment of the Fane household at times of festivity. My citations come from O'Connor 2006.

2 The scene has been attributed to Middleton, who presents Cupids in masques in *More Dissemblers Besides Women*, *The Nice Valour* and *Women Beware Women* (Jowett 2004). Yet as Robert C. Fulton demonstrates in a rare critical discussion of the *Timon* masque, it "enjoys a high degree of resonance with the play which incorporates it" (Fulton 1976: 283).

3 For a more extended discussion of Cupid's significant absence from the Shakespearean canon, see Kingsley-Smith, 2006. I am very grateful to Dr Kingsley-Smith for generously sharing with me drafts from her forthcoming book, *Lovestruck: Cupid in England, 1554–1634*, and for helpfully reading and commenting on a draft of the present essay.

9

DEATH BY NUMBERS

Counting and Accounting in
The Winter's Tale

Shankar Raman

A unit added to infinity does not increase it at all, any more than a foot added
to an infinite length. The finite dissolves in the presence of the infinite and
becomes pure nothingness. So it is with our mind before God, with our
justice before divine justice. There is not so great a disproportion between
our justice and God's justice as there is between unity and infinity.

Pascal 1995: 152

ONE AND NONES

I do not offer an alternative reading of *The Winter's Tale* as such, if by
that we mean that my assessment differs radically from much of what
has already been written about the play's concern with death and
time. I offer instead an alternative sense of the place of such readings,
a different way of arriving at what may seem similar or related
conclusions—and an alternative route necessarily discloses different
sights. The path taken here will lead through unexpected territory (at

least, for most literary scholars): a strange "world of figures" whose "form" has not yet been sufficiently attended to.[1] I hope to show a deep and abiding—I am tempted to say integral—connection between the language of Renaissance arithmetic and the (at first glance) unmathematical world of Shakespearean romance.[2]

I commence, though, at a remove from Shakespeare, joining voices instead with Catullus to echo the numerical challenge thrown down by his fifth song:[3]

> Let us live, my Lesbia, and love,
> and value [aestimemus] at one farthing
> all the talk of crabbed old men!
> Suns may set [occidere] and rise again:
> For us, when the short light [brevis lux] has once set [occidit],
> remains to be slept the sleep of one unbroken night.
> Give me a thousand kisses, then a hundred,
> Then another thousand, then a second hundred.
> Then, when we have made up [fecerimus] many thousands,
> we will confuse [conturbabimus] them [all], that we may not know
>   [the reckoning],
> nor any malicious person blight them with evil eye,
> when he knows that our kisses are so many.[4]

The mainspring of Catullus's remarkable *carpe diem* poem is the tension between the one and the multiple: the singularity of the plural (the couple as "us") distinguished from the plurality of the singular (the couple as a set of two distinct individuals, "my Lesbia" and him); the unitary value of what is said ("one farthing") versus the plurality of the saying ("the talk [rumores] of crabbed old men"); the unending repetition of habitual nocturnal rhythm versus the experiential singularity ("for us") of the night's event ("once" the short light sets); the multiple nights demarcated by the setting and rising of the sun against the single "unbroken" night shared by the lovers; the countable multiplicity of kisses given that "breaks" the single night; the opposition between kisses as enumerable, that is, discrete and countable, and innumerable, i.e. as indifferentiable mass.

The notion of the one operates in at least two senses here: as a discrete singularity that establishes multiplicity as a counting of units, and as a unifying principle that gathers up multiplicity as an agglomerate, a continuity, a mass. It is worth noting, too, how Catullus's exhortation ultimately evades the singularity of experience by avoiding the indicative tense. Instead, its pseudo-logical argument to get his lover to kiss him a lot rests upon the hypothetical: it imagines the multiplicity of the projected situation in such a way that it (may) lead to the singularity of a present experience—which implies, of course, the absence in the present of such an experience.

Nor does Catullus neglect the traditional gesture of the *carpe diem*: the association of such absence with death, menacing the very possibility of the experience desired. That evocation is a remarkably graceful one, borne primarily by the verb "occidere" (to fall, to set and to die) and the phrase "brevis lux," which points at the finitude of time in relation to the perpetuity of death. The constitutive ambiguity of lines five and six is therefore crucial: they set up the short light of our lives as prelude to the long sleep of death but transform that ever-present threat into the central motivation, an exhortatory cause aimed at bringing about the "real" event of the one unbroken night that the sun's setting has enabled—a night that will be broken up differently by the multiplicity of kisses. Thus, the poem rescues the lover from death's long shadow by entering it most fully, turning it into a perpetual night of an uncountable multiplicity of pleasures.

I evoke the Catullan game of numbers—rich in its own right—because his poem opens, too, an approach to Shakespearean arithmetic, and in particular to *The Winter's Tale* and its investment in counting, in ones and multiples. Polixenes' very first speech brings numbers to the fore:

> Nine changes of the wat'ry star hath been
> The shepherd's note since we have left our throne
> Without a burthen. Time as long again
> Would be filled up, my brother, with our thanks,
> And yet we should, for perpetuity,
> Go hence in debt. And therefore, like a cipher,
> Yet standing in a rich place, I multiply

With one "We thank you" many thousands moe
That go before it.

(1.2.1–9)[5]

Here, Polixenes likens himself to the well-positioned zero ("cipher") through whose agency he seeks to repay a "debt" of gratitude by turning a single expression of thanks into a multiplicity. As in Catullus, these lines express a tension between ones and multiples: the "nine changes" of the lunar cycle marking the single, continuous event of an unburdened throne; the individual person who thanks and multiplies while preserving his singular plurality in the royal "we"; the exceptionality of the zero or "cipher" whose singularly "rich" positionality generates a numerical series; the unity of gratitude that proliferates into the multiplicity of the thousands; the finitude of a time that could be "filled up" opposed to the "perpetuity" that must remain forever unfilled—unless arithmetic come to Polixenes' aid. Indeed, Polixenes even multiplies himself in his self-representation: he appears both as the one that asserts himself and the zero that multiplies that one. The sexual connotations of the zero's "standing in a rich place" and the multiplication it enables will not escape those who remember that this moment plays its part in triggering Leontes' jealous presumption that the child his wife bears belongs not to him but to Polixenes, the man now thanking him. If his wife's putative sexual availability results in her (single) body becoming both double and round, that transformation may affect Leontes most forcefully via the language of arithmetic, Hermione's multiplication prefigured in Polixenes'. Looking ahead in the scene, the ominous undertones of Leontes' reply ring louder: "Stay your thanks a while/And pay them when you part" (1.2.10–11). His subsequent insistence that Camillo "might'st bespice a cup/To give mine enemy a lasting wink" (1.2.318–19) suggests that the only departure that Leontes can imagine as an adequate expression of gratitude is the parting of Polixenes' soul from his body. For him, the perpetuity of a debt can only be filled by the perpetuity of death.[6]

It would not be too much to argue that the play's final scene replies to the zero's singularity—and its paradoxical connotations of a deadly absence that is nonetheless generative, potentially productive of multiplicities—with the equally paradoxical singularity of the one. Here, too, it is a matter of paying off debts, as we shall later see. Even as Leontes acknowledges that he "honour[s]" Paulina only with the "trouble" of royal visitation, he cannot help voicing a disappointment:

> Your gallery
> Have we passed through, not without much content
> In many singularities; but we saw not
> That which my daughter came to look upon,
> The statue of her mother.
>
> (5.3.10–14)

Hermione's statue would be, in other words, "that" singularity of singularities, the one object that stands out of the series of single objects, each distinct in its singularity but for that very reason indistinguishable, each a one of "many." Paulina's reply confirms Leontes' characterisation:

> As she lived peerless,
> So her dead likeness, I do well believe,
> Excels whatever yet you looked upon
> Or hand of man hath done. Therefore I keep it
> Lonely, apart. But here it is.
>
> (5.3.14–18)

The statue is incomparable no doubt in part because it reflects exactly Hermione's "peerless" condition in life—yet this exactitude equally provides the grounds for its unlikeness with regard to other artifacts, which are like each other in their singularity, but unlike this singular statue in their failure exactly to capture likeness. Hers is a singularity that excels, and therefore its state is to be kept singular: "lonely", sequestered, "apart" from other objects of which it might otherwise be considered a part. It is the One.

This overarching tension between the One and the Zero in Shakespeare's play draws into relief an important departure from the Catullus poem with which I opened. The departure rests upon a simple but momentous observation: the Roman system of numeration has no zero; its multiplicity emerges in relation to the primacy of the one.

As a correlate, death has no number, it is a-numeric, outside the space of number, which is the human space, the domain of counting and accounting. By contrast, in the arithmetical world of The Winter's Tale, death enters the domain of the numerical through the zero.

WORLD ENOUGH AND TIME

But with death also enters infinity: not—as in Catullus—as a countable infinity but as an uncountable one. This distinction is important. The confusion that Catullus's inventory of kisses produces does not result from their a priori uncountability: the kisses can indeed be enumerated in their thousands and hundreds, making up "many thousands". Rather, the confusion results from the failure of either participant or observer to keep track of the enumeration, so that the malicious person is reduced against his will to share the situation intentionally brought about by the lovers, that of only being able to see the kisses as an undifferentiated mass, a "so much". Nor is it necessarily the case that the sheer numerical size of the set of kisses is so large as to defy counting; instead, confusion derives from disordering, from the refusal of a simple sequential ordering. The alternation between hundreds and thousands renders impossible keeping track of what follows what.

Moreover, the premise of countability opens a connection to the economic world. The poem invokes the everyday business of buying and selling predominantly through three verbs: "aestimemus" (let us value"), "fecerimus" ("we have made up") and "conturbabimus" (we will confuse). Thus, in the opening lines, the speaker contemptuously discounts the gossip of "crabbed old men" for being worth no more than a single penny. But the dismissal does not extend to discounting the mode of economic valuation as such, for the speaker invokes that very mode later in the poem, in the "making up" of the many thousands and the "confusing" of the count. Not only are these verbs of valuation and reckoning linked to book-keeping jargon but it has been suggested that the verb "conturbare" conveys the shaking-up of the abacus to return it to its initial state (Levy 1941: 222–4).[7]

The Catullan conjunction of time, numbering and mercantile exchange is far from foreign to The Winter's Tale, which brings up these themes most insistently following the transition to Bohemia. As

Antigonus makes his remarkable exit, the Shepherd enters, searching for his lost sheep, and rails about the exploits of youth: "I would there were no age between ten and three-and-twenty, or that youth would sleep out the rest . . . Would any but these boiled brains of nineteen and two-and-twenty hunt this weather?" (3.3.58ff.). The discovery of Perdita, who takes the place of the sought-after sheep, accompanies the discovery of the gold and jewels that Antigonus has left with the child. As the Clown tells the Shepherd, he is a "made old man. If the sins of your youth are forgiven you, you're well to live. Gold! all gold!" (3.3.112–13). The Shepherd has already enumerated the sins of youth, and thus the gold is rightfully read as a sign that those have been paid for. Time enters thereupon to liken us to those wished-for youths who have indeed "slept out the rest"— "I turn my glass and give my scene such growing/As you had slept between" (4.1.15–16)—and to suggest that the passage of time is at least on one level a mercantile matter: "A shepherd's daughter/And what to her adheres, which follows after,/Is th' argument of Time. Of this allow/If ever you have spent time worse ere now" (4.1.27–30). The mercantile enumeration of expenditure parallels the sequential unfolding of a mensurable time.[8]

That we are entering a world in which time is measurable, countable and accountable is repeatedly stressed in this section of the play. In addition to Time's specifying the sixteen years that he slides over, Camillo reminds Polixenes of the fifteen years he has been away, and Polixenes in turn tries to convince Camillo that leaving him now would be tantamount to "wip[ing] . . . out the rest of the services" he has performed, for he would leave behind the "businesses" he has made, "which none without thee can sufficiently manage" (4.2.4ff.). This is a world of services rendered and debts paid, of profits and losses, of balancing ledgers, of book-keeping. Its nature is made explicit by the Clown, who enters soon after to tell us that he "cannot do't without counters" (4.3.35):

> Let me see; every 'leven wether tods; every tod yields pound and odd shilling; fifteen hundred shorn, what comes the wool to? . . .
>
> I cannot do't without counters. Let me see; what am I to buy for our sheep-shearing feast? Three pound of sugar, five pound of

currants, rice—what will this sister of mine do with rice? But my father hath made her mistress of the feast, and she lays it on. She hath made me four and twenty nosegays for the shearers ... I must have saffron to colour the warden pies; mace; dates? none, that's out of my note; nutmegs, seven; a race or two of ginger, but that I may beg; four pounds of prunes, and as many raisins o' the sun.

(4.3.31ff.)

The "note" or list the Clown clutches lays out his purchases in a (potentially) comprehensible order. The pleasures of the feast to come grow out of an accounting of sheep, people, goods and money, whereby income is balanced against outflow.[9] Of course, what also emerges in these lines is a confusion that seems to threaten the possibility of the count. Like Catullus's lovers who confuse the potentially malicious observer, Autolycus enters the play as the representative of deception, the one who will disrupt the reckoning. As he grovels upon the ground pretending injury, he tells the Clown that his ragged clothes offend him more "than the stripes I have received, which are mighty ones and millions" (4.3.55–6). The size of these figures—testimony once more to the power of the cipher—is sufficient to stretch to his limits the numerically challenged Clown: "A million of beating may come to a great matter" (4.3.57–8).

These instances draw attention to how *The Winter's Tale* returns over and over again to what is also central to Catullus's poem: an understanding that the everyday world of life and action is a measurable, countable, accountable one. Its confusions and deceptions take place within the homogenous sequentiality of enumeration: uncountability and unaccountability are pragmatic limitations that do not fundamentally throw out of kilter the principles of exchange and balance governing how human beings live from day to day. William Pratt's expansive definition extolling the utility of arithmetic seems especially pertinent here: "Arithmeticke is *The Art of Computation or Numbring*: by meanes whereof all reckonings and accounts in human affaires are truly and exactly made and rectified" (Pratt 1617: 1).[10] Even the play's miraculous events seem therefore balanced. When Autolycus reappears as a disguised salesman, "traffic[king]", as he says, "in sheets" (4.3.23), the absurd ballads he peddles nonetheless embody the everyday truth of accountability. Mopsa urges the Clown to buy some, as she "loves a ballad in print, a life, for then we are sure they are true" (4.4.255–6). And Autolycus's offer speaks to a moral balance through the very unreality of the song's "burthen": "Here's one to a very doleful tune, how a usurer's wife was brought to bed of twenty money-bags at a burthen" (4.4.257–9). Or again:

> Here's another ballad of a fish that appeared upon the coast on Wednesday the fourscore of April, forty thousand fathom above water, and sung this ballad against the hard hearts of maids. It was thought she was a woman and was turned into a cold fish for she would not exchange flesh with one that loved her. The ballad is very pitiful and as true.

> (4.4.270–5)

While Autolycus pokes fun at the genre of broadside ballads, his performance nevertheless takes comfort in numbers, which here become an absurd index of reality and truth. He parodically evokes a moral reckoning apt for the world of exchange: just as the woman's transformation into fish responds to her refusal of sexual commerce, so too does her song pay the debt she owes by encouraging maids to act otherwise than they do. As with Catullus, Autolycus's concerns are material and earthly: sex, money and exchange. Countability and accountability are central to this vision.

WRITING DEGREE ZERO

Evident as well, though, are the limits of envisioning the world thus. If Autolycus is excluded from the reconciliations that bring *The Winter's Tale* to a close, his omission suggests that the economic paradigm is ultimately and structurally inadequate. Polixenes cannot pay his debt of gratitude by simply filling up time with an enumerated series of "We thank you"s: such debts as he owes do not belong to the realm of sequential counting.[11] Enumeration belongs to the world of time and of temporality, measured and quantified, for instance, by the nine changes of the watery moon. But Polixenes' "burthen" is not like Autolycus's. While the responsibility he bears may be lightened by returning to fill a throne that has so long languished "without a burthen", that length of time is still not sufficient to answer his debt of gratitude. To pay the debt, to the extent that it is payable, demands something else: the zero.

"What belongeth to Numeration?" asks Thomas Blundeville's *His Exercises*, and answers as follows: "Two things, to know the shapes of the figures, and signification of their places." And how many figures are there? "These ten," Blundeville informs us, "1.2.3.4.5.6.7.8.9.0", but he immediately qualifies his list by insisting upon the zero's exceptional status: "whereof the tenth made like an o. as you see here, is called a Cypher, which is no number of it selfe, but serveth only to fill up a number" (Blundeville 1613: 1).[12] The two central distinctions made here—between the figure and its place, and between the cypher and the regular numbers—echo a farrago of earlier arithmetical treatises. Humfrey Baker's *The Well Spryng of Sciences*, for instance, describes the expression of value through numeration as deriving "partly by the diversity of the fygures, but chiefly of the places wherein they be orderlye set", a place being in turn defined— in language that resonates with Polixenes' opening speech—as "the seate or roome that a figure standeth in". There are, he continues:

> ten fygures . . . which are used in arithmetic, whereof nine of them are called signifyinge figures, and the tenth is called a ciphar . . . and of it self signifieth nothinge, but it beynge joyned with any of the other figures, encreaseth their value . . .
>
> (Baker 1568: 2)[13]

The cipher operates via a principle quite different from that governing the so-called simple numbers: eschewing the monotonic repetition of a singular unity or sign (the one "We thank you"), it relies on the emptiness of its signification to produce the fullness of its effects. Its positionality or its site, that is, its relationship to other elements that surround it (and, in particular, to the one that goes before) lends it its supernumerary powers, allowing it to suture the gap, manna from heaven. It is equivalent, in Cantor's set theory, to the empty or null set, "a pure mark . . . out of which it can be demonstrated that all multiples of multiples are woven" (Badiou 2004: 46).

The difference between the zero and the one in *The Winter's Tale* bespeaks a tension between the two different numbering systems, Arabic and Roman, to which the early modern era is heir.[14] In practice, no doubt, that tension can (and is) regularly resolved, since there is direct one-to-one mapping between these two modes of enumeration. But even a text such as Baker's, whose arithmetical level is not particularly sophisticated, expresses the conceptual difference between numerical systems in as (apparently) simple an operation as that of describing how one expresses the "value" of larger numbers on the basis of the "simple value" of any of the nine "signifyinge fygures when he is founde alone, or in the fyrst place of anye sume". To distinguish among the different places corresponding to the units, tens, thousands and so on, Baker resorts to words and Roman numerals, using the example of seven hundred thousand and seven million to teach the reader how the numerical sign expresses numerical value:

> In the syxte place everye fygure standeth for his owne valew, a hundreth thousande tymes. As 700000, is seaven hundreth thousande. The vii. place [is] a M.M. times, or a million: as 7000000, is vii.M.M, or vii. Millions.

> (Baker 1568: 3)

What Baker is trying to explain is precisely analogous to how Polinexes multiplies his one "We thank you" into the "many thousands more" by use of the "standing" ciphers that "go before" the one. That is, he wants to illustrate how the positionality of the pure, empty mark "which of it selfe is no number" can generate higher values from the simple values of proper numbers, so that each—as in De Flores' misogynistic vision of women—"spreads and mounts then like arithmetic—/One, ten, hundred, a thousand, ten thousand" (*The Change-ling*, 2.2.62–3; Middleton and Rowley 2002). But to denote the strange generative power of the a-numeric zero Baker has to bring its "place" under the control of the language of proper numbers: he therefore resorts to Roman numerals to denote the simple value of the columns or "places" where the zero stands, as well as to denote the multiplicative operation to which that placing is equivalent.[15] Thus must the cipher signifying nothing be brought back to the very fold of countable, simple numbers from which it otherwise marks a radical departure.

This "simple value" of the positive integer has its basis, and indeed its ideal type, in the One, out of which all positive numbers are generated. As Alain Badiou points out, the Greek conception of number expressed by Euclid makes the "being of number . . . entirely dependent upon the metaphysical aporias of the one". Early modern mathematical treatises faithfully follow the two sequential definitions available in Book 7 of Euclid's *Elements of Geometry*: number "is a multiplicity composed of units" (Definition 2) and a unit is "that on the basis of which each of the things that exist is called one" (Definition 1) (Badiou 2004: 59). Thomas Masterson's oft-reprinted *Arithmetick*, for instance, reproduces the Euclidean definitions thus: "Unitie, unit, or one is, by which every thing that is, is said one". The declaration that expands on this statement draws out more fully its epistemological and ontological implications:

> Unitie, unit, or one is, by which we distinguish, discerne, know, name, or expresse any thing that is, to be one: as one God, one spirit, one voice, one thing, one stroke, one world, one star, one house, one man, one yeare, one minute, one mile, one elle, one pound, one graine, one piece, &c. infinitely.
>
> (Masterson 1634: 1)

This remarkable sequence comes close to enumerating, one by one, a theological ladder descending from the essence of being, through language and time, to matter itself. Masterson's brief definition of number follows directly from his conception of unit and unity: "Number is, a multitude or a many of units". He further declares that a "number is that, by whiche we expresse what certaine quantity or multitude of those things, quantities, or magnitudes we desire to have named, knowne, or signified" (Masterson 1634: 1).

John Dee's discussion of numbers in his "Mathematicall Preface" to the English translation of Euclid's *Elements* is yet more complex, introducing a subtle metaphysical distinction between unit and number,[16] even as he echoes the Euclidean definition.

> Number, we define to be a certain Mathematicall Summe, of Units. And an Unit is that thing Mathematicall, Indivisible, by participation of some likeness of whose property, any thing, which is in deed, or is counted One, may reasonably be called One. We account an Unit, a thing Mathematicall, though it be no number, & also indivisible because of it materially, Number doth consist . . .
>
> (Euclid 1661: (a) ₁ʸ)[17]

It may be recalled that "things mathematical" constitute for Dee an ontologically intermediate state between the immaterial, incorruptible and unchangeable "things supernatural" and the material, compounded and changeable "things natural". Not only do things mathematical partake of both worlds,[18] but in the form of their immateriality point towards "the principal example or pattern in the mind of the Creator".

What follows is a remarkable paean to arithmetic:

> O comfortable allurement, O ravishing perswasion, to deal with a Science, whose Subject is so ancient, so pure, so excellent, so surmounting all creatures, so used of the Almighty and incomprehensible wisedome of the Creator, in the distinct creation of all creatures: in all their distinct parts, properties, natures, and vertues, by order, and most absolute number, brought from *Nothing*, to the *Formality* of their being and state. By *Numbers* property therefore . . . we may both wind and draw ourselves into the inward and deep search and view, of all creatures distinct virtues, natures, properties, and *Formes*: And also, farther, arise, clime, ascend and mount up (with Speculative wings) in spirit, to behold in the Glasse of Creation, the *Form* of *Forms*, the *Exemplar Number* of all things *Numerable*: both visible and invisible: mortal and immortal, Corporal, and Spiritual.
>
> (Euclid 1661: (a) ₂ʸ)

Notably, the zero does not enter Dee's *Preface*, except as the implicit correlate to the Nothing from which the Form of existence emerges through a repeated enumeration or counting that establishes and orders "distinct parts, properties, natures, and virtues". And nor should it, for Dee's numerology endows Number—and in particular the notion of the immaterial Unit (that is, the One) of which Number is composed—with a singular and formal generative power:

> *Number numbring* therefore, is the discretion discerning, and distincting of things. But in God the Creator, This discretion, in the beginning, produced orderly and distinctly all things. For his *numbring*, then, was his Creating of all things. And his Continuall *numbring* of all things, is the Conservation of them in being. And, where and when he will lack an *Unit*: there and then that particular thing shall be *Discreated*.
>
> (Euclid 1661: (a) $_2^{r\text{-}v}$)

Producing the lack of Unit, therefore, returns the existent One to the no thing from which the divine Number qua Unit brought it into its "being and state." And, as we have seen, the zero or the cipher is that sign which signifies no thing, standing in the place of and serving only to fill up a number, announcing the fullness of a lack.

Compare Dee's understanding of death as the lacking of a unit in God's mind, a refusal to conserve a thing in being by enumerating it as some (one) thing, with Leontes' acts of creation and dis-creation:

> Is this nothing?
> Why, then the world and all that's in't is nothing,
> The covering sky is nothing, Bohemia nothing,
> My wife is nothing, nor nothings have these nothings,
> If this be nothing.
>
> (1.2.291–5)

Leontes' rhetorical query fuses two questions that are at least in principle separable. To ask "Is this nothing?" is, on the one hand, to query the existence of the "this": does it, this thing, exist? On the other hand, it is also to ask whether we can deny the existence of the "this". The first question is directed at the object itself with regard to its existence, while the second concerns the subject's belief in or knowledge of something with regard to its existence. Briefly, the former question is ontological, the latter epistemological. Part of the point here, of course, is that for Leontes these two dimensions have become so entangled as either to become indistinguishable or to make the former (the existence of "this") dependent upon the latter (our apprehension or knowledge of the existence of the "this"). The logic is a consistent one, however curious, and consists of two related implications, the first assumed, the second deduced. If everything—sky, Bohemia, wife—exists, then "this" exists too. Consequently, if "this" does not exist, then neither does all of the rest. Buried is the assumption that existence of everything is of the same nature as the existence of the "this"—whereas the world exists as such, while the events he notes exist for him. As he will later claim, the nature of his own being is dependent upon the limits of his knowledge. There may be "in the cup/A spider steeped", but so long as the drinker knows it not, he may "drink, depart,/And yet partake of no venom, for his knowledge/Is not infected". But if he sees the "abhorred ingredient", the venom acts upon him to make him "crack[] his gorge, his sides/With violent hefts" (2.1.39ff.).

Presumably, this stance would make it more difficult to "bespice" Polixenes' cup "to fetch [him] off" (1.2.315, 333), as Leontes has already proposed, since Polixenes' demise would depend not only on his drinking poison but on his knowing that he has drunk poison. But I am nitpicking here, since the litany of negations is intended precisely to ensure that denying "this" its existence—to say that there was no whispering, no meeting of noses, no kissing with inside lip, and so on—makes no difference, since its existence has been made dependent upon the knowledge or belief in its existence. (Whether it is knowledge or belief that is at stake depends, the play suggests, upon perspective: what Leontes later calls the "infection" of knowledge, Camillo here calls "diseased opinion".) Since I know "this" to exist, therefore it does indeed exist, Leontes asserts. He is quite consistent in holding on to this position, for, as he tells Hermione later, "Your actions are my dreams./You had a bastard by Polixenes,/And I but dreamt it" (3.2.81–3). If I negate my knowledge of what exists, I thereby negate the existence of the thing. Consequently, in so far as the whole world and the people in it likewise depend for their existence on my knowledge of or belief in them, dis-creating them in my mind has as its necessary consequence their dis-creation as such. As with Dee's vision of divine power, creating or dis-creating something, as far as Leontes is concerned, is fundamentally a mental act that involves simply the active production of a "lack" of a unit, a making absence, a zero-ing out. Thus omnipotence seems virtually inseparable from a divine paranoia, prefiguring as it were both the extremity of the Cartesian experiment and Berkeleyan 'idealism.' To repeat: death enters the world of numbers—and thereby the world as such—through the zero.

SECOND PAYS FOR ALL, OR, O, WOULD HER NAME WERE GRACE!

But if the zero brings death, it also enables a different kind of compensation because it offers—as we have seen both in Polixenes' speech and in early modern arithmetical texts—the possibility of an infinite generation, an uncountable multiplication. There is, of course, another term (along with its relational cognates) that the play uses to denote the paradoxical operation of the zero: grace. Consider Paulina's welcome to Leontes in the play's final scene:

> All my services
> You have paid home. But that you have vouchsafed,
> With your crowned brother and these your contracted
> Heirs of your kingdoms, my poor house to visit,
> Is a surplus of your grace which never
> My life may last to answer.
>
> (5.3.3–8)

As in Polixenes' speech to Leontes, the theme is the familiar one of unpayable debts. Payable, enumerable, countable debts belong to the historical world. Here, services can be paid home, contracts specified and met. But the royal visit exceeds a debt that can be specified by contract and settled by "crowns". The crown royals and contracted heirs who descend upon Paulina's "poor" house demand instead the "surplus of . . . grace" that the time of human life—no matter how extended—can never "answer". It is the Christianised zero of grace that must redeem them thence. "Bequeath your death to numbness", Paulina will shortly tell Hermione, "for from him/Dear life redeems you" (5.3.102–3).

Nonetheless, if Hermione can re-enter historical time, be redeemed from death, pay off her debts to death in order to return to life, the requisite condition is doubtless a journey in the opposite direction, the death of that other "dear life", to whom is owed the very paradigm of grace and redemption. Such grace, unlooked for and undeserved, drops down upon them to reverse that "hereditary" "imposition"—which is also the imposition of heredity, namely, of living and multiplying—of which Polixenes and Leontes in their own ways wish to be "cleared":

What we changed
Was innocence for innocence; . . .
Had we pursued that life,
And our weaker spirits ne'er been higher reared
With stronger blood, we should have answered heaven
Boldly "Not guilty", the imposition cleared
Hereditary ours.

(1.2.68ff)

The struggles between the zero and the one in Shakespeare's play lead, I have been arguing, deep into its dense ruminations on the finitude of existence. This is no less true of Catullus's poem: it constitutes an archetype in which arithmetic and counting are tied to mercantile practice, to the time of living and exchange. But the poem does not generate a pressure to escape this frame; rather the poem plays its game within the parameters available, denying not countability as such, but rather its power. The gaze of the Other can be foiled, dust thrown in its eyes, because the Other is subject to the same constraints vis-à-vis numbers that merchants and lovers are. Rather than an omnipotent Cartesian demiurge, against whom there is only the final refuge of the *cogito*, we encounter the reduced figure of the near-impotent voyeur, whose quasi-magical invocations stumble on the "real" of counting.

The Winter's Tale develops differently, constructing a doubled relationship to arithmetic. On the one hand, arithmetic opens a connection to historical time, life and living, debt and bankruptcy. However, while the language of accounting may adequately provide the coordinates for the pleasures and deceits of the household, for the small world of sheep-shearers, it meets its limits in debts that are structurally unpayable. There are deaths—those of Mamillius and Antigonus, in particular—that no accounting can ever be fully adequate to—even if Leontes tries at the play's end to "match" one loss by insisting upon a second:

> Thou shouldst a husband take by my consent,
> As I by thine a wife. This is a match,
> And made between's by vows. Thou hast found mine;
> . . .
> I'll not seek far—
> For him I partly know his mind—to find thee
> An honourable husband. Come, Camillo,
> And take her by the hand, whose worth and honesty
> Is richly noted and here justified
> By us, a pair of kings.
>
> (5.3.136ff)

The very balance of the syntax echoes Leontes' intentions: Paulina should take a husband "by" Leontes' consent, "as" he has taken a wife "by" Paulina's; she "has found" his wife and therefore he must match her by "find[ing]" her a match. Camillo's acceptance is "justified" by the value of a royal guarantee ("richly noted") of her "worth". But these compensations cannot, it is clear, fully account for the "wide gap of time since first/We were dissevered". Paulina's mate is, as she notes, "never to be found again", and only her death can redress that loss, one absence filling in the other: "I, an old turtle,/Will wing me to some withered bough and there/My mate, that's never to be found again,/Lament till I am lost" (5.3.132–5). Such debts bespeak a fundamental imbalance that undoes the homogeneity of a world of numbers (infinity becomes, in a manner of speaking, uncountable and unaccountable). The rift can only be closed by recourse to the zero, the infinite supplementation of grace.

Now, were this gesture purely axiomatic (as is the fact of death in Catullus), then it might not be a problem. But—and this marks a fundamental theological fracture, an unclosed wound—Shakespeare also raises the (implied) question of how to justify the axiomatic. What this entails is a reversal of direction, as my reading of the singularity of Hermione's statue already suggests. The reversal is signalled by the return of the One, the paradigmatic unit: the fullness of a being whose sacrifice alone can fill the void at the very heart of human existence. Thus will one originary lack compensate for another, creating life out of a dead likeness.

But the paradox of this "solution" is expressed in its very instability, which takes the form of a singular and insistent division.[19] For the One is generative too. It will shortly divide into two Ones, the Hermione who is who she is in "not chiding, for she was as tender/ As infancy and grace" (5.3.24–5), and the statuesque Hermione who is "so much wrinkled", "[s]o aged as this seems" (5.3.26–7). And a little later, as the statue moves from the "dead likeness" (5.3.16) of life into life itself, she doubles herself once more: "Do not shun her/Until you see her die again, for then/You kill her double" (5.3.105–7). Hermione's statue evokes the double of her corpse (of which the statue was already a figure), but the uncertain suspension of "double" between adverb and noun renders the line even more complex. Do not shun her until you truly see her die, for if you do shun her before that event, you will kill her a second time, and thus bring about the event of her death yet again. Do not shun her until you truly see her die, for at that point you will be shunning not her, but her double, her dead likeness. And, between these instances, Hermione's singularity generates what her body had already done before, namely, produce the double who is her daughter: "O royal piece,/. . . which has . . ./From thy admiring daughter took the spirits,/Standing like stone with thee" (5.3.38ff.). Perdita is like her mother here in being petrified, hers is a "dead likeness" when compared to the "lively mock[ing]" of life that had earlier drawn a desirous Leontes to look on his daughter with an "eye [that] hath too much youth in't". The association of mother and daughter when Leontes meets Perdita for the first time becomes evident in his response to Paulina. When she admonishes him by recalling that Hermione "was worth more such gazes/Than what you look on now", Leontes equivocally replies: "I thought of her/Even in these looks I made" (5.1.243ff.). Consider, too, how the language of Florizel's earlier praise of Perdita resonates subsequently with the description of Hermione's statue in the play's final scene: "Each your doing,/So singular in each particular,/Crowns what you are doing in the present deeds,/That all your acts are queens" (4.4.143–6). In her "particular" singularity, Perdita thus uncannily anticipates and doubles the queen's singularity, One becoming Two.

And thus the play closes with bifurcation, as the one brought to life repeatedly divides, repeating on another register the crisis that opened the play: Leontes' paranoid refusal to relinquish his singularity in the face of the inevitable fact of his doubling. Closure, we might say, is only ever illusory. But is that not why we have the theatre: to make much ado of nothing, to tell us when nought is not naught?

NOTES

1   I appropriate Worcester's language expressing his impatience with Hotspur, in *1 Henry IV*, 1.3.207–8.

2   The exception is Stanley Cavell's suggestive "Recounting Gains, Showing Losses: Reading *The Winter's Tale*," in Cavell 1987. My argument progresses, however, in a direction very different from his analysis of the play as a study of scepticism and the recovery from sceptical doubt.

3   I would like to thank Hamish Robinson for reminding me of Catullus's poem, and Mary Crane for suggestions regarding its interpretation.

4   Translations of Catullus vary greatly in quality. I have lightly modified a fairly literal rendering that may be found at: www.vroma.org/hwalker/VRomaCatullus/005.html.

5   All citations are from the Pelican edition of *The Winter's Tale*, edited by Baldwin Maxwell. See Shakespeare 1971.

6   Cavell suggests that Leontes "wishes an evenness, or annihilation of debt, of owing, which would take place in a world without counting . . . And this sense of the unpayable . . . produces a wish to revenge oneself on existence, on the fact, or facts, of life as such" (Cavell 1987: 211).

7   Other mercantile connotations of "conturbare"—"to bankrupt" or "to default" on a debt—suggest the possibility of a different form of confusion: that reckoning the sheer number of kisses is rendered pointless by exhaustion, so that anyone trying to keep track will be rebuffed by the unpayability of the debt, such is its enormity.

8   Michael Bristol likens the play's two halves to the division in the Christian calendar and almanac between Christmastide and Midsummer, the symbolism of the latter "augmented by the practical temporality of rural life" (Bristol 1991: 154). The hinge connecting "these two fundamentally solstitial movements" is a "structuring absence"—the vanished Lent—which corresponds to Time's "swift passage" that "slide[s]/O'er sixteen years and leave[s] the growth untried/Of that wide gap" (4.1.5–7). The function of the zero, I suggest, is analogous to the "structuring absence" of the "temporal pivot" identified by Bristol.

9   To cite Cavell, "[t]he Clown's painful calculation reminds us that all the arithmetical operations—not alone multiplying, but dividing, adding and subtracting—are figures for breeding, or for its reciprocal, dying" (Cavell 1987: 215).

10 Bristol suggests that the gift economy which dominates the play's first half "must now coexist with an active and aggressive market in commodities and commodity exchange" (Bristol 1991: 163).

11 Bristol draws attention to the "distinction between a prisoner, who must pay fees, and a guest, who must return thanks." Accounts that can be settled, he suggests, are fundamentally dishonourable in that they reduce the relationship between kings to commodity exchange. "Polixenes' determination to depart entails . . . an obligation for Leontes to return the visit, so that, in the fullness of time, the imbalances that come to exist between giver and recipient, between host and guest, may be redressed" (Bristol 1991: 156).

12 Cavell notes that "[t]he last word of the Prologue [i.e., scene 1] is the word 'one' (in that context a pronoun for son); and the opening word of the play proper, as it were, is 'nine' [the duration of Hermione's pregnancy]" (Cavell 1987: 209). The scene is thus set for the appearance of the zero in Polixenes' speech.

13 One of the earliest English arithmetical texts, Robert Record's *The Ground of Arts*, is even more detailed in establishing the distinction between value and place. Having first identified the cypher, the "one [figure that] doth signifie nothyng", he lays out the double valence of other "signifiying figures":

The other ix are called signifying figures, and be thus fygured

| 1 | 2 | 3 | 4 | 5 | 6 | 7 | 8 | 9 |

And this is their value.

| i | ii | iii | iv | v | vi | vii | viii | ix. |

> But heere must you marke, that every fygure hath two values: One
> alwaies certayne that it signifieth properly, which it hath of his
> forme. And the other uncertaine, which he taketh of his place.
>
> (Record 1594: 43)

14 It would be untrue, of course, to claim that Roman numeration
lacked any sense of place-value notation. As John Durham points
out, a type of position-value is central to the use of the abacus as
well, where numbers are represented by the number of tokens in a
particular location (for instance, a fixed maximum number of "I"s or
"X"s on a line of the abacus). However, the fundamental conceptual
separation of an integer's place-value from its "simple" value depended
upon the representational paradigm enabled by the zero, which entered
Europe with the importation of the Hindu-Arabic system of numeration. This arithmetical notation came to Europe as early as the eleventh
century through translations of the work of the great ninth-century
Arab mathematician, al-Khwarizmi (to whose name we owe the word
"algorithm"). But its spread and popularisation required the further
impetus of commercial expansion, as well as the displacement of the
teaching of commercial arithmetic from the university curriculum
into the mercantile world. These conditions were met in late
fifteenth-century northern Italy, where the growth in the complexity
of commercial transactions and trade gradually led to widespread
adoption of the new notation (Durham 1992).

15 G. E. M. de Ste Croix argues that the alphabetic notations used by
the Greeks and Romans mitigated against the recognition of place-
value in its full sense. Despite advancements in property law and
commercial practice, accounts did not systematically tabulate debts,
receipts, payments and miscellaneous inventories; nor did they employ
the columnar arrangement central to balancing inflows and outflows
in modern accounting practice. He speculates that the introduction
and spread of the Hindu-Arabic numerals (and in particular the idea
of place-value embodied by the zero) provided the necessary "stimulus
towards the evolution of advanced concepts of debit and credit".
This innovation led to:

> producing accounts kept first in one column, and then in two,
> the separation of the figures into columns being of material
> assistance in bringing about that distinction between two "sides"
> of an account, which was an essential preliminary to a co-ordinated
> system of book-keeping by double or even single entry.
>
> (de Ste Croix 1956: 55–6)

16   This problematic distinction originates in part from the attempt to correlate Euclidean number with the Aristotelean point, as Thomas Hood's 1596 translation of *The Elements of Arithmeticke* makes explicit. As with Dee's "Preface", this text insists that in a rigorous sense:

> an unitie is properly no number, because it is no multitude, for multitudes only are numbred: neither is it part of a number because that every part of a number ought also to be a number. It answeareth in proportion to a moment, and to a point: whereof the one is the beginning of time, the other of magnitude, and yet no part of them . . .
>
> (Uristitius 1596: 1–2)

17   First published around 1570 to accompany Billingsley's translation of Euclid, Dee's preface was regularly reprinted through the seventeenth century.

   For an explanation of the page reference system here, see Chapter 5 note 4. [Ed.]

18   As Dee puts it, "[a] marveilous newtrality have these things mathematicall, and also a strange participation between things supernaturall . . . and things naturall" (Euclid 1661: (a) ₁ˇ).

19   That identity is divided from the outset is hinted at in Polixenes' conception of his pre-lapsarian identity: as one of the "twinned lambs that did frisk i' th' sun" (1.2.67–8).

10

HAMLET, PRINCE

Tragedy, Citizenship, and
Political Theology

Julia Reinhard Lupton

What is a prince? In Renaissance English, "prince," from *princeps*, meaning "first" (as in the German *Fürst*), could refer to the monarch as such, regardless of gender; Elizabeth was often called "prince." More often in Shakespeare's lexicon, however, a prince is a monarch-in-waiting, a future king: the *Henriad* is Shakespeare's royal *Bildungsroman*, charting the education of Hal from prentice prince to successful sovereign. Other princes in Shakespeare live in order to die, the very word coming to evoke the tender shoot of a blasted future, from the slaughtered princes of *Richard III* to young Mamillius of *The Winter's Tale*. To these sovereign, developmental, and elegiac senses of the prince we must add the distinctively Machiavellian turn impressed on the word by Renaissance political philosophy. For Machiavelli, *il principe* is he who makes a beginning—Machiavelli addresses the *new* prince, an innovator in search of legitimacy through the tactics of fear and love. The word itself derives from the Roman emperors, who called themselves *princeps*, meaning "first citizen," in order to retain a nominal relation to the constitutional order their office had eclipsed.

The Tragedy of Hamlet, Prince of Denmark is a meditation on the origins and destinies of princeliness. In *Hamlet's Heirs*, Linda Charnes's Hamlet is always a prince, never a king, pursuing the curriculum of the princely *Bildungsroman* but kept out of office by the Ghost's undead resistance to his own succession. Hugh Grady (2002) and Agnes Heller (2002: 8) are among the most recent critics to test Shakespeare's Machiavellian motives, finding in both Claudius and Hamlet traces of the Machiavel (see also Husain 2004). Responding to these recent reflections on Shakespeare's princes, this essay teases out the political possibilities embedded in the juridical conceit of *princeps* as First Citizen. What might it mean to encounter Hamlet as "First Citizen," understood not as the imperial terminator of representative rule, but rather as the initiator of the chance for constitutionalism, an emperor in reverse? The outlines of such a possibility take shape around Hamlet's friendship with Horatio, his Machiavellian moments, and his election of Fortinbras, political factors brought into literary focus by Hamlet's affiliations with Orestes, tragic subject of constitutional change.

The Shakespeare pursued here is "alternative" in several ways. I am looking for scenes of constitutionalism harbored only as experimental potentialities—as dreams, prophesies, and promises—in a play where courtly intrigue holds center stage. The speculative character of the project, brokered among distinct historical–juridical and literary–generic moments, is more formal and conceptual than historical or contextual. To read Shakespeare for citizenship is to enunciate an alternative genealogy of politics from the materialist variations that engage so much of contemporary academic criticism; my debts are to Aristotle and Arendt rather than Marx and Foucault. Reading *Hamlet* for citizenship also means rethinking the play's deep investments in political theology in relation to democratic futures as well as medieval pasts. In his essay *Hamlet oder Hekuba?*, Carl Schmitt, modern theorist of political theology and the state of exception, strove to dispel any liberal connotations that might accrue to "election" in the play. I take Schmitt's reading seriously, but I also take Schmitt to task, asking why he has to work so hard to defend the play against constitutional interpretations.

TRAGEDY AND CITIZENSHIP

In Book III of the *Politics*, Aristotle grants that definitions of citizenship will vary from polis to polis, but then puts forward a definition of citizenship "in the strict sense": "his special characteristic is that he shares in the administration of justice, and in offices" (1984: III.i, 1274b–1275a). The movement in Aristotle's thought points to an essential ambiguity of citizenship, which both adheres with passionate tenacity to a particular time, place, and regime, and aims beyond that local habitation to politics as a science transferable among regions and epochs. Citizenship is unabashedly restricted to those in its circle; one function of citizenship protocols is to police the limits of the polis. At the same time, citizenship names a broader, more mobile discourse that touches on human emancipation as such, insistently taking exception to its own exclusions. Citizenship makes this shift from the particular to the universal by shuttling a purely formal feature of its operations—the limited equivalence of persons conferred by rotating offices within a civic sphere—into categories of value concerning rights, equality, equity, and access. Releasing a fresh set of key words for critical musing, including office and duty, election and consent, friendship and fellowship, the discourse of citizenship invites us to reconsider power in its participatory and collective dimensions, the republican line historically in tension with the command–obedience model consolidated by Hobbes.[1]

Tragedy represents a foundational moment in the literature of citizenship (see Lupton 2005a, 2005b). Richard Seaford has uncovered the agon in Greek tragedy between the ancient stories of the great aristocratic houses, marked by self-destructive crises of incest and parricide, and the new institutions of Athenian citizenship, which challenged the charisma of authority based on kinship in order to reorganize political life around the equivalences conferred by civic participation (Seaford 1994). Jean-Pierre Vernant and Pierre Vidal-Naquet placed the education of the ephebes—young male citizens in training—at the mythic and ritual origins of Greek tragedy.[2] Deployed as scouts at the frontiers of the polis, the ephebes exercised ambiguous skills of ruse and surveillance.[3] At the end of their *ephebeia*, the Athenian youths would renounce the arts of cunning by joining the orderly army of hoplites, to whom they would swear their solidarity. John Winkler has speculated that the ephebes were given central seating along with members of the Boulê or Council in the central wedge of the theater, and he suggests that members of the Chorus may have been chosen from the ephebes, strengthening their ties with the young heroes on stage.[4]

The *Oresteia*, dramatizing the movement from an aristocratic revenge culture to a court of law that draws its jury from the citizenry, is perhaps the most classically "political" of the Greek tragedies in this regard. In the first play of the trilogy, *Agamemnon*, the title character returns home from the wars—and home from Homeric epic—to a humiliating death at the hands of his wife and her lover. Following the laws of aristocratic honor, in the second play Orestes avenges his father by killing Clytemnestra and Aigisthos, only to be driven mad and into exile by a swarm of Furies, archaic goddesses of blood right who revisit the rage of the slaughtered mother on her son. Resolution in the final dramatic installment occurs on the Aereopagus, site of the future high court of Athens, where Athena oversees the trial of Orestes. Ten jurors assemble to deliver their judgments. Athena breaks the tie among the ten, inserting the continuing necessity of a singular moment of sovereignty within the new constitutional order. Although Athena exonerates Orestes, the institutional consequence of the trial is to transfer adjudication of murder from the family to the court. Orestes both exemplifies and destroys the absolutism of kinship; he is the last revenger, declared innocent of wrongdoing but marking the ideal terminus of cyclical violence.

At the end of the trilogy, then, a set of passages has occurred: from boyhood to manhood, from aristocratic revenge to constitutional law, and from the world of maternal passion and violence to a normative relationship among cities and between men, figured in the alliance between Argos and Athens. Yet this series of epochal and subjective alterations retains a founding moment of mythic maternal power in the form of the Furies, now transformed into the "Eumenides" or "Kindly Ones" and given cultic place next to the court. Their sublime role, we learn, is to preserve fear of the law next to the law itself, sheltering a theological charge in constitutionalism as well as a feminine element in the suburbs of civic sociality (Conacher 1974: 339–40;

MacLeod 1982: 135–6). If Orestes, having reached his majority, returns to Argos as both sovereign and citizen by virtue of his new accord with the Athenian constitution, the feminine Furies have undergone civic naturalization in Athens itself, holding open a place for citizenships to come (Zeitlin 1984: 183–4).

Orestes is a *princeps* in the speculative sense that I aim to develop here: destroyer of his own aristocratic house and in pursuit of his majority, he survives the violent habits of his line by subjecting himself to a new constitutional moment that sets a limit to violence, at least for a time. *Princeps* is he who makes a beginning in a new constitutional order that will subsume him. Such a *princeps* is the last prince of the old order, and first citizen of the new. Another *princeps* closer to Shakespeare's immediate circuit of references is Lucius Junius Brutus, long seen as a classical analogue for Saxo Grammaticus's Amleth.[5] Avenging a crime by killing a tyrant-king who is also his uncle, and using madness as a cover (recalling the cunning of the ephebes), Brutus brings an end to monarchy in order to help institute the republic. If Lucius Junius Brutus is a comic *princeps*, Coriolanus is a tragic one, helping to found the new republic but unable to survive within its norms of civic equalization. The case of Coriolanus helps crystallize the singularity, the persistent "oneness" of the *princeps*, who may indeed enter the order of citizens, but always retains an exceptionality that keeps him apart from the circle into which he crosses. The *princeps* enters a profane or secular space, but he carries over a sacred character from the older mythic order, a charisma that does not illumine his person from within, but rather haunts and halos him as a symptom of epochal change.

Tragedy and citizenship are joint shareholders in Athenian democracy, but their alliance quickly faded in the post-classical period. Modern tragedy is shaped by Christian patterns of martyrdom and redemption rather than by the Greek agon between the *oikos* and the polis. Caught between the vertigo of subjectivism and the claustrophobia of Elsinore, Hamlet's problems feel worlds away from the open court of the Aereopagus. Yet, accompanied by Orestes and his fellows, we can recover within *Hamlet* a civic lining that reconnects his story to the passions of citizenship in classical tragedy, without dislodging his tale too absolutely from its proper situation on the late

Elizabethan stage. Critics have long noted the parallels between Hamlet and Orestes, young men sent away to school during the period when their mothers marry the men who have killed their fathers.[6] Whether arguing for mythical parallels or actual influence, these accounts tend to emphasize psychological and domestic similarities rather than constitutional ones. Yet the plays' familial crises take place on the public stage of states in emergency and in relation to constitutional mechanisms inviting us to use the *Oresteia* in order to read *Hamlet* for citizenship.

HAMLET AMONG FRIENDS

"Who's there?" "Nay, answer me. Stand and unfold yourself" (1.1.1–2). Both the *Agamemnon* and *Hamlet* begin with scenes of a night watch, commanded by a royal household in a state of traumatic transition from one sovereign to another. Both scenes dramatize the night watch as a sequence or rotation among equivalent elements. In the opening scene of Aeschylus's trilogy, a relay of lights, what we might call a pure sequence of signifiers, transmits the message of Agamemnon's imminent return from the ruins of Troy all the way to Argos. In the opening of *Hamlet*, the changing of the watch establishes equivalence among the men, who are soon joined by Hamlet's friend Horatio. Barnardo calls Horatio and Marcellus the "rivals of my watch," "rivals" implying here not competition but exchange, as rendered in Q1's "partners." The duties of the sentry place the young men on the edge of the castle; like the Greek ephebe sent to the frontier of the polis, the sentry is a *perípolos*, "the one who circles around the city without entering it," who scouts the *eschatia* or mountainous frontiers of the polis (Vidal-Naquet 1981: 148; Vernant and Vidal-Naquet 1981: 175). The citizen, writes Aristotle, is he who rules and is ruled in turn.[7] What makes citizens equal to each other is not identity of qualities, attributes, skills, or wealth, but rather the offices through which they rotate. The sentries combine the equivalence of office shared by adult citizens with the ambiguities of surveillance assigned to the scout. The inaugural uncertainties of the opening exchange are bred not only by the heavy night and the insecurities of state, but by the sentries' duties of suspicion and the equalizing function of office as such. As Paul Kottman has argued, when Horatio joins their circle in order to bear witness to the Ghost, the purely formal fellowship among guards is resealed through the act of shared testimony: "the relation between these three might be fairly taken as something like an emergent polity—a nascent company that will soon include Hamlet and that will come to be bound by an oath."[8] As if affirming the political nature of their association, Horatio secures consent from the sentries concerning Hamlet's membership in their group: "Do you *consent* we shall acquaint him with it/As needful in our loves, fitting in our duty?" (1.1.177–8; emphasis added).

This rotation of duties settles into an image of classical friendship when Horatio takes Hamlet onto the watch. Greek friendship both pre- and post-dates the institutions of democracy, yet it received a decisive philosophical and political imprint during the rule of the Athenian *demos*. In his chapter on friendship in the *Nicomachean Ethics*, Aristotle cites the proverb, "*philôtes isotês*," "friendship is equality," one of many points where he binds friendship (*philia*) and citizenship (*politeia*) around the measures of equality, reciprocity, and rotation.[9] Laurie Shannon has argued that Renaissance friendship inserted an experimental space defined by parity and likeness into the hierarchical scaffolding of early modern life. Classical friendship forms a kind of lozenge whose roots in Homeric bonds of reciprocity swell into properly political definition in response to democratic institutions, and then taper off into Hellenistic imperial and monarchic formations. In its aristocratic origins, democratic impress, and post-Athenian vicissitudes, Greek friendship carries its egalitarian ethos into Roman and Judeo-Christian scenes of sociability.[10]

Hamlet is, among other things, a young man among friends, ranging from his deep intimacy with Horatio, to the studied informality of his banter with the sentries, to the strategic, cynical friendships of Rosencrantz and Guildenstern. The play's awful longitudinals—parent–child, sovereign–subject, divine–human—are crossed by an equally dense network of civic latitudinals—brothers and sisters, comrades and sentries, foils and rivals—the pockets of equivalence created by their various feints and parries ringed about and further leveled by the politic convocation of worms in the great city of the dead. The play's sublimely vertical relationships usually take center stage in performance and criticism (and rightly so), but the horizontal strands also sustain our attention.

Hamlet's encounter with the Ghost, an Oedipal scene par excellence, has been the frequent object and emblem of critical attention (see, for example, Lyotard 1977: 395–411; Derrida 1994; Greenblatt 2001). Yet the spectral interview is framed more modestly by Hamlet's conversations with Horatio and Marcellus. Hamlet ventures alone onto Elsinore's *eschatia* ("the dreadful summit of the cliff" [1.4.70]) to meet his father, but he soon returns to his circle of friends, prefacing his request for secrecy by attesting to their community of interests: "And now, good friends,/As you are friends, scholars, and soldiers,/Give me one poor request" (1.5.146–8). When the Ghost cries, "Swear," Hamlet urges them, "Consent to swear" (1.5.159). The ghostly imperative reinforces the vertical command-and-obey structure of power that Hannah Arendt links to the Decalogue (1969/1970: 39), whose tablets loom behind Hamlet's commitment of the Ghost's "commandment" to the "tables" of his memory (1.5.13–17). Alone on the edge of Elsinore, Hamlet plays Moses to the Ghost's God, becoming, in Lyotard's telling phrase, the "Jewish Oedipus," "possessed by an Other who has spoken" (1977: 402). When Hamlet returns to his comrades, however, the ghosted sovereignty, issuing from the cellarage, not Sinai, loses its sublime edge. By enjoining his comrades not just to swear, but *to consent* to swear, Hamlet rebinds the circle of sentries in a collective agreement, instituting a provisional citizenship among them in order to carry out, but also to test and attenuate, the Ghost's commands. The *ephebia* has begun.

Hamlet shares with his fellows his proposed strategy, "to put an antic disposition on" (1.5.180). As critics have long noted, Hamlet's antic disposition affiliates him with Lucius Junius Brutus, the republican hero and first citizen of Machiavelli's *Discorsi* and late-coming avenger in Shakespeare's *Lucrece*. *Hamlet* plants itself firmly on the ramparts of monarchy and its discontents, yet it periodically opens onto the other scene of constitutionalism. And it does so in part by casting the prince as a philosopher-friend. Friendship, Aristotle writes, is realized by *philoi* "living together and sharing in discussion and thought" (Aristotle 1984: 1170b). Similarly, Seneca writes to his friend Lucilius, in an epistolary genre that prefigures the *essais* of Montaigne: "The first thing philosophy promises us is the feeling of friendship, of belonging to mankind and being members of a community" (Seneca 1969: 37). In the dedicatory letter to *The Discourses*, Machiavelli opposes the Prince and the Friend as the addressees of two very different forms—or *discorsi*—of political writing:

> Accept [this book], then, in the manner in which things are accepted amongst friends ... I seem in this to be departing from the usual practice of authors, which has always been to dedicate their works to some prince.
>
> (1983: 93–4)

Machiavelli's dedication decisively associates friendship and citizenship as part of what makes this particular book a set of "discourses": a commentary on Livy, but also a set of civil conversations with his contemporaries.

Participating in the humanist tradition shared by Aristotle, Seneca, Machiavelli, and Montaigne, Hamlet the prince, is also a philosopher and a friend. Returned from the ghostly encounter, he announces to Horatio, "There are more things in heaven and earth, Horatio, than are dreamt of in your philosophy" (1.5.174–5). The Folio reads "our philosophy," situating their discourse in the conversational sphere of friendship. The "more things" that represent the rational limit of philosophy bear not only on matters supernatural but on the untested resources of philosophy itself. Hamlet's philosophical language repeatedly touches on this "more," a potentiality caught between the social and the subjective, between civil publicity and psychic inwardness. Hamlet "eats the air, promise-crammed" (3.2.93–4), a phrase that binds a *soupçon* of the stage Machiavel with the promissory language of friendship in order to hollow out an inward space of pure expectancy. Hamlet would be "king of infinite space" if it were not for his bad dreams (2.2.255–6); he imagines an absolutism of reason, to which he assigns the name "king," and then finds its limits in the world of dreams, philosophy's other side. If the netherworld contains "more things" than philosophy, philosophy, too, is always more than itself, not simply a system of rational principles, but a discourse of social and political dreaming that overflows its own enunciation at any particular moment.

As the *perípoloi* prepare to reenter the castle, Hamlet reaffirms their bond:

> Rest, rest, perturbed spirit. So, gentlemen,
> With all my love I do commend me to you;
> And what so poor a man as Hamlet is
> May do t'express his love and friending to you
> God willing, shall not lack. Let us go in together.
> And still your fingers on your lips, I pray.
> The time is out of joint. O cursed spite,
> That ever I was born to set it right.
> Nay, come, let's go together.

$$(1.5.190-8)$$

Hamlet rotates here among several forms of address. He bids farewell to his father ("Rest, rest, perturbed spirit"), but his main energy is for his entourage. Twice he enjoins the group, "Let us go in together," "Let's go together," as if hungry for their companionship and sustained by their presence. And then there is the agonized couplet: "The time is out of joint. O cursed spite,/That ever I was born to set it right." We are tempted to hear this as a private cry, even an aside, but the couplet's placement allows it a more public currency as well. Hamlet finds himself "cursed" by the ghost's commandment, set on a mission that he will resist for most or even all of the play; he is, as many critics have argued, a reluctant revenger, a last action hero. Hamlet is doubly lonely, trapped by the secrecy and illegality of the Ghost's commandment, and isolated still again by the subjective terror of his own resistance to the generic machinery of revenge. Yet this double loneliness is nonetheless from the beginning accompanied by a fellowship of friends who lighten and lessen this isolation. These "friends, scholars, and soldiers"—a cohort bound by education, vocation, conversation, affection, and consent—shelter and support Hamlet's loneliness as he grudgingly shoulders the burden of the paternal past, providing an alternative scene—for both Hamlet and for criticism—to the drama of sovereignty played out on center stage. Throughout the play, Hamlet "plays the Machiavel," adopting a posture of frustrated ambition in order to cloak his agenda, which involves not so much carrying out the commandment to revenge as testing its provenance, its limits, and its meanings. When Hamlet assumes the mask of the Machiavel in the presence of friends and in the circle drawn by their collective consensus, il principe of tactical theatricality momentarily joins the res publica (public things) of the Discorsi.

Hamlet's fellowship with the sentries is thin, but his friendship with Horatio is substantial. Aristotle contrasts the "comradely way of friendship" (hetairikê philia), "always between two people," and the wider ties of political friendship (politikê philia).[11] Though linked to political friendship by the measure of parity, the friendship shared by two people is exclusive and intimate; in Laurie Shannon's formulation, "friendship discourse offers no comportment or affect to be generalized beyond the pair, no pattern to link all political subjects to one another" (2002: 18). Orestes, too, has such a friend, Pylades; early English versions of the Orestes story spell the hero's name "Horestes," who shares a syllable as well as a friendship discourse with Horatio.[12] In Louise Schleiner's analysis, Pylades provides "by his supportive presence and collaboration, male sanction and support for the supposedly necessary killing" (1990: 39). Horatio's role is a little different: his name implying ratio or reason as well as Horatian decorum, he supports not revenge per se but rather Hamlet's experimental path of evaluating and rerouting the Ghost's command. If Hamlet is the object and mirror of our imaginary fascination, Horatio directs the symbolic dimension of our subjective capture within the scenes before us. A late remnant of the classical chorus, Horatio performs this work in the mode of public opinion formation, as he goes about testing, weighing, and summarizing the state of the union throughout the drama. As such, Horatio is another figure for us, the audience, not a princeps or First Citizen like Hamlet, functioning at the head of the signifying chain, but rather situated discreetly within the devolution of public reason, a figure of normative consciousness within the play, between the play and its audience, and in the constitution of tragedy as a genre.

If the thin friendship of the fellowship of sentries is signed by the collective consent to swear, the thick friendship between the play's two philosophers is signed by the fact and act of election, a key term in the play's interlocking political and theological vocabularies. Hamlet and Horatio share a private moment:

> Hor. Here, sweet lord, at your service.
> Ham. Horatio, thou art e'en such a man
> As e'er my conversation cop'd withal.
> Hor. O my dear lord.
> Ham.   Nay, do not think I flatter
> [. . .]
> Since my dear soul was mistress of her choice,
> And could of men distinguish her election,
> She hath seal'd thee for herself.
>
> (3.2.53–65)

Horatio adapts a language of deference, but Hamlet responds by asserting their parity in friendship. Hamlet's "conversation"—his dealings, his social experience—has never met the match of Horatio, who in turn has become his partner in further conversation, in the *discorsi* of civil exchange. Hamlet goes on to say that he has "elected" Horatio as his special friend and confidant, the word implying the deliberative choice that distinguishes friendship from love. It also carries a Calvinist overtone: Hamlet deigns to "elect" Horatio much as God elects His saints, repeating, reversing, and rendering horizontal —profaning—Hamlet's own terrible election by the Ghost. The scope of "election" here is primarily private, but the word carries political connotations elsewhere in the play, and it is thence we must follow it, towards the temporal and conceptual *eschatia* of the drama.

PROPHESYING ELECTION

In Denmark, the king was elected by the Council, consisting of the major nobles of the land, a choice ratified by representatives of the common people. The reigning monarch played a substantial but not decisive role in shaping the election of his successor, and one sixteenth-century case involved the contested elections of an uncle and a nephew. Gunnar Sjögren describes the happier coronation of Christian IV in 1596:

> The Ordinator, the Bishop of Sjælland, asked the twenty Councilors to come forward and join simultaneously in putting the crown on

the head of the King ... The King was crowned with the following words: "Your Majesty, accept *from us* the Crown of this State in the name of God the Father, the Son, and the Holy Ghost."

(Sjögren 1983: 36, 38; his italics)

Neither a classical republic nor a hereditary kingdom (though closer to the latter than to the former), the elective monarchy of Hamlet's Denmark could hold a mirror up to England's own succession worries while also prophesying more distinctive forms of constitutionalism that might emerge from a genuine crisis in the crown.[13]

Various scholars have discounted the elections at Elsinore in order to tighten the play's analogies with the late Elizabethan scene, including James's own tortured family romance and the interest of the Essex group in furthering his claims to England's throne. The most interesting and symptomatic of these apologies is the one mounted by Carl Schmitt, the conservative Catholic jurist who became the legal architect of National Socialism by drafting Article 48 of the Weimar Constitution, and who recovered political theology for modernity by publishing *Political Theology: Four Essays on Sovereignty* in 1922. In his 1956 essay, *Hamlet oder Hekuba? Der Einbruch der Zeit in das Spiel* [Hamlet or Hecuba? The Intrusion of Time into the Play], Schmitt argues for a strong relationship between Hamlet and James, a coupling that enters the play not as an allusion or reflection, but as what he terms an *Einbruch*— an intrusion, a break-in, a traumatic incursion of real history into the space of the play.[14] In order to mount this argument (itself quite complex and sophisticated), Schmitt feels compelled to neutralize the "elective" character of Denmark's monarchy. The "dying voice" of the reigning monarch plays a major role in the choice of a successor, he notes, and the elections were always in-house: the king is

bound to name a member of his own royal clan, a son or brother or sundry fellow kin. The *dying voice* is, in other words, ordained by the old blood right; it had an originally sacred character . . . still recognized in James' writings on the doctrine of the divine right of kings.

(Schmitt 1956: 60)

It is not clear, however, that election in *Hamlet* can or should be kept so firmly apart from its liberal post-history. When Hamlet returns from his aborted trip to England, he declares to Horatio that Claudius "hath kill'd my king and whor'd my mother,/Popp'd in between th'election and my hopes" (5.2.65). Hamlet comes closest to subscribing to the Machiavellian persona that he elsewhere assumes as a pose in the same moment that he calls our attention to the elective character of the Danish monarchy. It is not his *succession* to the throne by primogeniture that has been stymied by Claudius, Hamlet tells Horatio, but rather his *election* to it. If this prince suffers from frustrated ambition, his foiled hopes reach beyond inherited blood right to include the chance for some form of political self-actualization on a broader public stage.

When he returns to the word again in his final speech, it is to "elect" Fortinbras:

> O, I die, Horatio,
> The potent poison quite o'ercrows my spirit.
> I cannot live to hear the news from England,
> But I do prophesy th'election lights
> On Fortinbras. He has my dying voice.
> So tell him, with th'occurrents more and less
> Which have solicited—the rest is silence.
>
> (5.2.357–63)

Schmitt, following J. Dover Wilson, insists that Hamlet's act is fully intelligible within the terms of England's own monarchy: "This is the *dying voice* with which Hamlet names Fortinbras, with which Elizabeth will name James and that, in the year 1658, they attempt to assume at Cromwell's death in favor of his son Richard."[15] Yet Hamlet, unlike Elizabeth, is not sovereign when he gives his dying voice to Fortinbras, for he himself has not been elected; Denmark is in effect headless once Claudius dies. Hamlet "prophesies" the election of Fortinbras, not naming his successor outright but rather initiating a political process by which Fortinbras will likely come to power. Election, though not "free" in the liberal sense, is nonetheless distinct from what Schmitt calls the political decision. Whereas decision names the extralegal judgment of the sovereign in a state of emergency, "election," as we saw in Hamlet's earlier musings on friendship, implies deliberation, rationality, and choice.[16] Whereas *decision* steps outside the law in order to make a sovereign judgment, *election* occurs within and fundamentally reaffirms the law. Election, unlike decision, implies *consent*: consent to a constitutional process, and consent to concur with the results of the process.[17] "Election" itself belongs to the people through its representatives, not to the monarch; if Hamlet predicts Fortinbras's election here, his voice issues from a place somewhere between that of the dying sovereign and that of the body politic that must ratify any new king. Turning to the phalanx of doubles and foils that have assembled around him in the course of the drama, the *princeps* as sovereign-in-waiting becomes the First Citizen, initiating an election that by definition exceeds the scope of his own life and will.

Moreover, the man whom Hamlet names, far from being a Danish clansman, comes from *out of state*. Schmitt writes, "a word like *Wahl* or *election* must only be understood in connection and collusion with the concrete order of a people and its dynasty" (1956: 59). For Schmitt, a "people" is a *Volk*, defined nationally and ethnically. But the English word "people" has two competing roots in Greek thought: the people as *ethnos* represents the national idea emphasized by Schmitt in this essay, while the people as *demos* suggests a group constituted by its institutions. While in many national formations (including ancient Athens), these two forms of the people overlap almost completely, citizenship steps forward as a discourse and a problem precisely at the moment when the two circles separate out around an alien element that requires either naturalization or exclusion.[18] Fortinbras, a new prince in the Machiavellian paradigm, introduces a measure of heterogeneity into the state, whose institutional and demographic circles cannot remain identical to each other under the late innovation of his coming rule.

A mixed social body shows up symptomatically throughout the play as a specter of election gone wrong. Laertes returns to Denmark "in a riotous head," the possible candidate of a popular election: "They cry: 'Choose we! Laertes shall be king!'" (4.5.101, 106). Meanwhile, "the distracted multitude" loves Hamlet (4.3.4), though "the people" is also "muddied"—mixed up and adulterated, rendered untransparent to itself—by the death of Polonius (4.5.81–2). And then there is "a certain convocation of politic worms": equal among themselves, they sublimely level "your fat king and your lean beggar" in the common communion of corpses (4.3.19–24). Hamlet thinks of the world itself as a "foul and pestilent congregation of vapors," an uncivil society of heterogeneous elements. Along with references to "the late innovation" (2.2.330) and "fine revolution" (5.1.89), the play assembles a multitude of phrases and images concerning political and social change. These images never cohere into a positive program of constitutional reform or popular rule, instead congregating distractedly around the undiscovered country of the play's political potentialities, "th'occurrents more and less" that Hamlet bequeaths unenumerated to Horatio.

Schmitt would like Hamlet to represent Denmark in the *volkisch* sense: "Hamlet's direct, unequivocal right to succeed to the throne arises from only one factor in the Nordic order of succession to the throne, the sacred blood right, in other words from the divine right of kings that James always appealed to" (1956: 61). Yet the declamatory energy of Schmitt's claim indicates that Hamlet's rights, as well as his commitment to those rights, may not be so unequivocal after all. Throughout the play, Hamlet commits the most extraordinary verbal abuse on the tropes of political theology: more than kin and less than kind, the king is a thing of nothing; Claudius, wed to the body politic through his marriage to Gertrude, is Hamlet's obscene mother (and the nation's, too). With the office of kingship already contaminated by the dubious virtues of Hamlet's father and further violated by the usurpations of Claudius, the prince takes sardonic pleasure in finding something rotten in the linguistic state of sovereignty.

Yet perhaps it is in the negation of these sacred tropes of kingship that Hamlet eventually finds the space for his own subjectivization, the "interim" he calls his own when he returns to Denmark:

> It will be short. The interim is mine.
> And a man's life's no more than to say "one."
>
> (5.2.73–4)

Opening up only to close again, life in and as the interim lasts no longer, Hamlet says, than a man can say "one." "One" is another name for the *princeps*, he who is "first" or "one," but it also suggests the unfolding of a sequence or series. In this interim, Christopher Pye has argued, Hamlet transforms the passivity of delay within the endless cycle of revenge into the activity of an anticipatory deadline, a call to action that allows the prince to become a subject (Pye 2000: 112). The subjectivizing "interim" marked by election orients Hamlet in a sequence of equivalent figures, his foils and doubles, his friends and his successors. If he accepts the beat of "one" as the space of his own life, it is not to remain sublimely apart, but rather to enter into a queue of fellows, to become *primus inter pares*. Hamlet's final words, I argue, announce not his accession to kingship in the moment of death, but rather his passage into the chain of friendship that will survive Hamlet and take up his story: "Horatio, I am dead./Thou liv'st. Report me and my cause aright/To the unsatisfied" (5.2.280–2). If so, he joins an uncommon commonwealth, sutured out of a grab bag of friendship styles whose conflicting social energies threaten to remain forever "unsatisfied." Hamlet can only address himself to the world at large through the singular voice of Horatio. Their intimacy creates an existential measure that must find weaker forms of fellowship wanting, but it may also leave us, as Paul Kottman has argued, with a renewed model of human plurality.[19]

The election of Fortinbras takes place on the other side of the sublime abjection and debasement of the sacral metaphors that buttress traditional sovereignty. Fortinbras stages the play's final tableau:

> Let four captains
> Bear Hamlet like a soldier to the stage,
> For he was likely, had he been put on,
> To have prov'd most royal; and for his passage,
> The soldier's music and the rite of war
> Speak loudly for him.
> Take up the bodies. Such a sight as this
> Becomes the field, but here shows much amiss.
> Go, bid the soldiers shoot.
>
> (5.2.400–8)

Here the pomp and circumstance of princely elegy—the bitter-sweet motif of sovereignty interrupted—put Hamlet to rest. Fortinbras strong-arms Hamlet's legacy into the mold of the soldier manqué, borrowing capital from the prince's lost future in order to fund his own military campaign. At the end of the play, *princeliness equals potentiality*, urged in a "royal" as well as military direction by the weight of history, narrative, and blood right, yet never fully disclosed or realized, and hence acting as a promissory note for a politics to come. In a Greek tragedy, these final lines were called the *exodos*, the "exit ode" delivered by the Chorus on its way off the stage. At the end of the *Oresteia* and the *Antigone*, the vacuum left by the terrible destruction of the royal house opens onto a scene in which political institutions stand to gain new scope and momentum. Shakespeare's Denmark is, of course, no Athens, and constitutional conditions and outcomes hang very far on the horizon indeed. At the end of *Hamlet*, the monarchy remains a monarchy, in the hands of a foreign strong-arm who is more thug than scholar, more a dictator seizing the occasion of emergency than either an anointed king or an elected magistrate. (There is a bit of Schwarzenegger in Fortinbras.) The political possibilities that attend election disappear even before they are enunciated. Yet an interim has opened up in a scene in which royal primogeniture is haunted by the suspect ghost of sovereignty past and displaced by the ambiguous prophesy of elections future. If the margin of subjectivity wrested by Hamlet by the end of the play is "sovereign," this hard-won sovereignty is not based exclusively on kingship and kinship (*pace* Schmitt), but rather on friendship and citizenship in their emancipatory promise.

If the move towards citizenship represents a set of gains (more equality, collectivity, and diversity in the social and political body), it also comes at considerable costs. One such casualty is Hamlet himself, who may become against all odds a political animal, but only at the cost of his own life. But Hamlet is intentional, not collateral damage; it is the women who must be counted among the play's civilian casualties. In their analyses of Greek tragedy, both Froma Zeitlin and John Winkler have emphasized the sexual stakes of the ephebes' transitions into citizenship: Winkler maps the varieties of manliness—competitive versus corporate, cunning versus honorable—required by the polis, as well as the intimate relationship between Greek citizenship and military discipline, while Zeitlin calls attention to the misogyny mobilized by the *ephebeia* in its struggle to purge itself of feminine attributes (Zeitlin 1984: 159–94). When Louise Schleiner makes the case for the impact of the *Oresteia* on *Hamlet*, she begins not with friendship but with matricide; the closet scene, she writes, preserves its "revision of matricide against intense psychic pressure," "releasing some of it through the sword thrust into the body of Polonius" (1990: 37). Hamlet's verbal cruelty to Gertrude is topped only by his verbal cruelty to Ophelia, and both are dead by the end of the play. Hamlet's sexual rage can certainly be linked, though not exclusively attributed, to the channels of friendship that allow him to drain off and manage some of the urgency of the Ghost's command. Bonding with the boys creates an easement from the pressure of the paternal, but it may also quicken his sexual fear and rage, at least through Act 4, while also laying the ground for the military solution at the end of the play.

Although citizenship and masculinity bear a deep affiliation, it is by no means a complete or exclusive one. Antigone holds the same relation to her house that Orestes holds to his, each marking the disastrous implosion of aristocratic kinship relations in the ancient past, as staged within the juridical landscape of the new democracy. As William Blake Tyrell and Larry J. Bennett have brilliantly demonstrated in their monograph, *Recapturing Sophocles' Antigone* (1998), Antigone's insistence on burying her brother appears to support a conservative aristocratic ethos of family obligation, but ends up affirming the values of the public funeral oration associated with Pericles. Antigone is last princess and first citizen in this brave new world; her name, meaning "against generation," places her at odds with the sexual economy, as does the erotic coldness and transitivity of the ephebes whom she resembles. To break with kinship is to make war with sexuality, at least for a period. But ironically, in Shakespeare's tragedy, written under a queen's rule, no such parallel space exists for women; we will have to wait for the Jacobean exercise of *Measure for Measure* for anything approaching a Shakespearean Antigone.

Hamlet, like Orestes, passes through but also out of the modality of revenge, discovering something like citizenship on the other side of reciprocal violence and sacral sovereignty. Both heroes find themselves caught up in an imperative for revenge that *comes from the grave*, echoing forth from what each play projects as a prior time, an aging genre, and an antiquated ethic. There is something formal and fantasmatic about this epochal precariousness. Literature always stages itself as the mediating moment between a Then and a Next, calculated in terms of psychic, political, ethical, and cultural regimes. As critics, we find ourselves ascribing to these repeated narratives of transition as if they were statements of fact: Hamlet is the first liberal subject, the first modern tragic hero, the first neurotic. Part of the princely script is to be counted as first (*princeps*); reading *Hamlet* in terms of tragic paradigms helps us recognize this script as precisely that. Still, the play was working *something* through: a civil war would eventually grip Britain, and a new constitutional arrangement would eventually be reached.

At the end of the play, we are left with two doubles of Hamlet on the stage. Fortinbras is the Double as Rival. He hearkens from international law, with its discourse of "just enemies," noble equals who could become friends through treaty and tribute; in this discourse friendship is a purely strategic category based on opposition to a common enemy.[20] Horatio is the Philosopher-Friend who hails from a more civic, humanist, and *ethos*-based tradition with its roots in Aristotle, Seneca, Cicero, and Montaigne. Both men have been "elected" by Hamlet as his representative, Fortinbras by receiving his dying voice and taking Hamlet's place as king, and Horatio by speaking for Hamlet and his cause as his elected friend. Both Fortinbras and Horatio survive the Danish prince, largely sharing the stage in the last fifty lines of the play. Each represents a face and future of princely potentiality, the one a "new prince" in the style of Machiavelli's *Il Principe*, and the other a public speaker and deliberator closer to the republican line of Machiavelli's *Discorsi*. Although Shakespeare leaves Denmark in the hands of Fortinbras, he entrusts Hamlet's story with Horatio, who in turn leaves it with us, "the unsatisfied." At the end of the play, *deliberative reason* (in the form of Horatio) has forged an uneasy alliance with *reason of state* (in the shape of Fortinbras). By virtue of status, rank, and sheer bravado, Fortinbras has the upper hand, but it is Horatio who continues to concern us, inviting us to process current dilemmas that differ in content while still recollecting in shape or urgency those that so vexed and stirred Shakespeare.

These once and future anxieties, I have suggested, concern citizenship: What are the costs and purposes of civic education, and civic membership? How does "election" differ from "decision"? What are the constitutional limits of emergency? What is a sustainable equilibrium between *ethnos* and *demos*, between nation and state? These are some of the questions with which Hamlet and Horatio leave us. The rest is *not* silence. We are enjoined rather to continue to engage, through the play, with matters of ongoing interest: to think with Shakespeare about the shapes, origins, costs, and limits of political community.

NOTES

1 See Arendt 1969/1970 for an attempt to recover a discourse of power allied with citizenship rather than command. Benhabib 2004 has developed the implications of Arendt's writings for contemporary citizenship debates in Europe and the United States.

2 Vidal-Naquet 1981; Vernant and Vidal-Naquet 1981. John Winkler notes that "Ephebe," meaning "those at *(ep')* their youthful prime *(hêbê)*," also came to be "the specific designation of the eighteen- to twenty-year old citizen in military training" (Winkler 1985: 27).

3 Vidal-Naquet 1981: 153 cites George Thomson.

4 Winkler 1985: 39. Other scholars state more simply that the chorus was always drawn from the citizenry, whereas actors and playwrights could be foreigners; see Sourvinou-Inwood 2005: 15.

5 Arden editor Harold Jenkins, for example, notes the parallels (1982: 86; Introduction to *Hamlet*); Hadfield 2003: 572 has developed the connection in relation to sixteenth-century tyrannicide discussions.

6 Readings of Hamlet and Orestes include: Murray 1914; Kott and Taborksi 1967: 303–13); Guilfoyle 1990: 61–5; and Schleiner 1990: 29–48.

7 "In most constitutional states the citizens rule and are ruled by turns, for the idea of a constitutional state implies that the natures of the citizens are equal, and do not differ at all" (Aristotle 1984: *Politics* III. 1259b).

8 Paul Kottman (2006) "Speaking as One Witness to the Scene: *Hamlet* and the 'Cunning of the Scene.'" Unpublished book chapter.

9 Aristotle 1984: *Nicomachean Ethics*, IX.8. 1168b. Shannon 2002: 3 cites Erasmus's *Adagia* for the Latin equivalent: "*Amicitia equalitas.*"

See Konstan 1998: 279–301 on the deep links among reciprocity, friendship, and the institutions of democracy in the ancient world.

10 On the Homeric origins of friendship and reciprocity and the egalitarian strains within the aristocratic ideal, see Donlan 1980.

11 Seneca develops both the distinction and dependence between political and comradely friendship, with a cosmopolitan emphasis absent in Aristotle:

> The assiduous and scrupulous cultivation of this bond, which leads to our associating with our fellow-men and belief in the existence of a common law for all humankind, contributes more than anything else to the maintenance of that more intimate bond I was mentioning, friendship. A person who shares much with a fellow human being will share everything with a friend.
>
> (1969: 97)

12 Schleiner 1990: 38 notes Caxton's spelling; Guilfoyle 1990: 62 cites Pikeryng's *Horestes*, a play produced in 1567–8.

13 Critics have mapped late Elizabethan succession worries onto the plot of Hamlet with varying degrees of allegorical precision, which often requires underplaying the elective character of the Danish monarchy (e.g. Charnes 2006: 59). Hadfield 2003: 566–70 summarizes the debates. I concur with Pye: if Shakespeare's Denmark manifests "a mixed form in which a vestige of lineal power is preserved in the form of prophetic knowledge," Hamlet's prophesy of election "equally anticipates a contradiction at the heart of the liberal subject, a subject defined by its freely contractual relation to the political/symbolic domain" (2000: 117).

14 Schmitt 1956. One section has been translated as "The Problem of the Tragic" in Schmitt 1987: 133–51. My student Jennifer Rust has translated the section on election and succession cited here, last accessed June 4, 2007 at www.thinkingwithShakespeare.org. On Schmitt and Hamlet, see especially Kahn 2003: 67–96 and Caverero 2002: 121–88.

15 Schmitt 1956: 59 follows closely J. Dover Wilson's *What Happens in Hamlet*, first published in 1935.

16 Schmitt 1922: 5 begins *Political Theology* with the famous formulation, "Sovereign is he who decides the exception." In their helpful critique of Schmitt, Heller and Fehér distinguish between decision as will and decision as choice:

Greek philosophy knew nothing about will. In Aristotle, decision is interpreted as choice and it follows the act of deliberation. If the act of decision is not the act of will but the act of choice, *popular sovereignty is possible under the conditions of social diversity and heterogeneity.*

(Heller and Fehér 1991: 412).

17 Cf. Archard 1998: 11:

Individual acts of voting are clearly, in the first instance, the formal expression of personal preferences for some candidate, party, or policy. Their full significance, however, is that individuals thereby participate in a process whereby an overall outcome is determined by the voluntarily expressed preferences of everyone who votes.

18 Balibar 2004: 8 distinguishes between "*ethnos*, the 'people' as an imagined community of membership and filiation, and *demos*, the 'people' as the collective subject of representation, decision making, and rights." On the figure of the foreigner in democratic theory and its narratives, see Honig 2001: 8.

19 On Hamlet and Horatio, Kottman (unpublished) writes:

Hamlet does not simply perish alone, after all, but dies *to* Horatio, who, it is decided, must survive him. Indeed, Hamlet is able to grasp his death only in terms of his living, dying relation to Horatio: "Horatio, I am dead,/Thou livest" (5.3.343–4), "O, I die, Horatio" (5.3.357).

Kottman further writes:

From the raw material of this ontological plurality [the sheer gathering of people in a theatre], the scene fashions a new plurality, a singular 'those' who were on the scene, a unique 'they' who are distinguished from all others in the world inasmuch as they alone can address one another as witnesses.

20 On the friend–enemy distinction in international law and modern politics, see especially Schmitt 1996.

11

MEMORY, IDEOLOGY, TRANSLATION

King Lear Behind Bars and Before History

Rui Carvalho Homem

In June 2005 a crowd of 100,000 thronged the streets of central Lisbon for an event that had complex political significance. That event was the funeral of Álvaro Cunhal, former secretary-general of the Portuguese Communist Party. To an outsider, it might seem surprising that the death of a communist leader in Western Europe should occasion such a massive tribute. After all, Cunhal's party had seen its vote dwindle inexorably over the three decades that followed the 1974 revolution, when it had enjoyed a brief but significant influence; and Cunhal himself had relinquished all formal political roles years before his death at the age of ninety-one. But the funeral was also a demonstration that brought together several generations of communists, fellow travellers, and democrats with broadly left-wing sympathies, who congregated around the memory of an era of resistance to dictatorship and political repression, a memory they believed was best embodied in the man styled, in a front-page obituary, "the last icon".[1] This would seem to prove Paul Connerton's suggestion, in *How Societies Remember*, that the master narratives that have informed our political world can retain their hold on the collective imagination long after they have ceased to determine our actual beliefs (Connerton 1989: 2 and *passim*). In fact, the tribute paid with such (last) rites was manifold: its object was a man whose firm ideals and determination, from early youth, had landed him in prison for eleven consecutive years, made him internationally renowned and the unquestionable leader of his party for several decades, until he chose to retire; but many in that crowd will also have been honouring the stern intellectual, the multi-talented artist and man of letters, the author of much-admired drawings, of a series of novels in the neo-realist mould, and of an acclaimed translation of *King Lear*—a version with a poignant origin and an intriguing publication history.

The textual specificities of Cunhal's rendering of *King Lear* will be considered only briefly in this essay. Attention will instead be focused on: (1) the reading of history (both *through* and *into* Shakespeare) that contributed to the translator's choice of a Shakespearean tragedy; (2) the arguably close connections between Cunhal's venture as a Shakespeare translator and other aspects of his work as an artist and man of letters; (3) (and ultimately) the possibility that the circumstances and intertexts summoned by Cunhal's *King Lear* highlight crucial aspects of the Portuguese national narrative, bringing out some of the ways in which, to gloss a Tom Paulin poem on history and memory, "we must remember who we are" (Paulin 1983: 29). In other words, I will be arguing that Cunhal's *Lear* can help us chart that narrative by pointing to some of its defining *topoi*, some of the images and representations that culturally and textually locate it. This choice of words (*topoi*, location) deliberately invokes the spatial rationale that has informed discourse on collective memory, its formation and transmission, after the influential work of sociologists such as Maurice Halbwachs (in particular through his proposed distinction and complementarity between autobiographical and historical memory) and, more recently, Pierre Nora and his study of *lieux de mémoire* (cf. Halbwachs 1992; Nora 1997).

The general framework provided by their writings indeed helps us read certain texts (with a particular bearing on those that have been dis-located through translation) as especially visible instances of those "specific places" where "we locate, or localize, images of the past", those "settings [that] provide us with our places of memory" (Hutton 1993: 77–8). When the texts under study bear Shakespeare's name, their critical consideration as sites of memory converges with a broader concern that has tended to find a focal point in Shakespeare studies: to what extent can those forms of historicism that have prevailed in the past two decades, with their tendency to highlight the unique and contextually specific, integrate an understanding of trans-historical elements in the human experience—including the perception and representation of human suffering in (or through) tragedy?[2]

The relevance of this concern to the particular object of this essay becomes apparent when one considers the genesis and history of the translation itself, as an element of a recent past that embeds the translator's biography. Cunhal translated *King Lear* between 1953 and 1955, during a period of intense intellectual activity that mitigated the quasi-absolute isolation in which he was kept for most of his long spell in jail (1949–60). This happened during the Salazar dictatorship, a highly repressive right-wing regime (founded and led for most of its duration by António de Oliveira Salazar) that lasted for forty-eight years (1926–74) and had a deep effect on twentieth-century Portuguese history. Again for political reasons, the text had to be published under an assumed name in 1962—two years after his sensational escape, together with other political prisoners, from the fortified prison in which they had been kept. Even after the end of the dictatorship, that translation was to remain a half-accidental secret for nearly thirty years until Cunhal was "reminded" of it by another translator and scholar who queried him on his Shakespearean venture (Torre 2002).

He decided to reissue his *O Rei Lear* under his own name in 2002, and it quickly became a bestseller for reasons that included the canonical status of the text, the high profile of the translator and the text's complicated history. This also made the translation a focal point for several lines of remembrance. It had been produced under violent repression and censorship, and its scholarly distinction further enhanced its value as a memorial to human assertion in the face of injustice—a "befitting emblem of adversity", to use the famous Yeatsian phrase

(Yeats 1990: 227). But its reception and its bearings on Portuguese political memory were rather more complex.

Highlighting the intellectual and literary distinction of the former communist leader also meant drawing attention, by contrast, to the declining influence of the party in the years following Cunhal's retirement—a decline that had one of its major causes in the demise of the Soviet Union. This recollection paradoxically entailed that praise for the aged communist's literary achievements, rekindled by the retrieval of a translation produced in the 1950s, was accompanied by a renewed memory of his unflinching support of Soviet policies, whose every move he followed right until the end with a persistence celebrated by some as loyalty to a cause and deprecated by many others as a sectarianism that was all the more surprising for being embraced by a distinguished intellectual. Further, Cunhal's decision to have his *Lear* reissued did not escape the remark, by some commentators, that it might involve a deliberate refraction[3]—or rather a sly, ventriloquised commentary on the ineffective management of the party by his political offspring (cf. Moura 2002).

Cunhal's interest in *Lear* and his decision to retrieve his version from oblivion should also be understood in the light of his historical materialism, which inevitably entails an interest in the forms taken by conflict and its representations in historiography, literature and the arts. This interest straddles the different genres and media of which Cunhal was a practitioner during his prison years, as is made clear by the connections that can be found between his reading of Shakespeare and his historiographic ventures in the years preceding the *Lear* rendering. It is especially visible with regard to his study of the late fourteenth-century crisis—a complex political juncture compounded by a dynastic conflict and war of independence against Castile, largely credited with having defined the conditions under which Portugal experienced the transition from the late Middle Ages to the Early Modern period. Cunhal's pronouncements on that moment in history are in fact served by a rationale that is not unlike the one that allows historicists to read topical or contextual implications into Shakespeare's *King Lear*. Such implications would hardly be unknown to Cunhal, in view of his familiarity with Marxist approaches to literature and drama and his awareness of the importance granted to Shakespeare in the Marxist tradition, from Karl Marx's much documented knowledge of the whole canon down to the present.[4]

The prominence traditionally accorded in the Portuguese national narrative to the political crisis of 1383–5 derives from its landmark, turning-point status, validated by broad historiographic consensus; but this is hardly separable from the conditions of its early recording. That crisis was a dominant object of the work of the fifteenth-century chronicler Fernão Lopes, widely regarded as the father of Portuguese vernacular prose and indeed the author through whom successive generations of Portuguese read about a defining moment in the history of their country. Lopes' distinction rests on his ability to offer a representation of late medieval Portuguese history that eschews the temptation to provide unquestioningly heroic profiles even of the monarchs whose chronicles are being written, assessing them rather in the complexity of their virtues, failings and motivations—as human rather than allegorical figures. Indeed, such qualities have arguably secured Lopes' *Crónicas* a comparable position in the canon of Portuguese writing, with regard to a national historical memory, to that enjoyed by Shakespeare's histories in the English canon[5]—despite their obvious generic, rhetorical and pragmatic differences. (In fact, Lopes' chronicles have even more in common with Shakespeare's histories: their galleries of characters often overlap, since the period they cover witnessed a strategic convergence between England and Portugal, and the establishment of dynastic links that culminated in a royal marriage and the signing of the Treaty of Windsor [1386], the oldest extant political alliance in Europe.)

A historiographic commonplace concerning Lopes' account of the popular uprisings in Lisbon in 1383–4 is that his hero is a collective one: the "common people" of Lisbon. This was certainly one of the factors that attracted Cunhal to Lopes' *Chronicle of King John I*, which he was actively reading during the first year of his imprisonment, taking issue (in the form of profuse annotation) with some dominant perspectives on the crisis it documented and producing a first version of his essay on *As Lutas de Classes em Portugal nos Fins da Idade Média* [*Class Struggle in Portugal in the Late Middle Ages*]. The whole study is informed by Cunhal's ideologically determined interest in contexts that foreground actual or latent conflict and in the complexities that characterise moments of swift change, as becomes apparent in his opening remarks on the coexistence, during the period in question, of "feudal relations" and the "dawning of capitalist relations", with a "broad range of intermediate situations" (Cunhal 1997: 13; my translation throughout). Cunhal is keen to point out the ironies and contradictions in the gradual dissolution of feudal bonds, as the serf is compelled "to renew again and again, 'freely' and 'by contract', the conditions of his own serfdom", and thus, supposedly "free from land and lord, [. . .] takes the first steps towards becoming the slave of capital" (1997: 13). Regarding the political crisis of 1383–5, the backdrop and catalyst for this process, he is vehement in arguing that it is a bourgeois revolution aimed at vindicating the interests of the rising bourgeoisie against the landed nobility—and he duly invokes the framework of Marxist theory to structure his research into specific Portuguese conditions. But he is equally vehement in underlining the decisive impetus the revolution derives from the "common people", both in the cities and in the countryside, and in stressing the "national betrayal" carried out by important sections of the nobility, who would have preferred a Castilian monarch (and hence the end of Portuguese independence) to the relinquishment of some of their political and economic prerogatives (Cunhal 1997: 99–100 and *passim*). No less central to Cunhal's argument is his quarrel with those historians that had derived the conditions for the crisis predominantly from the incompetent rule of a monarch, King Ferdinand—rather than from "class struggle" and a whole set of "deeper causes" than individual character (1997: 78–9).

The argument for collective rather than individual protagonism is obvious and predictable in a Marxist writer, but it introduces no less obvious complexities when one's focus is that same writer's decision to translate a tragedy—for, of course, discourse on tragedy has traditionally centred on the defining import of singular, exceptional assertion (Drakakis and Liebler 1998: 2–3, 6–11 and *passim*). One finds the issue of individual versus collective agency tackled with regard to the authorial condition in the opening sentence of a general "Translator's Note" (already included in the 1962 edition of Cunhal's *Lear*, and retained forty years later): "*King Lear* is an admirable example of the work of a great artist grounded in the creative spirit of his people, of the fusion of individual genius and popular genius" (Cunhal 2002: 11; my translation throughout). The compromise or mitigation that marks Cunhal's endorsement of the notion of genius, duly balanced by the popular and collective dimension, is paralleled in his remarks on the historicity of the play; having commented on the anachronisms that mark the text, Cunhal is wary of having those features invoked to wrest the play out of its context, and promptly adds: "King Lear is not, however, a timeless work: it is a critical work, and one that is typical of the Renaissance" (Cunhal 2002: 12).

This remark on the play's "critical" value and historical relevance, unspecific though it may sound, certainly reflects Cunhal's awareness of the way in which Marx and the Marxists always read Shakespeare as one of those especially complex writers they saw as emerging from transitional periods such as the Renaissance, styled by Engels "the greatest progressive revolution that mankind has so far experienced", and a "period of dissolving feudal ties".[6] This is an emphasis and a phrasing that one finds echoed in Cunhal's writings on late medieval Portuguese history, and (should one need further confirmation) in Marxist pronouncements on King Lear itself—some of them fairly recent, such as the following:

> If King Lear refers in any special way to early modern history, it must be to that same cataclysmic revolution in human affairs so eloquently described by Karl Marx in The Communist Manifesto, in which "The Bourgeoisie, wherever it has got the upper hand, has put an end to all feudal, patriarchal, idyllic relations" . . . Marx's view of the matter has been abundantly documented by social historians. If King Lear also documents it, then the older sisters must be meant to show us the breakdown of human relations with the coming of the cash nexus and Kent must stand for "feudal ties". Perhaps this is the reason why Shakespeare keeps him so much on stage, even when he has little to do but stand and wait.
>
> (Schneider 1995: 26–7)

But such possible representations of epochal change are offered for the sake of an ideological design that requires a prospective dimension, as is indeed emphasised by Gabriel Egan in his recent concise overview,

Shakespeare and Marx. His brief critical remarks on King Lear duly "[focus] on the play's exploration of the possibilities for future change"; and it is also this sense of design, together with the play's reputation for bleakness and pessimism, that account for the attention Egan pays to "historical inevitability" in connection with King Lear (Egan 2004: 4, 115ff.). Furthermore, the play's anachronisms are read as foregrounding its interplay of the retrospective and the prospective, and personal agency is argued to be qualified by the resulting prominence of historical complexities: "An analysis of King Lear that is concerned only with the king's character cannot account for the sense of historical dislocation that we feel in being brought to ancient Britain only to find characters anticipating futures radically unlike their own present" (Egan 2004: 148–9).

This is a recent instance of a critical approach that one might dub traditional, and that was certainly known—and congenial—to the prisoner kept in isolation in the Lisbon Penitentiary fifty years ago as he took up the translation of Lear. Cunhal would not have missed the irony, for a man in solitary confinement, of rendering the poignant suffering of a figure sent into a "houseless" condition (Lear 3.4.26, 30)—utter dispossession outdoors rendered from the perspective of utter dispossession indoors; and Edgar's closing soliloquy in 3.6 (in Q1) must have been found congenial: "Who alone suffers, suffers most i'the mind", "the mind much sufferance doth o'erskip,/ When grief hath mates and bearing fellowship" (3.6.101, 103–4). But it was obviously not just his personal plight that made the anticipation of "futures radically unlike ... [the] present" appealing to Cunhal. His insistence, in a variety of pronouncements, on the ultimate unimportance of individual concerns was of one piece with his wholehearted adherence to the historical materialist notion of an enhanced awareness of class struggle as a prime propelling force towards "les lendemains qui chantent" (the tomorrows that sing)— to name this particular utopia by a formula that was as famous as it was influential with Cunhal's generation.[7]

His version of Lear is not refracted in an obvious or pamphleteering way: Cunhal's intellectual stringency ensured that the translation would be scholarly and supported by a substantial body of notes. But, understandably, his mindset becomes apparent in some choices of lexicon and diction. A heightened sense of decorum characterises his approach to sexual and scatological references: strictures on foul language as unworthy of a good communist are well known,[8] and the reader has to progress no further than the opening exchange to find Gloucester's memorable "the whoreson must be acknowledged" (1.1.22–3) rendered as (the equivalent to) "the children of pleasure must be acknowledged" (Cunhal 2002: 24). Much more productive for the present argument, though, is the translator's decision to render Edmund's reference to "nations" ("The curiosity of nations," 1.2.4), as "*povos*" (peoples) (Cunhal 2002: 35); or Gloucester's reference to "the wisdom of nature" (1.2.104) as "*as ciências da natureza*" (the sciences of nature) (Cunhal 2002: 39)—in both cases, lexical options that are consistent with marked features of communist discourse, respectively its emphasis on internationalism and the appeal of the masses, and its fascination with the scientific. No less revealing is Cunhal's decision to paraphrase Lear's injunction "Take physic, pomp" (3.4.33) as "*Emendai-vos, grandes senhores*" (Mend your ways, great lords) (Cunhal 2002: 112), dropping the metaphor and sacrificing the passage's rhetorical curtness in order to make its verbal gesture of denunciation and admonishment considerably more explicit. And these are hardly accidental inflections: Cunhal's abundant notes prove that he is alert to the text's complexities, and exceptionally so for a translator who was not a scholar of English. In fact, he sometimes focuses on phrasings in the Folio or Quarto texts that lend themselves to occasional refraction through a discourse that he might practise in openly programmatic texts. An instance of this involves the "younger strengths" (1.1.39) on which Lear vows to confer his rule—"younger years" in Q1—, which become "*forças jovens*" (Cunhal 2002: 25), a phrasing that can also be read as "young forces" and might be used to represent the collective body striving towards the tomorrows that sing. And it is not surprising that the Fool's prophecy at the end of 3.2, the passage in *King Lear* (in F, though not in Q1) that is best known for countering the play's otherwise bleak world, should be rendered with a sense of the popular and the aphoristic that reveals gusto and commitment. These were, indeed, the same qualities that led Cunhal to render Edgar's epilogue-like pronouncement on "the weight of this sad time" (5.3.322) as "[*a*] *corrente destes tristes tempos*" (the current of these sad times) (Cunhal 2002: 199), associating time with flux (and hence progress) rather than burden and stasis.[9]

As Terry Eagleton begins by reminding us in his recent *Sweet Violence: the Idea of the Tragic*, which describes itself as "a political . . . study of tragedy", "tragedy remains a word of which the left is distinctly nervous" (2003: x). Eagleton deals at some length with this unease traditionally experienced by Marxist critics on account of tragedy's associations with fatalism and a transcendent design. Crucially, he queries the assumption that criticism informed by a radical politics entails an equally radical historicism and hence a rejection of the trans-historical; against this, Eagleton posits that there are aspects of experience whose breadth of representation can only be productively approached by criticism if we understand that they *are* trans-historical— and this is epitomised in human suffering, "a mightily powerful language" and indeed "a commonality of meaning" (2003: xvi). As he further argues, "oppression and suffering [. . .] are indeed contextually specific, but [. . .] the very rate of their recurrence in many different contexts means that the historical repeats itself into the trans-historical" (2003: xii). And this converges with a caveat regarding change: "Radicals are suspicious of the transhistorical because it suggests there are things which cannot be changed, hence fostering a political fatalism . . . But the truth is that there *are* things which cannot be changed, as well as some which are highly unlikely to change, and in some cases this is a matter to celebrate rather than lament" (2003: xiii). It is a caveat that grows out of the realisation that valuing change is not an intellectual exclusive of the left, and that indeed an "upbeat brand of historicism" that values the dynamic and metamorphic can be close to "becoming the opposite of radical politics rather than its intellectual ally"; or, in other and particularly apt words, "at its starkest . . . it is a choice between suffocating under history in Lisbon and stifling for lack of it in Los Angeles" (2003: xi).

Translating *King Lear* in his Lisbon prison cell fifty years before these remarks were made (and long before the perplexities of the postmodern moment that prompted them), starkly aware as he was of the forced stasis of his circumstances as much as of the historical paralysis to which the dictatorship was reducing his country, Cunhal could hardly afford to doubt the positive value of "change". His version, indeed, shows the translator overcoming the Marxist wariness of the tragic mould's potential fatalism by giving due emphasis to an envisaged change (and hence hope), even in such a bleak play as *Lear*. Cunhal's overall "progressive" stance, and its appertaining tendency to historicise, here involves reading tragedy into (or against the backdrop of) history. But historicising does not in this case mean stressing the unrepeatable and the irretrievably contingent—the intellectual assumption that over the past twenty years the "new contextualisms" have contributed to making increasingly familiar.[10] Rather, it involves trusting that sharp historical analysis inevitably yields a perception of patterns that will prove invaluable to those involved in positive efforts to transform the present. The remarks above on the affinities (and the chronological closeness) between Cunhal's *Class Struggle in Portugal in the Late Middle Ages* and his Shakespeare version concerned a particular instance of this process; but Cunhal's vision of history is one that appears marked by a sharp sense of design, the design provided by the objective causality of "History", as his biographer has cogently pointed out (Pereira 1999: 46). As he further argues, Cunhal and his generation "love history in the abstract, with a capital H": they "need History to have sense and make sense, because that is the only reason for all their actions". Indeed, "sense and direction, a vanguard and a rearguard" establish the difference between "those who are with History and those who are against History" (Pereira 1999: xi, 346, xiii–xiv; my translation). Although this need for design is felt and argued to be the opposite of a belief in the metaphysical conditions and inscrutable agency that characterise the universe of tragedy, it is no less ruled by a sense of necessity and inevitability—which in this case is afforded by a perception of supposedly "objective" causes and conditions. In fact, these affinities between tragic and historical design go further and deeper: they include the potential juxtaposition of the prevalence of *mythos* over *ethos* (action over character) as the prime object of representation in tragedy—in its Aristotelian understanding (cf. Butcher 1951: 27–31)—and the Marxist perception of individual acts as subordinate to a collective will that foregrounds the causal nexus of History.

This close involvement is arguably also present in the contradictory forms taken by Cunhal's self-representation. While invoking the limited relevance of the individual to justify his refusal to become a compliant object of (auto)biography, he wrote (under a pen name) a series of fictionalised accounts of the clandestine lives of persecuted militant communists, in which the austerity of his narrative diction does not prevent the heroic salience of a recognisably autobiographical central character (e.g. Cunhal 1974, 1975). Moreover, his "official" (i.e. party-approved) biographies, regularly rewritten to ensure the leader was never glimpsed on the wrong side of history (cf. Pereira 1999: xi–xiii), were blatant pieces of hagiography, endowing the figure of Cunhal with clear-cut exemplary value (e.g. Ferreira 1976).[11] His work as a visual artist adds a final note to the acknowledgment of these complexities: his drawings, equally a legacy of his years in prison, more often than not concern group scenes and offer an epic representation of suffering. They tend to feature images of the dispossessed that are meant to prompt redemptive political action, and, indeed, share in the aesthetics of socialist realism, on whose behalf Cunhal at times donned the critic's cloak to join some of his generation's most heated intellectual polemics. But it is a fitting confirmation of the argument above that among the few exceptional instances in Cunhal's prison drawings of an individual male face there is Lear's imagined one, the old man with a pained and poignant look that was to grace the cover of the play's translation in its quasi-posthumous 2002 re-publication (cf. Pereira 1999: 340–4; Pereira 2005: 187).

The attractions of singular, exceptional action and the possibility of self-representation thus seem to pervade the multifarious work of a public figure who ostensibly practised self-effacement and preached the unimportance of individual aspiration. Concomitantly, the refractions afforded by his version of a Shakespearean tragedy, and the complex circumstances that have framed this text, highlight the importance, for author and readers, of an extension of the autobiographical into the historical, those two areas that Maurice Halbwachs emphasised as distinct (though inevitably codependent) determinants of collective memory (Halbwachs 1992: 23–4 and *passim*). This duality is in fact operative both as regards the text's production and its belated reception, and it interlocks with another codependence, that between text and event. Indeed, the public response obtained by Cunhal's *Lear* has been shaped both by the historical implications read into the text and the lived experience that readers bear in their memory, which includes the enhancement of the translator's cultural distinction in his last years and the multitudinous commemorative event at his demise. Reading a Shakespearean text that has been thus refracted takes on a significance that largely overlaps with that of participating in those collective commemorations whose importance for defining the present through a construction of the past has been so thoroughly emphasised in the sociological study of identity and memory (Connerton 1989; Halbwachs 1992; Hutton 1993; Huyssen 1995; Nora 1997).

This sense of a coextension between reading and (collectively) commemorating is further enabled by the text's status as a translation, a rewriting that gives texts a new lease of life—or, as Ezra Pound famously put it, "bring[s] a dead man back to life" (Paige 1951: 148–9). Such a text should then be understood as a powerful counter to the conditions behind the current "lament about social, political, and cultural amnesia" (Huyssen 1995: 5), a lament produced by the same environment that has generated the recently renewed intellectual interest in memory and the construction of the past. On the other hand, the translation in question also contributed to refreshing the appeal of a man and (more tenuously) of a political group whose earlier loss of influence one has to associate with "the evident crisis of the ideology of progress", representative as they were of "a whole [fading] tradition of teleological philosophies of history" (Huyssen 1995: 6). This effect may prove to be short-lived, amounting to no more than a political epiphenomenon. Nonetheless, a version of *King Lear* has arguably bridged a significant cultural and ideological gap: from a standpoint in history when such teleologies would seem no longer tenable, it has helped recall and reinscribe the political gestures of a recent past whose appeal rested on a steadfast belief in the tomorrows that sing, and has made them resonate with both the present, culturally insecure moment and (through the historiographic intertexts highlighted here) a more remote and sturdily foundational stage in history.

A text like Cunhal's *O Rei Lear*, when considered against the complexity of its circumstances, offers us a place of reading from which we can approach a variety of contexts and issues. As seen above, it affords a challenging angle on the critical modes that have recently prevailed in Shakespeare studies, in particular by foregrounding the perplexities raised by historicist readings. These can be regarded as poised between two positions that prove hard to reconcile: on the one hand, a heightened sense of the historically specific that may render the past incomprehensible and hence irrelevant as an object of critical inquiry; on the other, the willingness to ground and justify such inquiry on the assumption of elements of permanence in human experience (and its representations), thereby allowing the past to enlighten the present and ultimately lay a pattern before the prospecting gaze. The understanding that experience conforms to an overarching order of some kind is, of course, the basis for a sense of tragic design. The difficulties this can pose to authors and audiences imbued with a belief in progress has been foregrounded by consideration of the contexts in which a Shakespearean tragedy was translated by a communist in the condition of political prisoner; and this work in turn was interrogated in the light of the scarcely linear relation between tragic pattern and the order of history.

Throughout this essay, however, these more general questions have hardly been proposed in abstract terms: they were prompted rather by an attention to some of the specific ways in which Cunhal's translation of *King Lear* has joined the gallery of textual inscriptions that inform Portugal's political memory. At a more immediate level, his text does so with regard to the recent past: the context in which it was reissued indeed made his Shakespearean version one of the aspects of the old communist's legacy that proved more consensually compelling in the final years of his life, commanding a latitude of admiration that could hardly be enjoyed by ideologically more explicit (or intellectually more taxing) texts. This perceived contrast also becomes an active reminder that the place held by Portuguese communists in the country's political memory is characteristically controversial. The credit for having organised a sustained opposition to the Salazar regime, and the hallowed memory of all those communists who were jailed, tortured and murdered during the dictatorship (of which, due to the grim site of its genesis, Cunhal's *Lear* becomes a token) was felt by many, in the past few decades, to be jeopardised by sectarian politics, difficulty in coping with the disappointment of election results, and adherence to the Soviet model long after it had ceased to enjoy favour. While Cunhal's *Lear* may have rekindled, in various combinations and readerships, a memory of these aspects of the recent past, it does not fail to relate to key moments in a more remote time; this is made possible by its adjacency, in chronology as in intellectual perspective, to Cunhal's best-known historical text (often used in schools), his essay on a defining juncture for the country's sense of its identity.

The bestselling success, in 2002, of Cunhal's translation of *King Lear* was primarily the result of a collective wish to memorialise its living but aged author; but the breadth and variety of the sites it can be seen to address in the nation's memory allow it to outgrow this personal or incidental significance. It confronts us, then, with an instance of a Shakespearean text turned into one of those "commemorative practices" that have long become "an essential mode of modern political representation",[12] arguably entitled to a place in the community's gallery of enabling textual *topoi*—texts with a privileged capacity to make us "remember who we are".

NOTES

1 The phrase appeared next to a picture of Cunhal in the prime of life (*Público*, 14 June 2005).

2 See Eagleton 2003: xiii-xvi and *passim*.

3 The word is here used in the sense it has acquired in translation studies—cf. Lefevere 2000: 241: "refractions—the adaptation of a work of literature to a different audience, with the intention of influencing the way in which that audience reads the work".

4 See Marx 1973: 163; 1979: 105, 142, 314. Shakespeare is also mentioned as a favourite poet in the *Confession* (Marx 1865), a semi-jocular questionnaire that Marx completed at his daughters' request. See also the passages on Marx's tastes in art and literature in Paul Lafargue's *Reminiscences of Karl Marx* (1890):

> He considered [Aeschylus] and Shakespeare as the greatest dramatic geniuses humanity ever gave birth to. His respect for

Shakespeare was boundless: he made a detailed study of his works and knew even the least important of his characters. His whole family had a real cult for the great English dramatist; his three daughters knew many of his works by heart. When after 1848 he wanted to perfect his knowledge of English, which he could already read, he sought out and classified all Shakespeare's original expressions.

Cunhal's familiarity with the cultural policies of the Soviet Union entailed that he would also be aware of the exalted position accorded to Shakespeare in that particular context of reception. Celebration of the dramatist, read as a forerunner of socialism, would also become a standard cultural feature in the communist regimes that emerged in Eastern Europe after the Second World War (cf. Shurbanov and Sokolova 2001)—exactly around the years when Cunhal was translating *King Lear*.

5 "John Churchill, the first Duke of Marlborough (1650–1722), is alleged to have said that he knew no English history but what he had learned from Shakespeare" (Hoenselaars 2002: 25).

6 Engels 1883; Engels 1859.

7 From the opening stanza of a song, "Jeunesse", by Paul Vaillant-Couturier, music by Arthur Honegger (1937): "Nous sommes la jeunesse ardente/Qui vient escalader le ciel/Dans un cortège fraternel/ Unissons nos mains frémissantes/Sachons protéger notre pain/Nous bâtirons un lendemain qui chante."

8 Verbal decorum was just a minor feature of a pattern of behaviour predicated as exemplary, a pattern that was indeed the basis for what Cunhal did not hesitate to call, in the title of one of his books, "the moral superiority of communists" (Cunhal 1975). As his biographer remarks:

> on sexual matters one finds in Cunhal two different and inter-penetrating registers: on the one hand, an exaltation of the body, health, vitality and virility; on the other, a moralism whose roots can be traced to the working class tradition that, from the 19th century, had condemned what it saw as the libertinism of the rich and powerful.
>
> (Pereira 1999: 446–7; my translation)

9 Although it is not a purpose of this essay to ground its conclusions on a sustained comparison between Cunhal's *Lear* and other

Portuguese versions of the play, the identification in this paragraph of a few ideologically determined features of this version is borne out by even a cursory glance at such other versions as: Ramos 1905; Álvaro 1967; Torre 2005.

10 The phrase "new contextualisms" is here borrowed from Howard Felperin (1990: vi and *passim*) who used it to describe the rise of new historicism and cultural materialism in the 1980s.

11 This is a Portuguese version of a Russian text by Yulia Petrova, originally published in Moscow. The Portuguese version aimed to expose Cunhal for having sanctioned a Soviet-style celebration of the leader's qualities.

12 Hutton 1993: 2, in a passage describing Philippe Ariès's fundamental work on commemoration and the history of mentalities.

12

THE MATERIALITY OF THE SCHOLARLY TEXT

What Our Books Reveal About Us

Mary Thomas Crane

In recent years, both British and American scholars have worried that the material conditions of scholarly evaluation and publication have led to a situation of "crisis," or at least serious concern, for literary scholars.[1] In the US, a number of prominent critics have addressed in print the "crisis in scholarly publication" caused by the decision of a number of American university presses to reduce severely, or even stop altogether, the publication of literary monographs.[2] In Britain, where many presses do still regularly publish literary monographs, scholars worry about the complex effects of the Research Assessment Exercise (RAE) on decisions about what and where to publish.[3] Opinion is divided, however, about whether there is an actual crisis, and there is particular disagreement, especially in the US, on whether the problem is that too many or too few literary monographs are being published each year.[4]

The field of Shakespeare and early modern drama makes an interesting case study for exploring the current state of scholarly publication, because it offers a full range of scholarly genres and extends from esoteric monographs through popular books such as Harold Bloom's *Shakespeare: The Invention of the Human*. Because I recently completed the annual review of "The Year's Work in Tudor and Stuart Drama" for the US journal *SEL: Studies in English Literature, 1500–1900*, I have read (or looked at) virtually all of the books published in this field over a calendar year, and still have them sitting in boxes in my office, so the basis for such a case study is conveniently to hand. In this field the number of scholarly monographs published each year has steadily increased. I received around 125 books, published roughly between November of 2004 and November of 2005, of which about 41 were scholarly monographs, and 17 were collections of essays (the rest were books for general readers, editions, lexica, guides, companions, etc.). In 1980, *SEL* received a total of 23 books in this field, 16 monographs and 2 collections of essays. In 1995, 63 books were received, including 39 monographs and 10 essay collections, and in 2000, 91 books, 35 monographs and 12 collections of essays.[5] It is true that American university presses published relatively few of these books in 2004–5: University of Delaware Press was the only American university press that produced a significant number of books, while British university presses and commercial presses such as Palgrave (as well as Ashgate and Routledge) produced the bulk of them.

This steady increase in the total number of scholarly monographs published each year is not unique to our field; *SEL* annual reviews in the fields of early modern non-dramatic literature, eighteenth-century literature, and nineteenth-century literature reflect similar numbers. Yet scholars on both sides of the Atlantic worry that not enough books are being published: in the US, there is concern that junior faculty will not be able to publish the book that is the usual requirement for tenure; in the UK, commentators sometimes worry that the RAE has led scholars to eschew the publication of scholarly books for more rapid forms of publication.[6] On the other hand, those close to the scholarly book trade also believe that the requirements of the tenure process in the US, and the RAE in the UK, have resulted in the publication of too many scholarly books: a "glut" that discourages scholars from reading each others' books, prevents them from writing textbooks or books for general audiences, and, in the opinion of some, has resulted in a lowering of quality.[7]

This difference of opinion about whether there are too few or too many scholarly books published each year can partially be explained in terms of the two rival dominant metaphors for the valuation of academic publication: the "benchmark" and the "gold standard." Those who believe there should be more opportunities to publish are operating in the world of the "benchmark," a metaphor derived from surveying where it denotes "a surveyor's mark cut in some durable material . . . to indicate the starting, closing, or any suitable intermediate point in a line of levels for the determination of altitudes over the face of a country" (OED). The benchmark is an arbitrary and relative standard, and as applied in measurements of scholarly productivity, it focuses on quantity of publication: you need one or two books for tenure, four publications in four years for the RAE.[8] Those who fear that too many books are being published are often, implicitly or explicitly, calling on a different common metaphor for a scholarly book, the idea that it represents a "gold standard." The gold standard is, of course, a "monetary system in which the standard unit of currency is a fixed quantity of gold or is kept at the value of a fixed quantity of gold" (Encyclopedia Britannica).[9]

In the US, the culprit that prevents publication of books needed to raise the benchmark is the "market," since the decision of US presses to stop publishing literary monographs resulted from the reduction in the market for these books, as libraries became unable to afford them, and individual scholars stopped buying them.[10] In the UK, critics of the RAE accuse its supporters of "commodifying" academic research, demanding higher production without concern for its quality.[11] "Benchmarking" and quantity of publication is valued by institutions on the way up and involves a fantasy that a university can work like a business, and achieve measurable success by producing "more" of whatever there is to be produced. The solutions for this version of the crisis in the US are to suggest that universities provide subventions to young scholars who need to publish books, that presses receive subsidies or that scholars learn to write for more general markets.[12]

Those who feel that the current state of "crisis" stems from the publication of too many books seem, at first glance, to be on shakier ground. If books are needed for tenure and for the RAE, why is their publication in increasing numbers a bad thing? The concept of the monograph as a "gold standard" that secures value reveals the logic behind this position. As Harvard University Press editor Lindsay Waters puts it:

> I hold books sacred and hate to see them losing their value, which is exactly what they are doing today, rapidly. The currency of books is becoming deflated in a way that is reminiscent of the decline of the German deutsche mark in the early 1920s, and the culprit is the same: hyperinflation. Our system of book publishing, which rests on the premise that we promote people who publish, is spiraling out of control.

(2001: B7+)

The idea of a book as gold standard is, of course, a fantasy about attaining stability of signification akin to the early modern insistence that the value of precious metal contained in a coin needed to be commensurate with its face value.[13] As Eyal Amiran has argued, publication is the "imaginary of the academic system": "the profession imagines itself living in palaces of publication, exchanging offprints (and journal issues) that have symbolic power only, because so few of the works so circulated are actually read with care, if at all" (1998: 3–4). Published works in this system function largely as symbolic capital. Amiran has suggested, for instance, that complaints about excessive and premature publication by graduate students really express worry about the devaluation of our symbolic capital, since publication "like gold bullion" is "symbolic and arbitrary; if too much of it is released to the market—by premature student investors, say—then the system itself is threatened" (1998: 4). Not surprisingly, in the US, at least, concern about over-publication is most often voiced by people associated with elite institutions and reflects a fear that if too many people have access to publication, its value will necessarily be diluted.[14]

Those who feel there are not enough books and those who feel there are too many both decry the influence of an outside force—

the government in the UK, the "market" in the US—on what is imagined as the previously "disinterested enterprise" of scholarship (Ryan 2004: 11). John Guillory has criticized the focus on publication (under the regimes of both benchmarking and the gold standard) as distorting "our understanding of the nature, scope, and value of scholarship" (Guillory 2005: 29). However, I believe that focus on "the market" or "the government" as outside forces disrupting the disinterested progress of literary scholarship misrecognizes the nature of scholarly publication. This misrecognition ought to have particular resonance for early modern scholars, because the system of scholarly publication is structured similarly to early modern publishing in that it superimposes a patronage system on a commercial market.

By patronage, I mean the whole range of ways in which scholarly publications are enmeshed in the making of careers and reputations. This includes, but is not limited to, a situation such as the one that existed within US university presses in the 1950s, when, according to Phil Pochoda, "university presses, though publishing many sound scholarly books, could be characterized fairly as academic vanity presses." These presses published books written by their own faculty and dissertations written by their own graduates, with minimal peer review (Pochoda 1997: 2). Patronage in my sense also includes series editors who publish books by their own students, or editors of collections who publish essays by their colleagues and friends. It includes the salutary influence that the prestige of the PhD granting institution of the author of a first book has on the prestige of the press that publishes that book.[15]

But beyond these obvious instances, I want to extend the term to mean any book or essay not published primarily to make a monetary profit for its author. Although such works may be published in the first place to make public the scholarly research or critical thought of their authors, a secondary aim is the advancement of the author's career: essays help land job offers, books are required for tenure and promotion, essays and books raise the RAE score of the authors' institutions. And considerations of marketability are largely irrelevant to "success" in this system. As Gordon Sayre argued in *Profession* 2005, "although certain publishers carry a good deal of prestige, tenure committees rarely consider whether the book has been profitable, how many copies it has sold, or whether it is available at most research libraries" (2005: 54). I mean "patronage," then, in the sense suggested by scholars such as Arthur Marotti, Daniel Javitch, and Frank Whigham, who argued in different ways that early modern texts were often written in order to attract attention and establish credentials for preferment: to gain employment or patronage from the court.

In this sense, virtually all scholarly essays and books are part of a patronage system. I do not mean this in a pejorative sense, and this essay is not meant to be an exposé of bad faith in scholarly publication. 'Patronage' in the sense I am using here is another word for our system of professional hierarchies and networks of relationships. The imperative to publish in order to attain professional rewards insures that faculty have incentives to remain immersed in their fields, that they continue to read, think, and write in ways that enhance broader understanding of the field as well as their own ability to teach at all levels.

Still, the fact remains that there is virtually no commercial market for our books. Those who describe the "crisis" in academic publishing argue that there was in the past a market for scholarly books, which has disappeared as libraries have drastically reduced the number of books that they can buy each year. However, this library "market" was in some sense a false one, since it was enabled by university subsidies. Graduate students and younger scholars, of course, read scholarship with real interest and engagement as they struggle to learn the field and find their own place in its ongoing conversations. They rely largely on library books because they rarely have the money to purchase increasingly expensive published volumes. Meanwhile, I think many established scholars come to experience the need to "read through" the relevant scholarship on a topic on which they are writing with feelings ranging from dogged determination to dread. Scholarly monographs found in libraries are, in a sense, partly raw material for still more publications, as Columbia University Press editor Jennifer Crewe suggests:

> in many monographs the core argument containing the original idea
> is about fifty to seventy pages long, and the rest of the book could

be described as filler to fit the form—the review of the literature, the arguments with other colleagues, the taking on of related issues, the reworking of the idea in yet another iteration.

(2004: 27)

There are currently two basic models for commercial success among scholarly presses. In one, used by prestigious US university presses, the press publishes large print runs (2,000 copies or more) of a relatively few titles that are judged likely to sell to a broad array of scholars across several disciplines, or to a general audience. These books are priced reasonably in hard cover and often published simultaneously (or after a delay) in paperback. In the other model, now followed by Oxford University Press and Cambridge University Press as well as by commercial presses, the press publishes small print runs (300–400 copies) of a large number of titles that have relatively high prices. Libraries account for the bulk of sales, and if production costs are kept down, and enough titles are published in a year, the press can make money.

The field of early modern drama is unusual, since the cultural status of Shakespeare offers opportunities for marketability that complicate our relation to the patronage system. Because of Shakespeare's status, and because there are recognizable academic "superstars" working in the field, there are books on Shakespeare that appeal to a large, non-academic reading public.[16] The potential market among general readers and students for books on Shakespeare is sometimes seen as eroding scholarly value of publications in the field. In an essay on the publication "crisis" in *Profession* 2004, Judith Ryan, a professor of French, disparages the salability of "books that engage in detailed readings of authors like Milton or Shakespeare . . . because there are always students somewhere who hope that these books will help them pass required courses" (Ryan 2004: 10). Her scorn may tell us something about the valuation of scholarly books: that their symbolic capital seems inversely proportional to their use value, if they are meant to be of use to students or general readers. "Companion" volumes have proliferated recently, perhaps because they function as crossover volumes: they retain some of the symbolic capital of scholarly publication for RAE and promotion purposes, but can potentially be sold to students. Literary biography is another crossover genre, combining respectability within the patronage system and appeal to a commercial readership.

As in early modern England, the interaction of patronage system and commercial publication currently works to affect the nature of the books being produced in interesting ways. I propose to turn the kind of scholarly attention to the history of the book that we direct at early modern books to our own books on Shakespeare and early modern drama in general. Attention to the ways in which these books present themselves to potential audiences, and to the language used to discuss the "crisis" of publication, reveals crucial slippages in concepts of value. The identification of the "crisis" as a crisis of the market conceals the ways in which "value" has become a slippery middle term, mediating our understanding of our professional roles in changing institutional contexts.[17] There is currently not a crisis of publication but rather a crisis of conflicting, and conflicted, valuation.

What do the books themselves tell us about their value? Just as scholars such as Arthur Marotti and Joseph Loewenstein have examined the prefatory materials of early modern books to register their mixed appeal to consumers and patrons, so we can note how the appearance, jacket blurbs, and acknowledgements of our scholarly books signal their multiple audiences and purposes.[18] An examination of these material features of the books on Shakespeare and early modern drama published in 2004–5 suggests that the subject matter and focus, the intended effect on readers, and the symbolic capital thought to accrue to a given book depends in large part on its intended audience. I want to emphasize that I am not attributing the "claims" these books seem to be making to their authors. I will be citing blurbs (written by other scholars), jacket copy (sometimes written by the author, sometimes by a marketing department), and acknowledgments (written by the authors) indiscriminately. My interest lies in how these books are presented to potential readerships, without making any claims about authorial intention.

Books for general readers present themselves very differently from student books and scholarly books: they emphasize the cultural status of Shakespeare, his "genius" or the "genius" of the author, and, most strikingly, the emotional effects of the book on its readers. Four such books in my SEL group are very similar. These are somewhat downmarket books intended as practical guides for the playgoing public.[19] All four book jackets, in both inside jacket copy and blurbs, stress the clarity and accessibility of the writing: "clear language" (Fallon), "clear, easy-to-use" (Butler), "down-to-earth, jargon-free" (Pinciss), and "inviting, conversational tone" (McCrea). Two of the three use the word "bard" on the cover (Fallon and Butler) and two refer to his "genius" (Butler and Pinciss). All present themselves as being calming, soothing, and reassuring: Fallon's book will "dispel some of [the] apparent strangeness" of the plays "to make modern readers and audiences feel comfortable with the Bard." Butler promises that his book will help readers to "engage with, understand, and appreciate the genius of Shakespeare" while Pinciss's book "demystifies Shakespeare."

More upscale books by well-known academics intended for general readers are also presented in terms that are strikingly similar among themselves, and that resemble and differ from their less ambitious cousins in interesting ways. Going beyond the SEL review books, I am thinking here of Stephen Greenblatt's *Will in the World*, Harold Bloom's *Shakespeare: The Invention of the Human* and Marjorie Garber's *Shakespeare After All*.[20] It is worth noting that all three authors are certified academic "superstars," having been the subjects of profiles in the *New York Times*.[21] These books seem subdivided into two categories, with Greenblatt offering a volume that appears closer to a scholarly book. Both Bloom's and Garber's books rely heavily on the fame of their authors. "Harold Bloom" has billing on the cover of his book only slightly smaller than "Shakespeare," and the back cover touts the book as "the culmination of a lifetime of reading, writing about, and teaching Shakespeare." Garber's book repeatedly refers to her Ivy League affiliations: "Marjorie Garber's Shakespeare courses at Harvard and Yale have played to packed houses for years"; the book is based on "her hugely popular lecture courses at Yale and Harvard over the past thirty years." Greenblatt's book gives Shakespeare top billing, emphasizing the author's skill at reading Shakespeare and knowledge of the period.

Like the downscale books, all of these volumes provide reassurance that they are readable: *Will in the World* is "clear-headed and lucid,"

Bloom's book is "scholarly yet accessible" while Garber's offers "erudition lightly carried." These books call attention not to the genius of Shakespeare, but to the intellectual qualities of the author: Greenblatt's "imagination is rich and interesting . . . he is a brilliant critic"; Bloom's readings are seen as "brilliantly illuminating each work with unrivaled warmth, wit, and insight"; Garber's "intellectual vigor and originality are in evidence on every page." Bloom and Garber, especially, offer excitement rather than comfort to their readers. Both are "exhilarating": Garber is also "breathtaking," offering a "bravura performance" while Bloom is "passionate," "heroic," and "dazzling." Greenblatt, limited as he is by the outlines of Shakespeare's life, is only "keenly enthusiastic," "dazzling," and, in an uncharacteristically somber note, "full of longing" to know Shakespeare better. Both Garber and Bloom are presented as necessary: "the indispensable introduction to the indispensable writer" (Garber) and "the indispensable critic on the indispensable writer" (Bloom). Greenblatt is, more modestly, "certain to secure a place among the essential studies of the greatest of all writers."

A different dynamic operates on the covers of works intended for students. These books are divided into books marketed for purchase directly by students, and books aimed at professors who will purchase them for a class. The latter category includes the proliferating "Companion" volumes, which seem to count as both scholarly publication and potential textbook. An example of a book intended for purchase by students would be the *Greenwood Companion to Shakespeare: A Comprehensive Guide for Students* (Rosenblum 2005). This book looks like a textbook, since it has a papercase binding. The back of the book promises that it has been "designed and written to meet the needs of students." While practical books aimed at general readers gently offer to make readers comfortable with Shakespeare's potential "strangeness," student volumes arouse anxiety about "Shakespeare's formidable canon" and "demanding plays" that the book promises to ease. Mainly, though, these books advertise themselves by listing the goods: "plot summaries, analyses of themes and characters," and "detailed explications of key passages." Here is a case where use value is thought to be self-evident once the contents are listed. In what may be a sop to teachers, the cover also promises that it "encourages students to engage in comparative studies and critical thinking"—although that would not be the goal of most students looking for a plot summary or detailed explication of a passage.

Books marketed to professors for use by students break the stranglehold of Shakespeare, and all three SEL volumes in this category consider his plays in the context of a larger body of works.[22] Sometimes the presence of Shakespeare is signaled on the cover, however, as in Rebecca Bushnell's *Companion to Tragedy*, which has a detail of a John Singer Sargent portrait of Ellen Terry as Lady Macbeth on the cover, although only 3 of 24 essays focus on early modern English drama and, even then, Shakespeare is only one among other playwrights included from the period. Like student books, the books marketed to professors arouse anxieties that they promise to alleviate, in this case professorial anxiety about critical and theoretical advances that he or she may not have kept up with. Bushnell's *Companion* notes that "the practice of reading tragedy has changed radically in the past two decades" making this book "an essential resource." Similarly, *Reconceiving the Renaissance* suggests that the "last two decades have transformed the field of Renaissance Studies," but, never fear, this book "maps this difficult terrain" offering the "only comprehensive overview of current thinking about the period." Unlike books for general readers that promise a Shakespeare that always stays the same (if only the jargon of professors is translated into clear, ordinary language), these books offer to "map" a larger field, imagined as always in motion.

These books also work to mediate the distance between scholar and student. Rather than emphasizing the personal brilliance of the authors, these books mention their solid reputations: "essays by renowned scholars from multiple disciplines" (Bushnell) or "each essay is written by a leading scholar" (Sullivan *et al.*). Unlike the passionate, exhilarating brilliance of stars such as Garber and Bloom, these writers have a greyer, corporate identity. On the other hand, these books take pains to depict the student-reader as active: Bushnell's book is for "anyone interested in exploring the role of tragedy" while Sullivan's will help students "expand their understanding." Most athletically, *Reconceiving the Renaissance* will pep up both the Renaissance itself, which "emerges wonderfully invigorated," and also students, who are given "the wherewithal and encouragement to do some reconceiving themselves."

When we turn to scholarly monographs, we find books that promise to do the reverse of the volumes examined so far: rather than offering to render texts clear and familiar, these books aim to show that the texts are more complex, and more unpredictable than readers have realized. Scholarly books often employ a spatial metaphor, promising to break new ground, uncover new territory, and explore previously uncharted places. These books make no claims about their emotional effects, offering only intellectual fare. It is possible to discern clear differences in subject matter and focus between presses at different levels, so that US university presses such as Chicago and Hopkins offer only books that extend over several traditional chronological fields, while commercial presses produce books that are generally confined to the early modern period. The prominence of Shakespeare can also be correlated with the status of the press. Acknowledgment pages offer important evidence about the authors' institutional affiliations and function similarly to dedications in early modern books, where the names of established scholars who are thanked invokes their authority in establishing that of the book.

The two books published by US university presses were a first book, Emily Wilson's *Mocked with Death: Tragic Overliving from Sophocles to Milton* (2004), published by Johns Hopkins University Press, and a book from an established scholar, Julia Reinhard Lupton's *Citizen-Saints: Shakespeare and Political Theology* (2005a), published by the University of Chicago Press. Although quite different in methodology, these books have in common a scope that extends from antiquity (Greek Tragedy in Wilson's book, the apostle Paul in Lupton's book) and includes chapters on both Shakespeare and Milton. Interestingly, Wilson's book lays claim to Sophocles and Milton in its title, but not Shakespeare, while Lupton's mentions only Shakespeare. The flyleaves of both books emphasize that they take up central and enduring questions: "Who is a citizen? What is a person? Who is my neighbor? These fundamental questions about group membership and social formation have been posed repeatedly between political and religious discourses through-out history" (Lupton 2005a); "In *Paradise Lost*, Adam asks, 'Why do I overlive?' Adam's anguished question is the starting point for a critical analysis of living too long as a neglected but central theme in Western tragic literature" (Wilson 2004).

This tendency for the most elite US university presses to publish books that cross traditional chronological field boundaries with explicit mention of canonical writers stands in a paradoxical relation to the job market, in which elite institutions tend to advertise for jobs in early modern studies, while less prestigious jobs cover a broader chronological range and mention Shakespeare and Milton explicitly.[23] On the other hand, books published by commercial presses, or less prestigious US presses, match the focus of more prestigious jobs, identifying their scope as "early modern England," or "early modern drama," with or without chapters on Shakespeare. These books virtually never include Milton.

There is a clearly identifiable shift, then, between these books and books published by presses that are lower down on the hierarchical scale. By "lower" I mean commercial presses such as Palgrave and Ashgate, and less prominent US university presses such as Delaware, Susquehanna, or University Press of America. The status of British presses such as Oxford and Cambridge is in transition, since they have adopted the same strategy—publishing a large number of individual monographs, in small print runs, for sale at high prices—as commercial presses, but are still widely viewed as more prestigious.

The majority of books from these presses cover some early modern topic, and include at least one chapter on Shakespeare, whether or not Shakespeare is mentioned in the title of the book. Fewer books are focused on Shakespeare alone, and still fewer on a playwright or topic excluding Shakespeare. In my group of SEL review books, volumes focused on Shakespeare alone came out from Delaware (2), Cambridge (3), University of Hertfordshire (1), Manchester University Press (1), Continuum (1), and University Press of America (1). Books on Shakespeare and other authors, with Shakespeare mentioned in the title, came out from Susquehanna University Press (1), Delaware (2), Cambridge (1), Palgrave (1) and the Chicago book discussed above. The largest category consists of books on some topic in early modern drama or literature that include discussion of Shakespeare but do not mention Shakespeare in the title, and these were published by Ashgate (1), Palgrave (3), Routledge (1), Delaware (2), and Cambridge (4). Books on some aspect of early modern drama excluding Shakespeare came out from Manchester (1), Cambridge (1), and Lund University (1).

These books are very similar in self-presentation. All are hardcover books, and many are first books. Paperbacks published by these presses are rare, and confined to works by established authors. Not surprisingly, the hardcover books all advertise their novelty, and, ironically, even books that critique early modern proto-colonialism present themselves as discovering and charting new territories. Philip Schwyzer's 2004 Cambridge University Press volume *Literature, Nationalism and Memory in Early Modern England and Wales* (2004) is "an important contribution to the expanding scholarship on early modern Britishness" and "the first study of its kind to give detailed attention to Welsh texts and traditions." A blurb on the cover of Daniel Vitkus's Palgrave volume *Turning Turk: English Theater and the Multicultural Mediterranean, 1570–1630* (2003) notes that he "is one of a handful of scholars currently redrawing the map of East–West cultural relations in early modern Europe," and that the book "offers a bold revision of widely held theoretical and historical assumptions." Jonathan Burton's Delaware University Press *Traffic and Turning: Islam and English Drama, 1579–1624* (2005) offers a "key assertion" that "Islamic figures in English drama were not only more numerous, but more complicated and varied than critics have previously allowed." Zachary Lesser's *Renaissance Drama and the Politics of Publication* (2004) is a "groundbreaking study."

Scholarly books from all presses signal their place in relation to networks of patronage in their acknowledgments. Lesser explicitly notes this: "like the early modern books I discuss in the ensuing pages, this book and its meanings are embedded in and shaped by a network of personal and professional relationships" (2004: ix). I will use Lesser as an example because his acknowledgments are typical, and because he seems aware of the complicated work they perform. Lesser follows the prescribed order, beginning with professional relationships and ending with personal.[24] It is the first paragraphs of an acknowledgment page that function as dedications sometimes did in early modern books, asserting the important connections of the author as both a sign of cultural capital, and also protection for the book. Lesser, for instance, explicitly refers to his graduate training at Columbia, thanking two very prominent advisors, David Kastan and Jean Howard, and also mentioning his "remarkable cohort of graduate students during my time at Columbia" (2004: ix). He then mentions the prominent Renaissance colleagues at the University of Illinois where he teaches, including Carol Neely. Finally, he refers to various supporting institutions—the Andrew W. Mellon Foundation, Folger Shakespeare Library—as well as to venues where pieces of the book have been published or presented. This is not to say that he is not genuinely thanking all of these people and institutions for their help, but it is to assert that these acts of thanking simultaneously provide a kind of pedigree for the book.

Acknowledgments, then, indicate very clearly the place of the author in hierarchies of prestige. There also seems to be some correlation between the status of doctoral program or teaching position of the author and the press that publishes the work. The scope of the book also seems to correlate with the prestige of the press that publishes it, with the most prestigious US university presses publishing only broadly focused books by authors with high status affiliations. Other presses that publish a high volume of books offer more specialized works, with Cambridge producing books by authors from more prestigious institutions, followed by Palgrave, Delaware, and Ashgate. Like early modern books, our own scholarly works make sure that the credentials of the author are clearly indicated.

Of course, the patronage contexts for scholarly books today also differ in important ways from early modern patronage systems. Most importantly, early modern writers were usually appealing to the taste and political interests of a single powerful patron, rather than to the collective judgment of an entire field of scholars on the value of their work. The survey of books published in 2005 makes clear that the commercial market, on the one hand, and our patronage system, on the other, require different things: different scope, different imagined effects, different deployment of Shakespeare. However, it would be salutary for us to acknowledge that both exert pressure on the form and content of our scholarship. There is no such thing as pure scholarship. Within these systems of scholarly evaluation, dishonesty stems not from the force of the market but from a disavowal of the role of institutions and status—in favor of some imagined "pure" standard of value.

My survey of the books published on early modern drama in recent years suggests that we are currently experiencing not a crisis in scholarly publication, since more books than ever are appearing in print, but rather a crisis of valuation. As presses change their goals and standards for publication and marketability, the book as an artifact changes in value. The "use value" of books changes when only 400 copies are in print, when all university libraries cannot be assumed to own it, when few scholars in the field will ever read it. The "cultural capital" of a book changes when the prestige of scholarly presses is in transition. In addition, our vocabulary for talking about the value of scholarly books has changed radically over the past thirty years, suggesting that what we mean by "value" itself is in flux.

Jeffrey Williams has recently argued that the "keywords" used to designate the value of scholarly work in literary studies have changed over the course of the twentieth century, from valuing "sound" philological or historical scholarship early in the century, to an emphasis in mid-century on "intelligent" readings of texts, to "rigorous" analysis during the "era of theory (roughly 1965–85)," and finally to our current term of approbation, "smart." Williams links these shifts to sociocultural changes and argues that "'smart' responds to the incommensurability of objects and methods in contemporary literary studies" (Williams 2004: 6). As our fields have expanded to include cultural texts of various kinds, and critical methodology often mixes and matches theories, "there are no uniform protocols of evidence across or even within literary periods," and "no overarching methodological standards." "Smart" values "the strikingness of a particular practice" and reflects current institutional valuation of the academic as "an autonomous entrepreneur in the market" rather than as "a brick in the edifice of disciplinary knowledge" (Williams 2004: 7). Williams argues, further, that "'smart' resides at the intersection of class and merit, or rather, of merit and its dissolve into class," since smartness is the quality that gains access to prestigious institutions, while affiliation with prestigious institutions functions as a guarantor of smartness.

Against this background of shifting terms of value, the desire for a "gold standard" that would serve as a bedrock of value seems understandable. John Guillory has argued that "benchmarking," or emphasis on the quantification of publication rather than on judgments about its quality, has become dominant in part because of a mistaken desire for "objectivity" in the evaluation of scholarly work. Guillory suggests that "the sheer fact of publication" has come to guarantee a kind of specious objectivity that is based on "black-boxing" the criteria for and act of evaluation (Guillory 2005: 34). Although Guillory's essay calls for a better articulation of the value of scholarship in the humanities, he does not suggest what its terms might be. This suggests to me that the "black box" that hides the scene of evaluation is necessary, not accidental, and is meant to conceal the fact that the "value" of literary and cultural studies is and always has been necessarily complex, subjective, ideological, influenced by institutional prestige, and in flux.

The RAE provides an interesting test case for this speculation, since its criteria for evaluation have changed over time in the interests of emphasizing quality rather than quantity. The guidelines for the assessment of research in English for the 1996 exercise began by promising that assessment would be based on the panel's "professionally informed judgement of the quality, not quantity, of cited publications and other forms of public output."[25] "Quality," in this case, is based on clearly identified external criteria: the "media" of publication, ranked in order from book down through lesser forms of publication; the "relative standing of publishers and journals," with "greatest weight" attached to "academic journals with rigorous editorial policies" (RAE 1996: 1). These criteria were criticized for exactly the kind of "black-boxing" that Guillory faults in the US. Broadhead and Howard noted that the criteria for assessment were "ostensibly set out for all to see, but actually open to a few—the panel—to interpret." For example, they note that publication in "prestigious journals" will be weighed heavily, but no ranked list of journals is included: "naturally, were such a list to be provided, it would be controversial and rightly condemned for its dictatorial audacity." They view the "vagueness" of the criteria as "an essential mechanism in the accommodation and consolidation of the ultimately arbitrary power and remit of the assessors to assess" (Broadhead and Howard 1998: 6).

Guidelines for the 2008 exercise emphasize that the panel will "assess all forms of output equally according to the published criteria, and give full recognition to the achievements irrespective of form or mode of delivery."[26] Rather than considering the "relative standing of publishers and journals," these guidelines claim that "place of publication will not influence the sub-panel's assessment of the quality of an output." Instead, the judgments of the panel will be based on three "descriptors": "originality: an intellectual advance or an important and innovative contribution to understanding and knowledge;" "significance: imaginative scope; importance of the issues addressed; impact or implications for other researchers and users;" and "rigour: intellectual coherence, methodological precision and analytical power." On the surface, this list of qualities might seem to answer Guillory's call for an articulation of value. They might even seem to correspond to Williams's generational keywords: "originality" standing for smartness; "significance" for soundness and intelligence; and "rigour" for itself. However, it seems unlikely to me that mode and place of publication could be so easily discounted, and also unlikely that a panel would be able to agree on the relative importance of these three criteria, let alone on the extent to which a particular book or article met them. Certainly British academics believe that the standing of the press or journal will continue to have impact on their assessment, although the guidelines now explicitly disavow this criterion. In practice, the revision of the guidelines seems like a reinforcement of the black box, in its insistence that the external criteria we all habitually use to judge a work of scholarship will be discounted.

Where does this leave us, then? It seems clear that the nature, scope, and purpose, and therefore the value, of the books we write on early modern drama are thus overdetermined in complicated ways by the interrelationship of market and patronage. The "value" of a scholarly book extends to include the contribution of its argument to knowledge of the field, the intellectual advances that the process of writing it helps its author to achieve, the job or promotion it helps its author to attain, and the benchmark or RAE rating it helps the author's institution to attain. "Value" here takes on multiple meanings whose slippages allow us to reconcile our intellectual and professional concerns. This slippage becomes a problem only if we refuse to recognize that it exists, and imagine that there ever was, or ever could be, a system for determining absolute scholarly value, apart from the pressures exerted by the academy, market, or government. We might be able to develop a clearer sense of relative value if presses provided basic information about their policies and review process. What is the average print run? What is the average price of a volume? How many readers are consulted for each manuscript? What percentage of manuscripts submitted are contracted and published? Do editors have an annual quota for the acquisition of books, and if so, what is it? What percentage of books come out in paperback? Perhaps an organization such as the MLA could make such information available, as it does for scholarly journals.

What is certain is that our decisions about what we write, how we write, and when we write, and our sense of what scholarship "is," do not emanate from an ivory tower. They emerge from the same institutions and affiliations that shape our professional careers. As artifacts, our books attest their entanglement with the material world as richly as do the early modern volumes they study.

NOTES

1   I would like to thank Erika Gaffney, Nigel Smith, and Laura Tanner for their help with this essay.

2   Letter to MLA Members from president Stephen Greenblatt, May 28, 2002, arguing that "The immediate problem, however, is that university presses, which in the past brought out the vast majority of scholarly books, are cutting back on the publication of books in some areas of language and literature." See also essays by Judith Ryan, Philip Lewis, Jennifer Crewe, and Domna Stanton in a "Publishing and Tenure Crises Forum" in *Profession 2004* (Feal 2004); and "Responses to the 2004 Publishing and Tenure Crises Forum" in *Profession 2005* (Feal 2005). Also, see Davidson 2003: B7+. The MLA appointed an Ad Hoc Committee on the Future of Scholarly Publishing, and its report was published in *Profession 2002* (MLA 2002: 172–86).

3   The Research Assessment Exercises are elaborate periodic evaluations of the research productivity of academic departments in the UK. Assessments were carried out in 1994 and 2001, and another is currently scheduled for 2008. Panels of academics in each field assess the productivity of every department and issue a rating, from 1 (worst) to 5* (best). Government funding is based on these ratings.

See Walford 2000: 13, 49–50; Peter Barry 1997: 189–91. Concerns have also been expressed about the impact of the RAE on hiring practices, decisions about the future of academic departments, and other issues; see Broadhead and Howard 1998. However, in 2006, the future of even the next scheduled RAE in 2008 was in question; see Donald McLeod 2006.

4 The scholars and critics referred to above generally believe that too few books are being published. The point that too many scholarly books are being published has been made by university press editors, most notoriously by Waters 2000: 315–17, and also by Crewe 2004: 25–31. Some US scholars share this concern, however: "our books are endangered as much by ubiquity and overabundance as by scarcity or obsolescence" (Sayre 2005: 52).

5 Although *SEL* did become more efficient and aggressive in soliciting review copies from presses over this period of time, Logan Browning, *SEL* Managing Editor, believes that the increase also reflects a real increase in the number of books published (email from Browning, January 26, 2006).

6 Walford has noted that "there seems, amongst all the academics I have spoken to, a view that publishing journal articles is the most effective way of getting a good rating in the RAE, and that other forms of publication will be less useful for this"(2000: 1). On the other hand, Barry argues that the "RAE seems particularly to favour what academics call the monograph, that is, the single-authored hardback book which aims to advance subject knowledge" (1997: 189). On concerns that junior faculty in the US will not be able to publish books for tenure, see, for example, Greenblatt 2002 and Ryan 2004.

7 On the "glut," see Crewe 2004. On the unfortunate dominance of monographs over books for students and general readers, see Barry 1997.

8 See Broadhead and Howard 1998: 6, for "getting your four" and issues of quantification related to the RAE.

9 See explicit reference to "The Book as the Gold Standard for Tenure and Promotion in the Humanistic Disciplines," the results of a survey by Leigh Estabrook conducted for the Committee on Institutional Cooperation (Estabrook 2003).

10 Greenblatt 2002 identifies the problem as "systemic, structural, and at base, economic." The MLA Ad Hoc Committee on "The Future of Scholarly Publishing" notes that while libraries could be counted on

to purchase 1,000 copies of a monograph in the 1970s, average sales were, by 2002, down to 300 copies; this drop occurred as the cost of journals, especially in the sciences, rose dramatically. At the same time, many universities stopped subsidizing presses (MLA 2002: 173–4). See also Pochoda 1997: 2.

11   Broadhead and Howard attribute to the RAE a larger tendency tending toward "the 'commodification' of academic research" (1998: 9).

12   For a suggestion that universities provide large subventions to junior scholars, see Stanton 2004: 35.

13   On the semiotic implications of this view of currency, see Waswo 1996.

14   Broadhead and Howard express a similar fear that the greater productivity prompted by the RAE has led to a dilution of scholarship: "Producing more articles, however, is now the same as doing more research. The regurgitation and multiple-placing of articles is on the increase. This process, although intellectually untaxing, is time-consuming, reducing time and energy available for both fresh research and course review" (1998: 10).

15   Editors explicitly acknowledge this influence, as Willis Regier, director of the University of Illinois Press commented in an interview with Jeffrey Williams of the *Minnesota Review*: "what is going to matter to the acquisitions editor most of all will be the credentials of the authors (is the project appropriate to the educational background of the author?)" and "most of the best books come through personal channels" (Regier 2004: 11).

16   On the phenomenon of academic "superstars," see: Shumway 1997; Bruce Robbins 1999; Tim Spurgin 2001.

17   See Guillory 2005, which discusses the problem of substituting quantity of scholarship produced for evaluation of its quality.

18   Arthur Marotti, in "Patronage, Poetry, and Print," has suggested that:

> one can detect, in the juxtaposition of dedicatory letters and epistles to readers, an interesting friction developing between the old-and new-style patrons, or at the least a complexity in the relationship of author, stationer, patron, and reader that was exploited by both writers and publishers to their own advantage.
>
> (Marotti 1995: 293)

Similarly, Loewenstein argues that Ben Jonson was "ambiguously engaged with the literary marketplace" because he "dedicates all of his newly recovered plays in the Folio either to people or to institutions, adapting the modern technology of dissemination to an archaic patronage economy" (1988: 273).

19 Fallon 2005; Butler 2005; Pinciss 2005; McCrea 2005. See the essay on "Shakespeare and the General Reader" by Tom Bishop 2004: 201–14.

20 Bloom 1998; Garber 2004; Greenblatt 2004; a British equivalent might be Kermode 2000.

21 On the importance of the *Times* profiles for establishing academic stars, see Shumway 1997 and Spurgin 2001.

22 Bushnell 2005; Sullivan *et al.* 2005; Fernie *et al.* 2005.

23 Based on the October 2005 MLA Job Information List, jobs at, for example, Yale ("Early Modern English including drama, 1500–1700"), Georgetown ("Early Modern Studies"), and University of California, Santa Barbara ("Renaissance Literary Studies") advertise for specialists in the early modern period. Heavy teaching jobs on the other hand, such as University of Atlanta at Huntsville (3/3 load, "Early Modern British Literature, especially 17th century, including Milton and Shakespeare"), San Francisco State University ("16th/17th century transatlantic literature including Shakespeare, Milton, Cavalier and Metaphysical poets, Colonial American literature"), Mount St. Mary's College (3/4 load, "British Renaissance Literature including Shakespeare, Western Civilization, and Freshman Seminars"); Kennesaw State University (3/4 load, "Pre-19th century British drama, Shakespeare, Medieval, Early Modern, Restoration and 18th Century, British Literature Survey") ask for broader chronological coverage with mention of specific major authors.

24 The acknowledgments for my own first book follow this order and similarly take pains to signal that I got my PhD at Harvard, and to associate the project with prominent scholars; see Crane 1993.

25 See RAE 1996.

26 UOA (Unit of Assessment) 57, English Language and Literature; see RAE 2006.

13

ALTERNATIVE COLLABORATIONS

Shakespeare, Nahum Tate, Our Academy, and the Science of Probability

Diana E. Henderson

There has been a boom in academic work on Shakespeare's afterlives during the past two decades, prompted by a variety of internal and external factors: cultural materialism's emphasis on the contemporary work art does; the poststructuralist recognition that readers (and by extension theatrical interpreters) create "meaning by Shakespeare" (Hawkes 1992); historicist studies and political challenges to canonical authorship; and, perhaps most importantly, creative multimedia revisions by modern artists (postcolonial and feminist, queer, populist, and apolitically experimental) that puzzle university students and have found enthusiastic advocates among like-minded scholars. These developments have all been, to a greater or lesser degree, controversial and contested, and the standpoints of their practitioners varied: while some have emphasized the power dynamics of appropriation and displacement, others hold on to the more Bardocentric vocabulary of adaptation, especially in reference to new art forms or media. Differences notwithstanding, amidst and alongside this exploration, there has been a fundamental expansion of understanding regarding Shakespeare's role as a collaborative artist.

Though scholarship in Shakespeare studies has become increasingly more welcoming of recent or contemporary collaborators, we have not so successfully addressed anterior collaborations of a particular type: later versions of presumed-to-be-familiar play scripts are still quite generally a site of (predominantly negative) judgment and bemusement. This response holds true especially for the cut-and-altered performance texts of earlier eras, and most particularly for the English Restoration revivals that pleased audiences for decades and even centuries after. In no instance has this critical attitude been more obviously expressed than in the treatment of Nahum Tate's revised *King Lear* of 1681, which held the stage for 150 years and was performed by the likes of Thomas Betterton and David Garrick. When I began studying Shakespeare, it was standard practice to mock Tate's *Lear* for its happy ending, and then move back (or, more accurately, on) to Shakespeare's version (in a modern edition conflating the Quarto and Folio texts that Tate read separately). Generally this is still standard practice. Although not necessarily a mistake in the classroom, such a response to a later reinterpretation raises important questions, among which one stands out: Given what we know about this revival and our profession's commitment (in theory, at least) to historicism and textual complexity, why are we still laughing?

I posit a multiple choice answer applicable to more instances than Tate's alone:

1   We are not reading the collaborative text itself.
2   We are not reading each others' scholarship.
3   We are less interested in the terms of explanation than in feeling superior.
4   The ways in which the work has been explained are not satisfying, either in illuminating the work for our students or in meeting our expectations of what matters in a text.
5   We could all use a laugh these days.
6   All of the above.

Each of these answers involves the current conditions of academia as well as our personal priorities, and for that reason alone I frame the case so bluntly. The limitations of time and the vast territories of material available for study certainly make it understandable that even committed scholars are not reading everything they might wish—although those conditions would seem to preclude the knowing snigger of recognition and dismissal that greets Tate's decision to create a love story for Edgar and Cordelia and to let Lear live. If we are indeed relying on the authority of others' accounts, should not those accounts include the paradigm-questioning work of scholars such as Christopher Spencer and editor James Black and the more recent contributions of Nancy Klein Maguire, C. B. Hardman, Sonia Massai and Peter Womack, all of whom have shed light on the political and textual conditions contributing to Tate's alterations? If not, why are we busily churning out new unread scholarship rather than enjoying a good read of Tate's three Shakespearean revisions (or, as my students say, whatever)?[1]

The third answer and especially the fourth answer aim at deeper concerns about our desires and disciplinary projects rather than at general public anti-intellectualism—although this phenomenon may be adding edge to the scholar's desire to feel superior and could well motivate the fifth response on the list. Even when Restoration texts are treated historically and sympathetically (as in Katherine Maus's more broadly noted study of Davenant and Dryden's *Tempest*, or Maguire's and Hardman's linkage of Tate's *Lear* to the politics of the Exclusion Crisis), the particulars of social or political history appeal to a sub-section of specialists more readily than to students or even to those not currently focused on overlapping research of their own: the contextual knowledge needed to make the material interesting, albeit not of the depth required to pursue archival research, takes time to attain, and its broader applications are harder to discern in this glut-of-information age. Confronted with such difficulty and less evident payoff, it is easier (at least with Tate) to make a quick gesture at historical understanding and then play for the punchline. If this is true in the classroom, then exaggerated fears of scholarly relativism are less pertinent than concerns about a continued failure to inspire a truly historical imagination. For those at a more advanced level of engagement, another dimension of scholarship's failure (more frequently noted) involves oversimplifying the artwork into a perfectly reflective rather than refracted mirror of ideology, thus denuding it of interest and the need for detailed scrutiny.

What follows represents one attempt to wrestle with these problems intellectually, speaking from within a specific academic environment as well as disciplinary culture, in a manner that connects professional research with classroom experience and the pressing changes within higher education. I am only secondarily interested in redeeming Nahum Tate as worthy of close analysis, or in exploring another reading of the play for its own sake—but I do try to capture my enjoyment of such tasks as one strand contributing to the larger project of better integrating historical understanding with artistic imagination (both of which include a large measure of contingency and probabilistic rather than a priori knowledge). I hope a recombinant exploration of material historical change, history of ideas revisited, linguistic specificity, and reflection beyond disciplinary boundaries may challenge the remnant of an evolutionary positivism in Shakespeare studies that still presumes we in the twenty-first century are less benighted than artists past, be it by our getting back to the "original" or by having gone beyond the intervening alterations to some more radical revision. Moreover, I hope to do so without losing a political edge in the present thereby. Like postcolonial work geographically challenging the center, this form of reading performance and collaborative history has ramifications for our current interpretive practices.

THE ART OF THE PROBABLE

Let us first turn back to a word, "probability," reconsidered in light of the seventeenth-century upheavals that shaped English Restoration theory and culture—and not only those disruptions in the monarchy and religious authority more familiar to humanities scholars, but also the world-reshaping debates in mathematics and scientific experimentation. The vocabulary, anxiety, and energy evinced in those debates carry over into Tate's "altered" revival and other over-judged, under-read Restoration plays; they help make more sense of his *Lear*'s enduring appeal as well. More profoundly, they prompt us to think historically and critically about what is possible, popular, and—especially—probable.

Once noticed, probability (like the phrase "persons of quality") turns up everywhere from the 1630s onward. The reiteration of the same word, however, masks fundamental debates over its truth status and shifting referentiality. One radically new idea of probability, its mathematical study, was initiated by the work of Pascal, Fermat, and other mid-seventeenth-century thinkers, as a means of rationalizing expectations. They began humbly enough, trying to figure out a fair gamble in games of chance, but Pascal soon expanded the horizons of their mathematical method (at least rhetorically) towards infinity itself, in his famous wager on the wisdom of believing in God.[2] Looking to ground personal choice and make sense of the future, these mathematicians' notion of probability involved a temporal shift of attention; their gaze forward took it in a different direction (one conventionally associated with modernity) than was encouraged by the descriptive, evaluative use of the word in Aristotle's *Poetics*— Aristotle's usage being, appropriately enough, the presumed frame of reference for the aesthetics underwriting Shakespearean adaptation throughout the Neoclassical era. Both models saw in cause-and-effect analysis a means to advance the ends of justice, but the Pascalian method was more ambitious in hoping to understand the actual workings of a deterministically conceived present and—perhaps against the spirit of Pascal himself—suggested a future that, even without *certain* knowledge, men could master.

Nevertheless, even before this mathematical turn to the future, Aristotle's legacy in defining probability was far from simple, and the *Poetics* only a small part of that inheritance. Without rehearsing the word's complicated elaboration by medieval philosophers, it is worth recalling that Thomas Aquinas had invoked it as that which, because grounded in authority, made an opinion worthy of approbation. As such, the probable had social and moral if not absolute epistemological value, and pointed to the communal foundations underpinning beliefs shaped by human authorities. It was this association with authoritative proponents that would be extended quite distinctively by Jesuit casuistry and empirical science, to the disgust of Pascal and Hobbes respectively. In Pascal's scalding parody of the Jesuits' "double probability," for example, because "the affirmative and negative of most opinions have each, according to our doctors, some probability," both became allowed as "safe" grounds for moral action; moreover, the greater difficulty of "discovering probability in the converse of opinions manifestly good" made it a "feat which none but great men can achieve" (1941: 391, 396)—contorted ingenuity thus having the effect of licensing grotesquely "incorrect" behavior and indirectly giving birth to libertinism. The seemingly more benign example of the Royal Society's reliance on multiple witnesses and repeated experiments to attain probable results was no less repugnant to Thomas Hobbes; he found the insertion of subjective epistemology into the study of natural philosophy anathema (even if adherents made limited claims for their understanding). The specter of relativism loomed, as the common sources of social authority appeared increasingly corrupt or incapacitated while inherited forms of argumentation premised on their robustness continued to be invoked, prompting rigorous critique and new methods of calculation from more absolutist and mathematically inclined truth-seekers.

Hints of this looming moral and epistemological crisis involving probability and design appear in England by the start of the 1630s, as in John Ford's Caroline tragedy *The Broken Heart* (Ford 1995). There, a discussion between the hot-tempered, love-thwarted Orgilus and his temporary tutor, the appropriately named Tecnicus, illustrates probability's properly subordinated place within the old scientific order and vocabulary. Like a well-trained Aristotelian schoolman, or for that matter Hobbesian, Orgilus earlier explained his retreat from society in cause-and-effect terms—the cause, his troubled mind, needed "information" (that is, its incoherent matter needed shaping, in-form-ation). When Orgilus then decides to return to society for reasons of honor, the learned Tecnicus worries that he might not yet be adequately informed. Recalling an epistemology of certainty based on a priori knowledge, in which probability signaled a disappointing compromise, Tecnicus claims:

> ... honor must be grounded
> On knowledge, not opinion—for opinion
> Relies on *probability* and accident,
> But knowledge on necessity and truth.
> (*The Broken Heart* 3.1.45–8; my italics)

For the philosophical Tecnicus, even the best of socially grounded opinions remains inadequate in its contingency, and distinct from true knowledge. Like so much generalized language in Ford, however, the clarity of this traditional formulation is undermined by its context (including its only nominal setting in ancient Sparta rather than Caroline England). For the lovelorn Orgilus is actually lying about his reason for retreat, and his search for "information" leads not to certainty but to red-herring intrigue and a grotesque, apparently dishonorable form of revenge. While upright Tecnicus—translated in the cast list as "artist" and capable of spiritual interpretation as well as classical *techné*—understands the dire portents of an oracular missive and leaves Sparta to serve Apollo at Delphi itself, most of those who remain at court prove unable to overcome their violent passions and waste away (if female) or destroy one another and themselves (if male).

In a most remarkable such instance, Orgilus replicates the very form of cruelty that victimized his own beloved Penthea by killing her brother Ithocles and thus contributing to his beloved Cleantha's titular broken heart. Because Ithocles had misused his fraternal control over Penthea's marital choice and denied Orgilus's suit, the angry young man feels justified in denying the repentant brother's happiness in turn. Indeed, twisting Tecnicus's high-minded theory to fit his fractured world, Orgilus will defend his murder of the trapped, unarmed man (in a chair that is also a "machine") by invoking the *necessity* of the *effect*. Orgilus could not brook the unreliability of honorable combat precisely because he distrusts "fortune": this is no longer a world for Shakespearean trial by combat, for virtuous-Edgar-beats-evil-Edmund and fortune's wheel come full circle. Of course, arguably neither was the world of *King Lear*, in which that archaic moment of justice simultaneously enacts fratricide, and where the metaphorical wheel becomes a fiery torment and a rack. Nevertheless, Shakespeare at least attributes his final tragic turn to bad timing and good men's forgetfulness. For John Ford's courtiers, the world of social interactions and codes has become so uncertain that one cannot infer just outcomes even to properly willed and motivated actions: hence the need for Pascal's new science, as well as baroque ethical explanations.

That the Aristotelian cosmos was unraveling is not news; but in England during the reign of Charles I, when loyalty and honor were being sorely tested on and offstage, these gaps between theories and practice, both epistemological and social, further strained coherence. Such uncertainty echoes in one document that we might expect to be certain in its rhetoric, even if benighted in its logic: the proclamation, too often still presumed to be definitive and absolute, closing the theaters in 1642.[3] With florid personification and rhetorical figures dressing its legal structure, it reads in part:

> Whereas the distressed Estate of Ireland, steeped in her own Blood, and the distracted Estate of England, threatened with a Cloud of Blood by a Civil War, call for all *possible* Means to appease and avert the Wrath of God, appearing in these Judgements . . . and whereas Public Sports do not well agree with Public Calamities, nor Public Stage-plays with the Seasons of Humiliation . . . It is therefore thought fit, and Ordained . . . That, while these *sad causes* and set Times of Humiliation do continue, Public Stage Plays shall cease, and be forborn, instead of which are recommended to the People of this Land the profitable and seasonable considerations of Repentance, Reconciliation, and Peace with God, which *probably* may produce outward Peace and Prosperity, and bring again Times of Joy and Gladness to these Nations.[4]

Probably? That rhythmically intrusive and semantically plaintive "probably," appearing in a position of such periodic importance, reminds us that this was far less than a conclusive statement at the time: not only as an act of theatrical closure, which would be repeatedly subverted and defied during the next five years, but also as a statement of God's involvement in world affairs, registering as it does the ever-stronger sense of doubt at being able to count on His corrective intervention even when His wrath seemed clear enough. The interpretive crisis of understanding divine as well as human cause-and-effect sequences, success, and succession, would become spectacularly traumatic with the beheading of Charles I, that deeply unpopular action that—even in hindsight and when re-shaped by the Restoration's most triumphalist rhetoricians—took an awfully long time for God to address.[5] The execution would, of course, play a major role in shaping the Restoration imaginary—and indeed, the British imaginary through to the days of Dickens, long after eyewitnesses such as Samuel Pepys had come to dust.

What was now certain, or even probable? Ascribing Cromwell's rise to power to "fantastic chance," Shakespeare's would-be son William Davenant wondered that those "so young and new in judgement" could believe that "the glorious Robe, Authority," could last when they wore it "in all weathers and in ev'ry Throng"—his language combining echoes from the stories of both *Lear* and *Richard II*, two of the three Shakespeare plays that Nahum Tate would later attempt to stage (Maguire 1991: 31).[6] For Davenant during the years of the Republic as later for Tate writing during the Exclusion Crisis (when Parliament attempted to exclude Charles II's Catholic brother James from the royal succession), the foundations had toppled with King Charles I's head, and the future was unknowable and unreliable; they did not yet have a reasonable calculus upon which to base political choices. The old methods for determining approbation had collapsed: tellingly, Tate would excise Shakespeare's exchange in which the disguised Kent easily identifies the "Authority" "which I would fain call master" in his dishonored King's countenance (*King Lear* 1.4.28–30). Dangerous times created life trajectories as improbable as the fictional Edgar's—or Edmund's. Davenant, Charles I's poet laureate at the closing of the theaters, found a way to serve and entertain Cromwell before becoming a mainstay of Charles II's Restored theatre; Nahum Tate, the son of Faithful Teate, a Puritan minister in Ireland, eventually wrote Royalist drama while professing absolute "Loyalty" as his code. No wonder that they, like the authors of the Parliamentary proclamation, would strive to equate the word "probable" with the concept of the "ideal," rather than with the "necessary" or even just the "likely."

Hence Tate's pleasure, announced in the preface to his revived *King Lear*, that he has (by "good Fortune") discovered a new model of dramatic probability:

> *'Twas my good Fortune to light on one Expedient to rectifie what was wanting in the Regularity and Probability of the Tale, which was to run through the whole* A Love *betwixt* Edgar *and* Cordelia, *that never chang'd*

> *word with each other in the Original. This renders* Cordelia's *Indifference and her Father's Passion in the first Scene probable. It likewise gives Countenance to* Edgar's *Disguise, making that a generous Design that was before a poor Shift to save his Life.*[7]

Probability, in the form of Cordelia's love for Edgar, motivates her to fail the speech-test intentionally, thus avoiding an unwanted state marriage. Although this results in some oddly insincere moments for the actress asked elsewhere to emblematize "Piety," it consistently serves to ennoble Edgar as an agent of justice, rescuing damsels in distress, a despairing father, and a king imperiled—here, by his eldest daughter's death warrant against him. Thus altering the roles—with more schematic gender implications than in *Lear*—allows Edgar to participate as a fundamentally loyal, if estranged and tested, courtier who aids in his King's eventual "blest Restauration" (5.6.118). For many a Stuart courtier and their kings, such consistency was a state devoutly to be wished.

In both his prologue and epilogue as well, Tate makes explicit his awareness that the times do not conventionally confirm his idealizing order. He begins by arguing that "Morals were alwaies proper for the Stage,/But are ev'n *necessary* in this Age" (Prologue 19–20; emphasis added). This quite un-Aristotelian sense of necessity, whereby the playwright must urgently combat religious immorality rather than neutrally describe a deductive syllogism, locates Tate's play as squarely in sympathy with certain types of social reform (an anti-libertine strain that might hearken back to his Puritan upbringing) while at the same time upholding conservative courtly hierarchical relations. Similarly, in the epilogue his Cordelia, played by Mrs Berry, counters libertine skepticism (advocated throughout the play by evil Edmund, and associated offstage with Charles II's illegitimate son the soon-to-be-rebellious Duke of Monmouth) when she asserts:

> *Inconstancy, the reigning Sin o' th' Age,*
> *Will scarce endure true Lovers on the Stage;*
> *You hardly ev'n in Plays with such dispense,*
> *And Poëts kill 'em in their own Defence.*

> *Yet One bold Proof I was resolv'd to give,*
> *That I cou'd three Hours Constancy Out-live.*
> (Epilogue 1–6)

Amazement at three hours' constancy can look like frivolous, slyly winking fun from a distance, but the wit aims at a deeper skepticism, bordering on despair. Anticipating his audience's disbelief that love could in fact endure and hence prove a possible, much less probable, means to a happy ending, Tate counters that tragic conclusions are themselves a form of poetic self-defense; he thereby implies that his plot alterations both provide a counterargument or "Proof" of constancy *and* constitute a bolder, riskier artistic choice.

A close reading of his *Lear*'s latter acts testifies to Tate's full consciousness that a fortunate conclusion is far from necessary: it is not even probable in the mathematical sense, but rather a source of deep wonder. This is not, in other words, Aristotelian plotting by numbers: more apt to call it a miracle, requiring reiterated assertion before a deeply doubting Lear will believe he is not "gull'd/With Lying Hope" (5.6.66–7). To Cordelia's conclusion that "Then there are Gods, and Vertue is their Care," Lear replies:

> Is 't Possible?
> Let the Spheres stop their Course, the Sun make Hault,
> The Winds be husht, the Seas and Fountains Rest;
> All Nature pause, and listen to the Change.
> (5.6.96–100)

The *cause* of this wondrous change is Albany's explicit recognition of human empathy, acknowledging the kinship between his own and Lear's abuse by Goneril. The unlikely *effect* is a traditional form of social justice. *Is't Possible?* Three years later the Monmouth rebellion, and three years after that the "Glorious Revolution" would each hinge on filial ingratitude, or at least induced disloyalty; those events imply that such probability and notions of orderly succession were the stuff of stage fiction, serving increasingly as a realm of compensatory justice for what could not so successfully be enacted offstage.

A SPRING IN THE AIR, A KING ON HIS THRONE

It was in this climate of uncertainty and disillusionment with social justice and absolute knowledge, as well as God's inscrutability, that Robert Boyle had begun to experiment with an air pump. Rather than, like Tate's Lear, command Nature pause, his experiments seemed to listen anew to what changes she might reveal. Boyle famously incurred Thomas Hobbes's wrath by expressing complacency regarding uncertain causation and by preferring to focus on effects alone, the "matters of fact" that, when demonstrated through reliance on instruments that improved and corrected for errors introduced by the (human) senses, would undergird the development of empiricism.[8] Boyle's apparently humbler method and claims finessed what had been a topic of vigorous philosophical debate: whether Nature might not abhor a vacuum after all, unsettling the premise that "Nothing will come of nothing" so fundamental to Aristotelian cosmology and King Lear alike. For Hobbes, Boyle's "solution" of bracketing the question of whether any form of matter remained within the air pump meant the denial of causation and hence of "knowledge" itself; he regarded Boyle's experimental accounts describing the "springe of the air" (later known as air pressure) as mere "opinion"—rather like an anecdote in contradistinction to an historical master narrative. Nevertheless, Boyle's results became news, and his method caught on. Published accounts of the experiments, like printed stage plays, recorded and disseminated events performed before small audiences to a wider public, and paved the way for a new kind of celebrity, the experimenter—later to become the scientist—as hero. Moreover, Boyle himself would be able to generalize so effectively from his experiments that his mathematical formula known as Boyle's Law still remains basic training for scuba divers and physicists alike.

In Carolean culture, the disciplinary walls we moderns have constructed between philosophy, politics, science, and drama did not exist. Hobbes had been Charles II's tutor and was kinder in his judgments of William Davenant than of Robert Boyle. For a time, Boyle's neighbor in Pall Mall —very likely his nextdoor neighbor— was Nell Gwyn.[9] Boyle's older brother Roger, Earl of Orrery, was the most popular playwright of the 1660s, author of many of those now-unread heroic dramas that delighted audiences in the newly Restored public theatres. Pepys, who as a youth had witnessed Charles I's beheading on the "tragic scaffold" outside Whitehall, was a member and eventually became president of the Royal Society, where the experimentalist Boyle put on a show by repeating for a non-specialist audience those actions he had carried out "backstage" in his sister's home with the aid of Robert Hooke: each of these scientific actors would soon have a Law named after him, the beginnings of a new regime of knowledge that would control interpretation of phenomena and provide a set of rules that trumped those attributed to Aristotle. Indeed, like Aristotle, much of what they hypothesized as mere observation of effects or probable theories would eventually be enshrined with near-absolute authority. They might plead philosophical humility, but their own effects and legacy were anything but. In time, all the world became their stage.

Awareness of the Hobbes/Boyle debate, like awareness of Pascal's mathematics and contemporary work with infinitesimals, provides another pathway towards understanding at least some of Tate's dramaturgical choices and his *Lear*'s popularity. For example, his habit of concocting verbal tableaux describing hypothetical future events has understandably been deemed melodramatic—end of discussion. Two examples from a single scene, 3.2, capture Tate's rhetorical extremity. First, Cordelia (riffing off Edgar's contemplation of "the worst" in Shakespeare's version) considers the "probable" fate of her father on the heath:

> *Cordelia* Or what if it be Worse? can there be Worse?
> As 'tis too probable this furious Night
> Has pierc'd his tender Body, the bleak Winds
> And cold Rain chill'd, or Lightning struck him Dead;
> If it be so your Promise is discharg'd,
> And I have only one poor Boon to beg,
> That you'd Convey me to his breathless Trunk,
> With my torn Robes to wrap his hoary Head,
> With my torn Hair to bind his Hands and Feet,
> Then with a show'r of Tears
> To wash his Clay-smear'd Cheeks, and Die beside him.
>
> (3.2.80–90)

As she thus imagines a bleak future and sets out to find her father, she is overheard by Edmund, who begins his soliloquy by quoting her subsequent words and reflecting on the "lucky change" he anticipates will follow from this chance encounter:

> *Bastard* Provide me a Disguise, we'll instantly
> Go seek the King: —ha! ha! a lucky change,
> That Vertue which I fear'd would be my hindrance
> Has prov'd the Bond to my Design;
> I'll bribe two Ruffians that shall at a distance follow,
> And seise 'em in some desert Place, and there
> Whilst one retains her t' other shall return
> T' inform me where she's Lodg'd; I'll be disguis'd too.
> Whilst they are poching for me I'll to the Duke
> With these Dispatches, then to th'Field
> Where like the vig'rous *Jove* I will enjoy
> This *Semele* in a Storm, 'twill deaf her Cries
> Like Drums in Battle, lest her Groans shou'd pierce
> My pittying Ear, and make the amorous Fight less fierce.
>
> (3.2 111–24)

Edmund's scheming "Design" contorts the vocabulary of divinity (confirmed in his Jovial removal of his "Semele"'s will), and reveals his distance both from God and the mathematically deterministic philosophers who would soon regard "luck" as merely a sign of insufficient knowledge: by 1717, for example, Abraham de Moivre of the Royal Society could argue in *The Doctrine of Chances* that probabilistic analysis could "cure a Kind of Superstition, which has been of long standing in the World, viz. That there is in Play such a thing as Luck, good or bad," and furthermore that his book "inforced" recognition that "the Notion of Luck is meerly Chimerical" (1718: iv).

What fascinates me most here, however, is that in each instance these melodramatic imaginings substitute for what does not come to pass within Tate's fiction: Cordelia and Lear are reunited and live, after Edgar rescues first her from Edmund's "Ruffians" and then both of them from Goneril's would-be murderers. In other words, the verbal tableaux enact the limits of predictability from the perspective of the characters within their fictional world, even as the playwright, deploying compensatory logic, rigorously restructures Shakespeare to fit his idealized notion of a probable solution to the story of a kingdom turned upside down. In foiling the despair of Cordelia and Edmund's villainous design, he emphasizes the gap between their subjective epistemologies and his own creative authority, and as playwright labors to reclaim a just world beyond their ken. Those like de Moivre would soon attempt to restore a predictable order through mathematics, whereby one might learn

> to distinguish the Events which are the effect of Chance, from those which are produced by Design: The very Doctrine that finds Chance where it really is, being able to prove by a gradual Increase of Probability, till it arrive at Demonstration, that where Uniformity, Order and Constancy reside, there also reside Choice and Design.
>
> (1718: vi)

But when Tate wrote, such dramatic demonstrations were more difficult to attain: these scenes in context reinforce his awareness that his version of probability involved an act of faith and immense will. Hence, rather than rape, the double-death of Lear and Cordelia, or Gloucester's exploding heart—all imagined as future events within the text—we are awarded that notorious happy ending.

For that, Tate has become the object of our satirical barbs. Perhaps he would not be surprised that history has made him a critics' whipping-boy. Tate had already faced the difficulty of having his storytelling misinterpreted, or at least not interpreted as he wished, when his adaptation of *Richard II* was banished from the stage; for him, the royal refusal to read closely was an improbable insult to common sense. (So feel many of us, in the classroom and out, when close reading is rejected.) But in a world still topsy-turvy and politically chaotic, Shakespeare's views of history and the nobility's corruption could still cause trouble, justifying discontent among the populace. That Tate struggled to idealize order and suppress random injustice is ultimately less surprising than that he chose three of Shakespeare's least consoling tragedies (*Richard II*, *Lear*, and *Coriolanus*) for his experimentation. These were far from easy choices.

Tate wrote at a time when his own King had lost much of that "Authority" Kent found in Lear's face, in a year when many feared or hoped that 1641 had come again, forty years on—he did not write with the complacency we may still impose upon him, because in hindsight we know that the bastard Duke of Monmouth's rebellion would fail and that the fall of James II would be deemed (comparatively) "bloodless." As luck (or design) would have it, the Stuarts' would-be kings soon were called Pretenders, while the pretend world of the stage continued to represent Tate's play celebrating "the King's blest Restauration." Shakespeare, for Tate—like the behavior of air, for Boyle—both resisted easy explanation and proved the unlikely basis for a new civility, even without certainty. His "altered" Lear seems to have served those needs for his audiences as well. And although literary historians have not treated him so civilly, judged in theatrical terms, one hit out of three—and a hit with "legs" at that— is not such bad odds.

Nor is it only in his success rate (further enriched by his lasting contribution to opera as the librettist for Purcell's Dido and Aeneas) that Tate's drama gestures at a future based on numbers. In his Preface to Lear, he also makes a case for his ending based on theatrical knowledge:

> This Method necessarily threw me on making the Tale conclude in a Success to the innocent distrest Persons: Otherwise I must have incumbred the Stage with dead Bodies, which Conduct makes many Tragedies conclude with unseasonable Jests. Yet was I Rackt with no small Feare for so bold a Change, till I found it well receiv'd by my Audience.
>
> (Tate 1681, Prefatory letter, lines 34ff.)

Arguing that Shakespeare's dead bodies defied probability, arguing from experience that a large number of such falling bodies often produced giggles from an audience, Tate adapts the experimental vocabulary of Boyle more exactly, though perhaps less consciously, than he does those insights of Aristotle that some considered Laws.

To say this is to recognize that the mechanistic model and probabilistic conception of Tate's dramaturgy both responds to a particular mid-century political rupture and participates in and gestures towards a future that was discovering new ways to cope with disrupted causation. King Charles's death continued to haunt Shakespeare's seventeenth-century afterlife—leaving its overt trace in the published quartos of Tate's adaptation, where Lear suffers not "bareheaded" but "beheaded"on the heath. Tellingly, that seeming mistake was reiterated in the subsequent four quarto editions published within Tate's lifetime (after 1681, 1689, 1699, 1702, 1712). Was this a sign of sloppy reprints or a sign of the times—or both? But lest we begin to resemble *David Copperfield*'s Mr Dick, we should look not only at King Charles's head and the troubles that came before but also at the Restoration's emergent epistemologies and ceremonies for seeking a more stable common ground. Secularization, as Peter Womack describes it, captures some of the change in Tate's *Lear*; crucially and consequentially, experimental science and mathematical probability would be the methods of that new philosophy. They are methods with which we, and our students, need to reckon.

NOW WHAT?

Tate's *Lear* continued to hold the stage for 150 years. The empire of chance would grow mightily in those ensuing centuries, and the quantitative study of probability and eventually statistics would grow with it, struggling to control the random and unpredictable. Chaos has come again, and with it a simultaneous skepticism and absolute reliance upon a rational calculus and algorithmic reasoning. Evidence of this un-Aristotelian study of probability saturates even pop culture: witness the US hit television drama *Numb3rs* (2005–) starring a mathematician as a detective-pop hero. Quantum physics confirms that ordinary matter—the 5 per cent of matter in the universe that we actually understand—operates in accordance with probability theory. As students of Shakespeare we may not think this is our territory, but in trying to describe the popularity of an author in the present day, it is hard to avoid numbers or make claims that cannot be substantiated using the tools of science, or at least social science. Increasingly subject to quantitative measures of assessment, qualitative analysis is in dire need of better rhetoric and argumentative defense, at the very least. Otherwise it will be dismissed as merely "anecdotal"—and not in the revelatory New Historicist sense. For these pragmatic as well as more intellectually adventurous reasons, it seems time to look again at the scientific paradigms too many of us turned away from when we turned to Shakespeare.

For in its confusing proliferation of meanings both past and present, as well as in its denotations, "probability" speaks directly to our moment: the misrecognition or blindness to differences of definition has become one of the most persistent problems in the current academy, aggravated by disciplinary specialization. At the same time, it points out our distance from an era when natural philosophy and moral philosophy were more involved than our "arts and sciences" have become. Indeed, now even within the "hard sciences" (still so called, unproblematically, by most of their practitioners), the professoriate is just beginning to realize that hyperspecialized vocabularies in science and mathematics lead to confusion for students: engineering majors studying biology discover (or more likely are baffled when) "vectors" and "expression" mean different things in the two subjects—and neither mean anything close to what literature students may presume they mean.[10] The difficulty of determining "common sense" parlance today makes all the more important an understanding of the context in which such verbal assumptions as "common sense parlance" came into being.

Increasing numbers of scholars in the humanistic disciplines are now working to lower those disciplinary boundaries that began to rise with the death of Hobbes and with Robert Boyle's success. Given my location at MIT, I am probably more inclined to see our reentry into those experimental spaces as a matter of urgency, especially if the humanities wish to reclaim more authority in discussions of public policy and education. Although at other schools the pressures are greater to focus exclusively on educating English majors and eventually English PhDs, looking no further, unless we all also change the market economy in which we churn out both them and more of ourselves, the endgame will not be pretty. By pursuing linguistically and historically sensitive readings while also voyaging beyond our normal disciplinary comfort zones and looking towards the future, however, we might increase our cultural capital without compromising our priorities.

We might also learn more about the particular possible causes for that shape-shifting phenomenon known as the Shakespeare effect, at a time of social fractiousness. Rather than rehearse the Augustan afterlife of Shakespeare in terms of an aesthetic competition between the critical acuity of Nahum Tate and Joseph Addison, in other words, it seems a good time to supplement our appreciation of Lear's "compelling anguish" with more sympathy for, or at least willingness to debate the merits with, those who react to global crises by seeking representations of a stable moral order and a just ending. We may even find new sources of enjoyment: as Rodney Brooks, head of MIT's Computer Science and Artificial Intelligence Lab, put it to my co-teacher Janet Sonenberg, a theater professor who happens to be his wife, "if you'd taken five courses in mathematics, you'd feel more secure in the world because you could better assess risk" (they were debating the merits of MIT's core requirements). Maybe, maybe not—but by placing collaborations with Shakespeare in a broader disciplinary context, the conversation about them certainly becomes less predictable.

In citing these instances of my own experience at MIT and in drawing here on materials that I also share in the classroom, I hope to contribute to those dialogues and encourage others to do the same, as befits their particular institutional environments and conditions of employment. In the words of the late Gloria Anzaldùa, "A bridge (made up of stories, ideas, theories) is knowledge. It is public; it is communal; it is where our paths converge." If we in the humanities want to keep engaging the public imagination seriously, we need to talk across the disciplinary barriers that keep our paths from crossing, much less converging. We also need to reconsider the reasons we are asking ourselves and others to produce interpretations for publication at such a rate that the publishing industry and our own friends cannot keep up—much less the public implied in publication. Nothing feels particularly easy for a committed teacher/scholar these days: not only publishing expectations but staffing reductions, challenges to tenure lines, and diminished respect for expertise of any kind (that is not obviously instrumental or market-rewarded) all conspire to eat up our days and limit our horizons. But such conditions make it all the more important that we consider the root *causes* for our field's diminished prestige and reorient our internal rewards structures and our academic *effects* (or, in management-speak, outputs and outcomes) to improve our collective condition.

Why are we, who pride ourselves on subtle knowledge of cultural studies and the politics of language, advertising ourselves as unnecessary luxury goods (the new boredom)? As much as we enjoy the process, do we truly believe that delving with more specificity into more unknown manuscripts—or the umpteenth instance of a popular Shakespeare allusion—will or should inspire the public to return their focus from genetic engineering or cancer research back to us? Even if they should do so, is it *probable* that this is the best way in which to exert our collective energies and knowledge as the twenty-first century proceeds? Despite the provocative tone of these questions, my answer is that I cannot be sure, but I think we should pay attention to the odds and the public a bit more. That includes spending more time learning about disciplines and events not immediately obvious for their instrumental value to us, although in the long run they might be—and might allow more cross-fertilization of a sort witnessed less frequently in the modern academy than at the birth of the Royal Society. Call it a Pascalian wager. This does not mean turning away from our traditional delights and skills, but it does mean making more efforts to recontextualize broadly as well as deeply. In doing so, what some deem "service teaching" may turn out to serve us all well—but only if we can hear what students in those classes are challenging us to reconsider and can learn from what they and their disciplinary-specialist teachers tell us.

In these efforts, more humility in our cultural accounts of past collaborations with Shakespeare likewise could play its part. Humility rather than smugness when faced with Tate's *Lear* may not be so different a stance, after all, than one would wish to see practiced more often by political and religious leaders of all faiths who presume they know what the Word and words mean. Practicing that attitude of respect and pursuing a wider frame of reference—while maintaining our skepticism and ability to analyze carefully—might well be the best form of education we can now provide, as well as the most likely way to keep our own and Shakespeare's best potentialities in play. I would argue it *is* probable.

NOTES

1 The institutional reasons for individual faculty wishing to retain or improve their working conditions to continue writing largely unread articles are obvious, as are the particular scholarly obsessions and mental rewards of thinking through writing that spurred many to enter and remain in academia; but as a collective rather than individualized response at the systemic level, it is inadequate merely to cite these motivations.

2 See especially Hacking 1975 and Gigerenzer *et al.* 1989 on early notions of probability and the historical shifts in its truth-value.

3 See the books by Clare 2002 and Butler 1984, and their and other essays in Milling and Thomson 2004.

4 Emphasis added. From *Acts and Ordinances of the Interregnum I,* 26–7, as cited by Butler 2004: 439.

5 See Henderson 1998/1999 on the representational crisis caused by Charles's seemingly unpunished "martyrdom" as rendered in elegiac poetry.

6 Davenant's 1657 poem was (by "fantastic chance"?) addressed to Roger Boyle, later Earl of Orrery—the elder brother of the natural philosopher Robert Boyle discussed below, who is best known for his Law measuring air pressure.

7 Throughout, I cite the first edition from the Furness Collection at the University of Pennsylvania as transcribed online by Jack Lynch, checked against James Black's 1975 Regents edition, http://newark.rutgers.edu/ ~jlynch/Texts/tatelear.html; I use Black's act-scene-line divisions. This passage comes from the prefatory letter to Thomas Boteler, line 23ff.

8 On the Hobbes-Boyle debates, see Shapin and Schaffer 1985; on the larger epistemological context, see also Poovey 1998 and Shapin 1994.

9 Steven Shapin in conversation, MIT, spring 2005.

10 http://web.mit.edu/newsoffice/2006/communication-gap-1122.html. The link summarizes an article by Kathleen Cushman and Jennifer Donovan in the *Howard Hughes Institute Bulletin* on the pedagogical work of biologist Graham Walker.

14

AFTERWORD

Alternativity at the Theatrical Core

A Conversation with Michael Boyd, Artistic Director of the Royal Shakespeare Company

[The following is redacted from a wide-ranging interview held in London in July 2005, when Boyd was preparing the RSC's 2006 *Complete Works* festival and working on the architectural negotiations for the new theater complex at Stratford. I began by asking him what connections and use he saw to academic scholarship, and progressive or "alternative" scholarship in particular. Ed.]

MB: We're trying to be more responsive to academic research . . . I'm personally really grateful for the balance the academic world gives to the really quite weak situation we have at the moment in terms of journalistic criticism: the levels of investment into inquiry (in mainstream journalism) are quite minimal. So a comparison I would make right away would be between scholarly criticism, which involves a great deal of personal investment, and journalistic criticism, which is more formulaic and forced to pursue a quite shallow agenda. Even our printed material, for my (2004) *Hamlet*, has really good little essays by Greenblatt and Jonathan Bate as well as a popular historian who has written about Arbella Stuart. I was very interested in her as a prism through which one could see Hamlet's madness and Ophelia's madness and the whole marriage game at the time. I think there is a place—without getting too highbrow—where that is useful. We have entered into relationships, all different kinds of inquiry, with universities both in the States and here; the key thing is always the personal relationship.

I think there's an awful lot more work on the plays for scholars to be doing. I think there's a great deal more work to be done on the language. Something I would love to do would be to analyze what I would call the stylistics of censorship. I'm very interested in it partly because of my time as a training director in the Soviet Union in 1979, but partly as a director of Shakespeare. It's decoding, it's the Kremlinology of reading Shakespeare's plays, the use of a word such as "more" in Shakespeare's language, in his sonnets—for people to be alert to that. But actually I mean much more than that—I mean that the kind of cryptic nature of the sonnets is partly borne out of a habit of concealment. It's not just a meretricious playfulness. There is a necessity to crypticism in the plays and in the poems, just as there is a necessity to rhyme and meter in terms of memorizing—you know, that's really why they're there, so the lines are memorable, first of all for the artist or the story re-teller, and then later for memorability for the listener. And I think there's a lot more to be done on that . . . What I do every single time I read a play—a Shakespeare play, or indeed any Renaissance text—is try to find the way they're expressing what they're not allowed to express. And I think that is quite . . . that is one very important x-ray to put on the piece.

In terms of us generating what you might call progressive or alternative work, that means so many different things. It is progressive, I believe, to return to the founding ambitions of the RSC, and to explore the ideals and approaches of the great European ensembles, in the context of an English and, indeed, American theatrical culture that is very wary of intellectual inquiry or moral or spiritual seriousness, and that is dominated by economic considerations and short-term contracts because of celebrity. I think it's very progressive to revisit the traditions of collective theater-making whether they be the touring ensembles or the London ensembles of Shakespeare's time or the Eastern European ensembles born out of totalitarianism and, indeed, the great British attempt to explore that territory in the early days of the RSC. I think that's progressive—partly aesthetically, but also partly it's an important thing to do right now, to explore viable collectives. And I think the RSC's one of the best places to do it. The achievement of contingent consensus in a sort of profoundly complex way is a major achievement now, and to do it at a national institution would make me happy to die. That would be fine.

Why? Because it does a really important job of providing benign social glue—*genuine* social glue because it reasserts moral and spiritual values, because it provides a gathering place for (hopefully) an ever-widening constituency that frankly no longer goes to church: the gathering place is the shops, and that won't do: it won't do. I don't think that the internet societies provide alternative communities yet that can rival the flesh-and-blood gathering in an auditorium dealing with birth, marriage, and death, together.

Other kinds of progressive I suppose depend where you are. I think it's progressive for theater to assert its right to deal with ideas, again, and for a classical theater company to reassert its right to address contemporary culture. There will always be a tension there, and a proper tension, between accommodating the work and the culture it is trying to address. But if you don't maintain that tension and you don't take a risk of breaking that tension, you're nowhere. So next year (2006), for instance, when we're collaborating with Sulayman Al-Bassam on his pan-Arabic *Richard III*, where he is saying that there is a valid analogy to be drawn between the barons of the emergent English nation and the power brokers of pan-Arabia, I think he's right: there is a process of revelation and indeed restoration of Shakespeare's work that can be involved there, and a restoration of the relationship of Shakespeare's work to his audience, which is equally important, and I think that collaboration will be very important to us. I think the Royal Shakespeare Company can accommodate and absorb the shock of textual intervention in those kinds of things as well. In the *Al-Hamlet Summit* that Sulayman did, he completely rewrote Claudius's prayer and became an author in the work. I think that's absolutely fine and completely appropriate territory for the Royal Shakespeare

Company. If we were doing nothing but that, and we were never revisiting the original texts, we would be risking drift. We would be risking getting caught in a different patch where we would be talking only to ourselves and not taking advantage of the conversation with Shakespeare and with our history.

Another kind of progressive, alternative, theater that relates very closely to what Sulayman's doing but from completely different motives is the project I am working on with *Romeo and Juliet*, a two-hander for two 75-year-olds, using exclusively Shakespeare's language. It's on the evening of their decision to die, and it's a celebration of their life. That is more Duchamp, using Shakespeare as pretext: it is frankly making something new out of the carcass of *Romeo and Juliet*. I think that is legitimate and appropriate both in its own right and, well, as dissection is appropriate in a biology lab, or particle acceleration is appropriate in a nuclear physics program—you smash things into each other and you find things out. It might just be a boring implosion, it might fail, but it might have a virtue of its own, and it hopefully will also have a virtue in revealing something different about the material.

[The following is in response to a question about the project's origins, and whether it had been suggested by the major media attention to "right to die" cases such as Terri Schiavo's:]

MB: The most important question for theater, and indeed any art form to address, is our mortality. It is the most important question, and the greatest art comes from addressing that, because it's the worst thing we have to deal with and the greatest task we can give ourselves. It's especially urgent now, in a secular age . . . or at least a secular culture that we live in.

I think in Britain and America it is alternative to offer continuous training in theatrical skills, and work towards a theatrical culture and a Shakespeare culture where physical theater is not deemed inevitably the enemy of the spoken or written word. We've had a fantastic and very famous voice department for a very long time and now we are building a movement department alongside it. We have always celebrated the work of movement directors on each show, but now we are evolving a more coherent, if pluralist, vision for physical work in the company, which will hopefully push our work deeper into the bones and muscles of the actors we're working with.

At the Royal Shakespeare Company, it's quite a hard cultural trick to be honest about the degree to which your work has been peripheralized by the culture, and to use that to your own ends, because you have to play both games at the same time. You have to not frighten the conservative forces at the same time as pursuing a progressive agenda, and actually the key to it for me has been learning and training, because, looking from the right wing, they are the preservation of tradition, and looking from the other way, you see the next step.

[DH: Does working with conservative donors bring restraints and external pressure to the theatrical process?]

MB: No, I don't find that a huge issue. It's really what they represent; they're only symptoms of the culture, and actually they're some of the more benign symptoms—they don't *have* to invest 6 million dollars anywhere near the arts. But they are symptoms of a fearful, retrospective, moribund Western culture that loves ... well, when you're dealing with Shakespeare, you're dealing with a particular thing. You're dealing with what it (the culture) thinks of as an ancient unifying cultural oak, and if you try to dramatize, to highlight the extent to which Shakespeare dramatizes dissonant noises and cultural splits, schisms, you could be smearing shit on their Gainsborough, whereas they will accept a performance artist who bleeds for a living as part of the culture in a way that Elizabethan culture would accept a fool. There is something odd there, in terms of the management of expectations.

[DH: And pressures from within the theatrical community?]

MB: There have been decades of an apolitical RSC that has thought: "thank God for the humanism of Shakespeare among all this clunky conceptual art, agitprop, and likeable but really rather shallow sort of polemicizing among artists these days," and thought we could return to issues of the soul, the spirit, emotions, and all the things that are summed up in that lowbrow *Daily Telegraph* advert "the times change, values don't"—obviously being aggressive towards the *Times*, and setting itself up as the steady solid voice of a kind of conservatism that doesn't get distracted by fashionable shifts, and endorsing the notion that there are values that are universal. ... There's been a while when the RSC fell away from an engagement with the culture to some extent. It chose to be blind to the relationship between the daub of paint on canvas and its place in the rest of the world.

Even the Royal Court disappeared into, you know, love-and-semen plays that were sort of sensationalist ... the drawing pins in the foreskin, suicidal, almost human vivisection plays where it was an implosive thing, Sarah Kane, etc. ... even the Court went into retreat for a while ... I mean, the most important people, Robert Wilson triumphing in a way over Peter Sellars, with Sellars' method engaged and Robert Wilson aloof. And I'm on Peter Sellars' side. There's another stylistic censorship in a way with something like the Wooster Group, where it gets very convoluted in its conceptual style lest it should make a vulgar or oppositional statement: it constantly goes back on its own terms of reference and becomes a bit monotonous, even though it is mesmerizing in its virtuosity ... I found their work inspirational but incomplete. And of course there's another burden with being a Shakespeare company, it's this bloody demand for completeness that your house playwright saddles you with. But it's quite a good demand because it's to do with the potential for a broad cultural address, and it's why we can come to the masses, actually, because it has a voice historically and in the future—it can make a *noise*. And the price you pay for that is an intolerance of experiment, and therefore your experiment has to be subversive. But that's okay!

[DH: What are the biggest roadblocks to experimentation with actors?]

MB: It's the investment people have in the work of the past, you know? Which is lovely. But always at every step of the journey you make, when you try to get some investment in some putative work of the future, it's not always there. There's a skepticism and vulnerability to deal with, when you ask people to experiment or train, because it's one thing them watching and standing outside and being invited to move in a new direction; it's another thing altogether to risk personal failure. But that's okay, because we all do that—every time some engineer goes on a continuous personal development program, they risk humiliation, so why shouldn't *artists* do that? Sorry! I mean, sometimes I think that accountants working in the arts are more courageous than the artists themselves, because an accountant working in the arts is *by definition* undergoing humiliation on a daily basis, and risking ridicule, regularly. And they do it. And actually they know *why* they're doing it: they've made clear, fundamental choices in their lives, whereas a lot of us who call ourselves artists stumble into the world of the arts. It's very interesting to discover the extent to which the arts community is an institutionally reactionary community. I mean, take ethnic diversity, racial diversity: the financial institutions in the City are *streets* ahead of the Royal Shakespeare Company in terms of ethnic diversity. And *we're* supposed to be radicals?

You don't want to—you can't—suddenly lose the skills of previous generations—you can't. I think in America it can lead to moments of overindulgence in the past, which is at the same time forgiven because of the many-headed monster of consumerism in the States, but I just feel that—oh, I don't know—that Harold Bloom gets away with murder . . . And the reception of the launch of our Complete Works Festival here . . . it's fantastic, but a lot of it depended upon . . . it tapped into a sort of conservative yearning—astonishing among the classes that work in the newspapers and in the media.

[DH: So how do you change it?]

MB: Well, by doing things: by seducing people into new places, by treating them with respect, and sometimes just by insisting. And in the end—yes—it is by experience that people will judge whether to follow or to go . . .

BIBLIOGRAPHY

Abbot, George (1600) An Exposition Upon the Prophet Ionah. London.

Abbot, John (1623) Iesus Praefigured. [Antwerp?].

Abel, Richard (1984) French Cinema: The First Wave, 1915–1929. Princeton NJ: Princeton University Press.

—— (1987) "Before Fântomas: Louis Feuillade and the Development of Early French Cinema." Post Script, 7 (1): 4–26.

—— (1988) French Film Theory and Criticism: 1907–1939, Vol. 1. Princeton NJ: Princeton University Press.

Acland, Charles R. (2003) Screen Traffic: Movies, Multiplexes, and Global Culture. Durham and London: Duke University Press.

Adelman, Janet (2003) "Her Father's Blood: Race, Conversion, and Nation in The Merchant of Venice." Representations 81: 4–30.

Adorno, Theodor and Horkheimer, Max (1972) "The Culture Industry: Enlightenment as Mass Deception." In Dialectic of Enlightenment, trans. John Cumming. New York: Continuum: 120–67.

Allestree, Richard (1667) The Causes of the Decay of Christian Piety. London.

Álvaro, Gervásio (trans.) (1967) William Shakespeare, Rei Lear. Lisboa: Presença.

Amiran, Eyal (1998) "The Publishing Imaginary and Electronic Media." The Minnesota Review, N.S. 48–9. Accessed at www.theminnesotareview. org/ns48/ on February 2, 2006.

Andrew, Dudley (1984) *Concepts in Film Theory*. Oxford: Oxford University Press.

Andrews, John (ed.) (1991) *The Merchant of Venice*. London: J. M. Dent.

—— (2002) "Textual Deviancy in *The Merchant of Venice*." In John W. Mahon and Ellen Macleod Mahon (eds) *The Merchant of Venice: New Critical Essays*, London: Routledge.

Anon. (1611) *The Crib of Joy*. London.

—— (1638) *Miserere mei Domine*. London.

Archard, David (1998) *Sexual Consent*. Boulder CO: Westview Press.

Arendt, Hannah (1954) "On Education." In Hannah, Arendt *Between Past and Future: Eight Exercises in Political Thought*. New York: Penguin.

—— (1969/1970) *On Violence*. New York: Harcourt Brace.

Ariès, Philippe (1962) *Centuries of Childhood: A Social History of Family Life*. New York: Vintage.

Aristotle (1984) *Complete Works of Aristotle*, 2 vols, ed. Jonathan Barnes. Princeton NJ: Princeton University Press.

Austin, J. L. (1962) *How to Do Things with Words*. Oxford: Clarendon Press.

—— (1975) *How to Do Things with Words*, eds J. O. Urmson and Marina Sbisà. Cambridge MA: Harvard University Press.

Badiou, Alain (2004) *Theoretical Writings*, ed. and trans. Ray Brassier and Alberto Toscano. London: Continuum.

Bagwell, Richard (1890) *Ireland Under The Tudors, vol. III*. London: Longmans, Green, and Co.

Baker, Humfrey (1568) *The Well Spryng of Sciences*. London.

Balibar, Etienne (2004) *We the People of Europe: Reflections on Transnational Citizenship,* trans. James Swenson. Princeton NJ: Princeton University Press.

Ball, Robert Hamilton (1968) *Shakespeare on Silent Film*. New York: Theater Arts Books.

Baret, John (1573) *An Alvearie or Triple Dictionarie*. London.

Barnes, Julian (1989) *A History of the World in 10 1/2 Chapters*. New York: Alfred A. Knopf.

Barry, Peter (1997) "Editorial Commentary." *English* 46: 189–91.

Barton, D. Plunket (1919) "The Celtic Note in *Cymbeline* and in Barton D. Plunkett *The Tempest*." In *Links between Ireland and Shakespeare*. Dublin: Maunsel and Company: 235–40.

Bazin, André (1951) "Pour en finir avec la profondeur de champ." *Cahiers du Cinema*, April, 18–19.

Beck, R. Theodore (1974) *The Cutting Edge: Early History of the Surgeons of London*. London: Lund Humphries.

Belsey, Catherine (1985) "Disrupting Sexual Difference: Meaning and Gender in the Comedies." In John Drakakis (ed.) *Alternative Shakespeares*. London: Methuen: 166–90.

—— (2006) "Review of *Shakespeare: National Poet-Playwright* by Patrick Cheney." *Shakespeare Studies*, 34: 170–6.

Benhahib, Seyla (2004) *The Rights of Others: Aliens, Residents and Citizens*. Cambridge: Cambridge University Press.

Berger, Harry Jr (1989) *Imaginary Audition: Shakespeare on Stage and Page*. Berkeley CA: University of California Press.

Berger, Thomas L., William C. Bradford, and Sidney Sondergard (1998) *An Index of Characters in Early Modern Drama: Printed Plays 1500–1660*. New York: Cambridge University Press.

Bergeron, David (1980) "*Cymbeline*: Shakespeare's Last Roman Play." *Shakespeare Quarterly*, 31 (1): 31–41.

Berry, Philippa (2006) "Incising Venice: The Violence of Cultural Incorporation in *The Merchant of Venice*." In Lena Cowan Orlin (ed.) *Center or Margin: Revisions of the English Renaissance in Honor of Leeds Barroll*. Selinsgrove PA: Susquehanna University Press: 40–53.

Billerbeg, Franciscus de (1584) *Most Rare and Straunge Discourses, of Amurathe the Turkish Emperor That Now Is* [London?].

Bioscope (1911) *Supplement*, June 15.

Bishop, Tom (2004) "Shakespeare and the General Reader." In Graham Bradshaw, Tom Bishop, and Mark Turner (eds) *The Shakespearean International Yearbook 4: Shakespeare Studies Today*. Aldershot: Ashgate: 201–14.

Blake, William Tyrell and Larry J. Bennett (1998) *Recapturing Sophocles' Antigone*. Lanham MD: Rowman and Littlefield.

Blayney, Peter W. M. (1997) "The Publication of Playbooks." In John D. Cox and David Scott Kastan (eds) *A New History of Early English Drama*. New York: Columbia University Press: 383–422.

—— (2005) "The Alleged Popularity of Playbooks." *Shakespeare Quarterly*, 56: 33–50.

Bloom, Harold (1998) *Shakespeare: The Invention of the Human*. New York: Riverhead.

Blundeville, Thomas (1613 edition) *His Exercises*, London.

Boesky, Amy and Mary Crane (eds) (2000) *Form and Reform in Renaissance England: Essays in Honor of Barbara Kiefer Lewalski*. Newark NJ: Delaware.

Boling, Ronald J. (2000) "Anglo-Welsh Relations in *Cymbeline*." *Shakespeare Quarterly*, 51 (1): 33–66.

Bonde, William (1526), *The Pylgrimage of perfection*. London.

Bordwell, David (1996) "La nouvelle mission de Feuillade; or, What was Mise-en-scène?" *Velvet Light Trap*, 37, Spring, 10–29.

Bourdieu, Pierre (1984) *Distinction: A Social Critique of the Judgment of Taste*, trans. R. Nice. Cambridge MA: Harvard University Press.

Bowers, Fredson (1955) *On Editing Shakespeare and the Elizabethan Dramatists*. Philadelphia PA: University of Pennsylvania Library for the Philip H. and A. S. W. Rosenbach Foundation.

Boys, John (1610) *An Exposition of Al the Principal Scriptures Vsed in our English Liturgie*. London.

Bradbrook, Muriel C. (1936) *A Study in the Literary Relationships of Sir Walter Raleigh*. Cambridge: Cambridge University Press.

Bragg, Melvyn (1988) *Rich: The Life of Richard Burton*. London: Hodder and Stoughton.

Braunmuller, A. R. (ed.) (1997) *Macbeth*. Cambridge: Cambridge University Press.

Brewster B. and Jacobs L. (1997) *Theater to Cinema*. Oxford: Oxford University Press.

Bristol, Michael D. (1991) "In Search of the Bear: Spatiotemporal Form and the Heterogeneity of Economies in *The Winter's Tale*." *Shakespeare Quarterly*, 42 (2): 145–67.

—— (1996) *Big-Time Shakespeare*. London: Routledge.

Broadhead, Lee-Anne and Sean Howard (1998) "The Art of Punishing: The Research Assessment Exercise and the Ritualisation of Power in Higher Education." *Educational Policy Analysis Archives 6.8*. Accessed at http://epaa.asu.edu/epaa/v6n8.html on May 1, 2006.

Brockbank, Philip (1980) *On Shakespeare: Jesus, Shakespeare and Karl Marx and other essays*. Oxford: Blackwell.

Brockes, Emma (2006) "Fail Again, Fail Better." *Guardian*, 28 June.

Brooke, Nicholas (ed.) (1994) *Macbeth*. Oxford: Oxford University Press.

Brooker, W. and Jermyn, D. (2003) *The Audience Studies Reader*. London: Routledge.

Brown, John Russell (1965) "Three Kinds of Shakespeare: 1964 Productions at London, Stratford-upon-Avon and Edinburgh." *Shakespeare Survey*, 18: 147–55.

—— (1981) *Discovering Shakespeare: A New Guide to the Plays*. New York: Columbia University Press.

Bruster (2003) *Shakespeare and the Question of Culture*. New York: Palgrave.

Bullein, William (1564) *A Dialogue . . . Wherein is a Goodly Regimente Against the Feuer Pestilence*. London.

Bulman, J. C. and H.R. Coursen (eds) (1988) *Shakespeare on Television: An Anthology of Essays and Reviews*. Hanover NH and London: University Press of New England.

Burton, Jonathan (2005) *Traffic and Turning: Islam and English Drama, 1579–1624*. Newark NJ: Delaware University Press.

Bushnell, Rebecca (ed.) (2005) *A Companion to Tragedy*. Oxford: Blackwell.

Butcher, S. H. (ed. and trans.) (1951 [1894]). *Aristotle: Poetics*, 4th ed. Mineola NY: Dover Publications.

Butler, Colin (2005) *The Practical Shakespeare*. Athens OH: Ohio University Press.

Butler, Martin (1984) *Theatre and Crisis, 1632–1642*. Cambridge: Cambridge University Press.

—— (2004) "The condition of the theatres in 1642." In Jane Milling and Peter Thomson (eds) *The Cambridge History of British Theatre, vol. I: Origins to 1660*. Cambridge: Cambridge University Press: 439–57.

Callow, Simon (2002) *Actors on Shakespeare: Henry IV, Part 1*. London: Nick Hern Books.

Calvin, John (1583) *Sermons on Deuteronomy*, trans. Arthur Golding. London.

Cambini, Andrea (1562) *Two Very Notable Commentaries*, London.

Cartelli, Thomas and Katherine Rowe (2007) *New Wave Shakespeare on Screen*. Oxford: Polity Press.

Castaldo, A. (2002) "The Film's the Thing: Using Shakespearean Film in the Classroom." In Courtney Lehmann and Lisa Starks (eds) (2002) *Spectacular Shakespeare: Critical Theory and Popular Cinema*. London: Associated University Presses: 187–204.

Catullus, Gaius Valerius. *Song V*. Accessed at http://www.vroma.org/hwalker/VRomaCatullus/005.html on December 16, 2006.

Cavell, Stanley (1987) *Disowning Knowledge in Six Plays of Shakespeare*. Cambridge: Cambridge University Press.

Caverero, Adriana (2002) *Stately Bodies: Literature, Philosophy, and the Question of Gender*, trans. Robert de Lucca. Ann Arbor MI: University of Michigan Press: 121–88.

Caws, Mary Ann (2002) "Taking Textual Time." In Elizabeth Bergman Loizeaux and Neil Fraistat (eds) *Reimagining Textuality: Textual Studies in the Late Age of Print*. London: University of Wisconsin Press.

Charnes, Linda (2006) *Hamlet's Heirs: Shakespeare and the Politics of a New Millennium*. London: Routledge.

Clare, Janet (2002) *Drama of the English Republic 1649–1660*. Manchester: Manchester University Press.

Clark, Beverley Lyon (2003) *Kiddie Lit: The Cultural Construction of Children's Literature in America*. Baltimore MD: Johns Hopkins University Press.

Cloud, Random [i.e. Randall McLeod] (1991) "The very names of the Persons: Editing and the Invention of Dramatick Character." In David Scott Kastan and Peter Stallybrass (eds) *Staging the Renaissance: Reinterpretations of Elizabethan and Jacobean Drama*. London: Routledge: 88–96.

Clowes, William (1588) *A Prooued Practise for All Young Chirurgians*. London.

Cohen, Walter (1985) *Drama of a Nation: Public Theater in Renaissance England and Spain*, Ithaca NY: Cornell University Press.

Collick, J. (1989) *Shakespeare, Cinema, and Society*. New York: Manchester University Press.

Conacher, D. J. (1974) "Interaction between Chorus and Characters in the *Oresteia*." *American Journal of Philology*. 94 (4) Winter: 339–40.

Connerton, Paul (1989) *How Societies Remember*. Cambridge: Cambridge University Press.

Conquergood, Dwight (1991) "Rethinking Ethnography: Towards a Critical Cultural Politics." *Cultural Monographs*, 58: 179–94.

—— (1992) "Ethnography, Rhetoric, and Performance." *Quarterly Journal of Speech*, 78: 80–123.

—— (1995) "Of Caravans and Carnivals: Performance Studies in Motion." *The Drama Review—The Journal of Performance Studies*, 39 (4): 137–41.

Cooper, Thomas (1578) *Thesaurus Linguae Romanae & Britannicae*. London.

Cotgrave, Randle (1611) *A Dictionarie of the French and English Tongues*. London.

Cowper, William (1616) *The Bishop of Galloway*, London.

Crane, Mary Thomas (1993) *Framing Authority: Sayings, Self, and Society in Sixteenth-Century England*. Princeton NJ: Princeton University Press.

Crewe, Jennifer (2004) "Scholarly Publishing: Why Our Business is Your Business Too." In Rosemary G. Feal (ed.) *Profession 2004*. New York: Modern Language Association of America: 25–31.

Crooke, Helkiah (1631) *Mikrokosmographia: A Description of the Body of Man*, London.

—— (1634) *Somatographia Anthropine*. London.

Crumley, J. Clinton (2001) "Questioning History in *Cymbeline*." *Studies in English Literature*, 41 (2): 297–315.

[Cunhal, Álvaro; as] Tiago, Manuel (1974) *Até Amanhã, Camaradas*. Lisboa: Avante.

Cunhal, Álvaro (1975a) *A superioridade moral dos comunistas*, 2nd ed. Lisboa: Avante.

—— (1975b) *Cinco Dias, Cinco Noites*. Lisboa: Avante.

—— (1997) *As Lutas de Classes em Portugal nos Fins da Idade Média*, 3rd ed. Lisboa: Caminho.

—— (trans.) (2002) *William Shakespeare: O Rei Lear*. Lisboa: Caminho.

Curran, John E., Jr (1997) "Royalty Unlearned, Honour Untaught: British Savages and Historiographical Change in *Cymbeline*." *Comparative Drama*, 31: 277–303.

David, Richard (1953) "Shakespeare's History Plays: Epic or Drama?" *Shakespeare Survey*, 6: 129–39.

Davidson, Cathy N. (2003) "Understanding the Economic Burden of Scholarly Publishing." *Chronicle of Higher Education*, Oct. 2003: B7+.

De Chauliac, Guy (1542) *The Questyonary of Cyrurgyens*. London.

De Grazia, Margreta and Peter Stallybrass (1993) "The Materiality of the Shakespearean Text." *Shakespeare Quarterly*, 44: 255–83.

de Moivre, Abraham (1718) *The Doctrine of Chances: or, a Method of Calculating the Probability of Events in Play by A. de Moivre. F.R.S.* London: W. Pearson.

de Ste Croix, G. E. M. (1956) "Greek and Roman Accounting." In A. C. Littleton and B. S. Yamey (eds) *Studies in the History of Accounting*. London: Sweet & Maxwell.

Deats, Sara Munson. (2004) "*Dido, Queen of Carthage* and *The Massacre at Paris*." In Patrick Cheney (ed.) *The Cambridge Companion to Christopher Marlowe*. Cambridge: Cambridge University Press: 193–206.

Derrida, Jacques (1982) *Margins of Philosophy*, trans. Alan Bass, Brighton: Harvester.

—— (1994) *Spectres of Marx*, trans. Peggy Kamuf. London: Routledge.

Desai, R. W. (2002) "'Mislike Me Not for My Complexion': Whose Mislike? Portia's? Shakespeare's? Or That of His Age?" In John W. Mahon and Ellen MacLeod Mahon (eds) *The Merchant of Venice: New Critical Essays*. New York and London: Routledge.

Dessen, Alan C. and Leslie Thomson (1999) *A Dictionary of Stage Directions in English Drama, 1580–1642*. Cambridge: Cambridge University Press.

Dodd, A. H. (1938) "Wales and the Scottish Succession." *Transactions of the Honourable Society of Cymmrodorion*, Session 1937: 201–25.

—— (1944) "North Wales in the Essex Revolt." *The English Historical Review*, 59 (235): 348–70.

Donaldson, Peter (2002) "'In fair Verona': Media, Spectacle and Performance in *William Shakespeare's Romeo+Juliet*." In Richard Burt (ed.) *Shakespeare after Mass Media*. New York: Palgrave: 59–82.

Donlan, Walter (1980) *The Aristocratic Ideal in Ancient Greece.* Lawrence KS: Coronado Press.

Donne, John (1640) *LXXX Sermons,* London.

Drakakis, John (ed.) (1985) *Alternative Shakespeares.* London: Routledge.

—— (2000) *"Jew.* Shylock is my name: Speech Prefixes in *The Merchant of Venice* as Symptoms of the Early Modern." In Hugh Grady (ed.) *Shakespeare and Modernity.* London: Routledge: 105–21.

—— and Naomi Conn Liebler (eds) (1998) *Tragedy.* London and New York: Longman.

Durham, John (1992) "The Introduction of 'Arabic' Numerals in European Accounting." *The Accounting Historians Journal,* 19 (2): 25–55.

Eagleton, Terry (2003) *Sweet Violence: the Idea of the Tragic.* Oxford: Blackwell.

Edwards, Philip (1998) "Shakespeare, Ireland, Dreamland." *Irish University Review,* 28: 227–39.

Egan, Gabriel (2004). *Shakespeare and Marx.* Oxford: Oxford University Press.

Ellmann, Richard and Ellsworth Mason (eds) (1959) *The Critical Writings of James Joyce.* New York: Viking Press.

Elsaesser, T. (ed.) (1990) *Early Cinema: Space, Frame, Narrative.* London: British Film Institute.

Encyclopedia Judaica (1971/73) 16 volumes. Jerusalem: Keter Publishing House, first printing 1971, 2nd printing 1973.

Engels, Friedrich (1859) "Letter to Ferdinand Lassalle" (18 May). Accessed at www.marxists.org/archive/marx/works/1859/letters/59_05_18a.htm, on September 24, 2006.

—— (1883) "Introduction." In Friedrich Engels *The Dialectics of Nature.* Accessed at www.marxists.org/archive/marx/works/1883/don/ch01.htm.

Engle, Lars (1986) "'Thrift is Blessing': Exchange and Explanation in *The Merchant of Venice.*" *Shakespeare Quarterly,* 37: 20–37.

—— (1993) *Shakespearean Pragmatism: Market of His Time.* Chicago IL: University of Chicago Press.

Enterline, Lynn (1995) *The Tears of Narcissus.* Stanford CA: Stanford University Press.

Erne, Lukas (2003) *Shakespeare as Literary Dramatist.* Cambridge: Cambridge University Press.

—— (ed.) (2007) *The First Quarto of Romeo and Juliet.* Cambridge: Cambridge University Press.

Esslin, Martin (1980) *The Theatre of the Absurd*, 3rd ed. Harmondsworth: Penguin.

Estabrook, Leigh (2003) "The Book as the Gold Standard for Tenure and Promotion in Humanistic Disciplines." *Committee on Institutional Cooperation.* Accessed at http://lrcsurvey.lis.uiuc.edu/surveys/99EZJ2/99EZJ2 0001.html on May 2, 2006.

Euclid (1661 edition) *Euclides Elements of Geometry . . . whereunto is added. The Mathematical Preface of Mr. John Dee.* London.

Fabricius Hildanus, Wilhelm (1674) *Fabricius's Cistus Militaris, or, A Military Chest.* London.

Fallon, Robert (2005) *How to Enjoy Shakespeare.* Chicago: Ivan R. Dee.

Farmer, Alan B., and Zachary Lesser (2005) "The Popularity of Playbooks Revisited." *Shakespeare Quarterly,* 56, 1–32.

Feal, Rosemary G. (ed.) (2004) *Profession 2004.* New York: Modern Language Association of America.

Feal, Rosemary G. (ed.) (2005) *Profession 2005.* New York: Modern Language Association of America.

Feerick, Jean (2003) "A Nation Now Degenerate: Shakespeare's *Cymbeline,* Nova Britannia, and the Role of Diet and Climate in Reproducing Races." *Early American Studies,* 1 (2): 30–70.

Felperin, Howard (1990) *The Uses of the Canon: Elizabethan Literature and Contemporary Theory.* Oxford: Clarendon

Fernie, Ewan, Ramona Wray, Mark Thornton Burnett, and Clare McManus (eds) (2005) *Reconceiving the Renaissance.* Oxford: Oxford University Press.

Ferreira, Francisco (1976) *Álvaro Cunhal, herói soviético.* n.p.: F. Ferreira.

Fienberg, Nona (1998) "Circumcision in *The Merchant of Venice,*" *PMLA* 113 (3): 452.

Florio, John (1598) *A Worlde of Wordes.* London.

Floyd-Wilson, Mary (2002) "Delving to the Root: *Cymbeline,* Scotland, and the English Race." In David J. Baker and Willy Maley (eds) *British Identities and English Renaissance Literature.* Cambridge: Cambridge University Press: 101–15.

Ford, John (1995) *Tis Pity She's a Whore and Other Plays,* ed. Marion Lomax. Oxford: Oxford University Press.

Freinkel, Lisa (2002) *Reading Shakespeare's Will: The Theology of Figure from Augustine to the Sonnets.* New York: Columbia University Press.

Friedman, Jerome (1987) "Jewish Conversion, the Spanish Pure Blood Laws and Reformation: A Revisionist View of Racial and Religious Anti-semitism." *Sixteenth Century Journal,* 18: 3–29.

Friel, Brian (1989) *Making History*. London, Faber and Faber.

Fulton, Robert C. (1976) "Timon, Cupid and the Amazons." *Shakespeare Studies*, 9: 283–99.

Fuller, Thomas (1653) *The Infants Advocate*. London.

Gale, Thomas (1563) *Certaine Vvorkes of Chirurgerie*. London.

Galileo (1983) *The Discourses*, ed. Bernard Crick, trans. Leslie J. Walker. London: Penguin: 93–4.

Garber, Marjorie (1981) *Coming of Age in Shakespeare*. London: Methuen.

—— (2003) "Groucho Marx and 'Coercive Voluntarism' in Academe." *The Chronicle of Higher Education*, 49 (18): B20.

—— (2004) *Shakespeare After All*. New York: Pantheon.

Gataker, Thomas (1624) *A Gagge for the Pope, and the Iesuits*. London.

Gigerenzer, Gerd, *et al.* (1989) *The Empire of Chance: How Probability Changed Science and Everyday Life*. Cambridge: Cambridge University Press.

Ginzberg, Louis (1909–38) *The Legends of the Jews*, 7 vols. Philadelphia PA: The Jewish Publication Society.

Grady, Hugh (2002) *Shakespeare, Machiavelli, and Montaigne: Power and Subjectivity from* Richard II *to* Hamlet. Oxford: Oxford University Press.

Greenblatt, Stephen (ed.) (1997) *The Norton Shakespeare: Based on the Oxford Edition*. New York: W. W. Norton.

—— (2001) *Hamlet in Purgatory*. Princeton NJ: Princeton University Press.

—— (2002) *A Special Letter from Stephen Greenblatt, 28 May 2002*. Accessed at www.mla.org/resources/documents/rep_scholarly_pub/scholarly_pub on May 26, 2005.

—— (2004) *Will in the World: How Shakespeare Became Shakespeare*. New York: Norton.

Greg, W. W. (1942) *The Editorial Problem in Shakespeare: A Survey of the Foundations of the Text*. Oxford: Clarendon Press.

—— (1951) *The Editorial Problem in Shakespeare: A Survey of the Foundations of the Text*, 2nd ed. Oxford: Clarendon Press.

Griffiths, Huw (2004) "The Geographies of Shakespeare's *Cymbeline*." *English Literary Renaissance*, 34 (1): 339–58.

Griffiths, Paul (1996) *Youth and Authority: Formative Experiences in England 1560–1640*. Oxford: Clarendon Press.

Grigely, J. (1995) *Textualterity: Art, Theory, and Textual Criticism*. Ann Arbor MI: University of Michigan Press.

Guilfoyle, Cherrell (1990) *Shakespeare's Play within Play: Medieval Imagery and Scenic Form*. In *Hamlet, Othello, and King Lear*. Kalamazoo MI: Medieval Institute Publications, 61–5.

Guillemeau, Jacques (1598) *The Frenche Chirurgerye*, trans. A. M. Dort.

Guillory, John (2005) "Valuing the Humanities, Evaluating Scholarship." *Profession 2005*: 28–38.

Gunning, Tom (1989) "The Cinema of Attractions: Early Film, Its Spectator and the Avant-Garde." In T. Elsaesser and A. Barker (eds) *Early Film*. London: BFI.

Gurr, Andrew (2004) "A New Theatre Historicism." In Peter Holland and Stephen Orgel (eds) *From Script to Stage in Early Modern England*. Basingstoke: Palgrave Macmillan.

Gussow, Mel (2004) *Gambon: A Life in Acting*. London: Nick Hern.

Gyer, Nicholas (1592) *The English Phlebotomy*. London.

Hacking, Ian (1975) *The Emergence of Probability: A Philosophical Study of Early Ideas About Probability, Induction and Statistical Inference*. Cambridge: Cambridge University Press.

Hadfield, Andrew (2000) *The Vanishing: Shakespeare, the Subject, and Early Modern Culture*. Durham NC: Duke University Press.

—— (2003) "The Power and Rights of the Crown in *Hamlet* and *King Lear*." *Review of English Studies*, 54, 217: 566–86.

Hageman, Elizabeth H. and Sarah Jayne Steen (1996) "From the Editors." *Shakespeare Quarterly*, 47 (4): v–viii.

Halbwachs, Maurice (1992) *On Collective Memory*, ed., trans., and introduced Lewis A. Coser. Chicago IL and London: University of Chicago Press.

Hall, Kim F. (1992) "Guess Who's Coming to Dinner? Colonization and Miscegenation in *The Merchant of Venice*." *Renaissance Drama* (new series), 23: 87–111.

Hall, Peter (1963) "Avoiding a Method." In *Crucial Years: The Royal Shakespeare Company*, London: Max Reinhardt: 14–19.

—— (1964) "Shakespeare and the Modern Director." In John Goodwin (ed.) *Royal Shakespeare Company 1960–1963*. London: Max Reinhardt: 41–8.

Halpern, Richard (1997) *Shakespeare Among the Moderns*. Ithaca NY and London: Cornell University Press.

Hammond, Anthony (1992) "Encounters of the Third Kind in Stage-Directions in Elizabethan and Jacobean Drama." *Studies in Philology*, 89: 71–99.

Hansen, M. (1991) *Babel and Babylon: Spectatorship in American Silent Film*. Cambridge MA: Harvard University Press.

Harbage, Alfred (1962) "*Love's Labor's Lost* and the Early Shakespeare." *Philological Quarterly*, 41: 18–36.

Hardman, C. B. (2000) "Our Drooping Country Now Erects Her Head: Nahum Tate's *History of King Lear*." *The Modern Language Review*, 95 (4): 913–23.

Harris, Bernard (1966) "'What's Past is Prologue': *Cymbeline* and *Henry VIII*." In John Russell Brown and Bernard Harris (eds) *Later Shakespeare*. London: Edward Arnold: 203–34.

Harris, Jonathan Gil (2000) "The New New Historicism's Wunderkammer of Objects." *European Journal of English Studies*, 4: 111–23.

—— (2001) "Shakespeare's Hair: Staging the Object of Material Culture." *Shakespeare Quarterly*, 52: 445–57.

—— (2004) *Sick Economies*. Philadelphia PA: University of Pennsylvania Press.

Harris, Wendell V. (2005) "Of the Making of Books." In Rosemary G. Feal (ed.) *Profession 2005*. New York: Modern Language Association of America: 47–51.

Hawkes, Terence (1992) *Meaning by Shakespeare*. London: Routledge.

—— (ed.) (1996) *Alternative Shakespeares 2*. London: Routledge.

—— (2002) *Shakespeare in the Present*. London and New York: Routledge.

Hayles, N. Katherine (1999) *How We Became Posthuman: Virtual Bodies in Cybernetics, Literature, and Informatics*. Chicago IL: University of Chicago Press.

Heller, Agnes (2002) *The Time Is Out of Joint: Shakespeare as Philosopher of History*. Lanham MD : Rowman and Littlefield.

Heller, Agnes and Frances Fehér (1991) *The Grandeur and Twilight of Radical Universalism*. New Brunswick NJ: Transaction Publishers: 412.

Henderson, Diana E. (1998/99) "King and No King: 'The Exequy' as an Antebellum Poem." *The George Herbert Journal*, 22, (1& 2): 57–75. [Also published in Eugene D. Hill and William Kerrigan (eds) (2000) *The Wit to Know: Essays on English Renaissance Literature for Edward Tayler*. Fairfield CT: 57–75.]

—— (ed.) (2006a) *A Concise Companion to Shakespeare on Screen*. Malden MA: Blackwell Publishing.

—— (2006b) "Introduction: Through a Camera, Darkly." In Diana E. Henderson (ed.) *A Concise Companion to Shakespeare on Screen*. Malden MA: Blackwell Publishing: 1–7.

Higginbotham, Jennifer (2003) "Shakespearean Girlhoods: Gender and Childhood in Shakespeare's England." Unpublished paper presented to the "Shakespeare's Children/Children's Shakespeare" conference, Roehampton University.

Hinman, Charlton (ed.) (1996) *The Norton Facsimile: The First Folio of Shakespeare*, 2nd ed. New York: Norton.

Hirota, Atsuhiko (2004) "Forms of Empires: Rome and Its Peripheries in *Cymbeline*." *Shakespearean International Yearbook*, 4, 279–93.

Hodgdon, Barbara (2003) "Re-incarnations." In Pascale Aebischer, Edward J. Esche, and Nigel Wheale (eds) *Remaking Shakespeare: Performance Across Media, Genres and Cultures*. New York: Palgrave Macmillan: 190–209.

—— (2007) "Shakespearean Stars." In Robert Shaughnessy (ed.) *The Cambridge Companion to Shakespeare and Popular Culture*. Cambridge: Cambridge University Press 46–66.

—— and W. B. Worthen (eds) (2005) *Companion to Shakespeare and Performance*. Oxford: Blackwell.

Hoenselaars, A. J. (2002) "Shakespeare and the Early Modern History Play." In Michael Hattaway (ed.) *The Cambridge Companion to Shakespeare's History Plays*. Cambridge: Cambridge University Press: 25–40.

Holderness, Graham (2002) *Visual Shakespeare: Essays in Film and Television*. Hatfield: University of Hertfordshire Press.

Honig, Bonnie (2001) *Democracy and the Foreigner*. Princeton NJ: Princeton University Press.

Hopkins, Lisa (1999a) "How Far to Milford Haven? A Response to Garrett Sullivan's 'Civilizing Wales: *Cymbeline*, Roads and the Landscape of Early Modern Britain'." *Early Modern Literary Studies*, 5 (1): 16. 1–5. Accessed at http://purl.oclc.org/emls/05-1/hopkread.html

—— (1999b) "It is Place Which Lessens and Sets Off: Perspective and Representation in *Cymbeline*." *Shakespeare Yearbook*, 10: 253–68.

Husain, Adrian (2004) *Politics and Genre in "Hamlet."* Oxford: Oxford University Press.

Hutton, Patrick H. (1993) *History as an Art of Memory*. Hanover NH and London: University Press of New England.

Huyssen, Andreas (1995) *Twilight Memories: Marking Time in a Culture of Amnesia*. New York and London: Routledge.

Itzin, Catharine and Simon Trussler (2005) "Interview with Peter Hall" (*Theatre Quarterly*, 16, 1974). In Ian Smith (ed.) *Pinter in the Theatre*. London: Nick Hern: 131–57.

Jackson, Shannon (2004) *Professing Performance: Theatre in the Academy from Philology to Performativity*. Cambridge: Cambridge University Press.

James, Heather (1997) "*Cymbeline*'s Mingle-Mangle: Britain's Roman Histories." In Heather James, *Shakespeare's Troy: Drama, Politics, and the Translation of Empire*. Cambridge: Cambridge University Press, 151–88.

Jenkins, Harold (ed.) (1982) *Hamlet.* The Arden Shakespeare (2nd series). London: Methuen.

Johnson, Nora (1997) "Body and Spirit, Stage and Sexuality in *The Tempest.*" *ELH,* 64 (3): 683–701.

Jones, Emrys (1961) "Stuart *Cymbeline.*" *Essays in Criticism,* 11: 84–99.

—— (1977) *The Origins of Shakespeare.* Oxford: Oxford University Press.

Jonson, Ben (1600) *Every Man Out of His Humour.* London.

Jordan, Constance (1997) "*Cymbeline.*" In Constance Jordan, *Shakespeare's Monarchies: Ruler and Subject in the Romances.* Ithaca and London: Cornell University Press, 69–106.

Jowett, John (ed.) (2004) *The Life of Timon of Athens by William Shakespeare and Thomas Middleton.* Oxford: Oxford University Press.

Jowett, John (2006) "From Print to Performance: Looking at the Masque in *Timon of Athens.*" In Peter Holland and Stephen Orgel (eds) *From Performance to Print in Shakespeare's England.* Basingstoke: Palgrave Macmillan: 73–91.

Joyce, James. (1956) *A Portrait of the Artist as a Young Man,* first published 1916. London: Jonathan Cape.

Kahn, Victoria (2003) "Hamlet or Hecuba: Carl Schmitt's Decision." *Representations,* 83: 67–96.

Kastan, David Scott (1999) *Shakespeare after Theory.* London: Routledge.

—— (ed.) (2002) *King Henry IV, Part 1.* The Arden Shakespeare. London: Arden.

Kennedy, Richard F. (1998) "Speech Prefixes in Some Shakespearean Quartos." *Publications of the Bibliographical Society of America,* 92: 177–209.

Kermode, Frank (2000) *Shakespeare's Language.* New York: Farrar, Straus, and Giroux.

Kernan, Alvin (1987) *Printing Technology, Letters, & Samuel Johnson.* Princeton NJ: Princeton University Press.

Kerrigan, John (2006) "The Romans in Britain, 1603–1614." In Glenn Burgess, Rowland Wymer, and Jason Lawrence (eds) *The Accession of James I: Historical and Cultural Consequences.* Basingstoke: Palgrave Macmillan: 113–39.

Kidnie, M. J. (2000) "Text, Performance, and the Editors: Staging Shakespeare's Drama." *Shakespeare Quarterly,* 51: 456–73.

King, John (1599) *Lectures Vpon Ionas.* Oxford.

King, Ros (2005) *Cymbeline: Constructions of Britain.* Aldershot: Ashgate.

Kingsley-Smith, Jane (2006) "Love's Labours Scorned: The Absence of Cupid on the Shakespearean Stage." Unpublished paper presented to the International Shakespeare Association conference, Stratford upon Avon.

Knight, G. Wilson (1947) *The Crown of Life: Essays in Interpretation of Shakespeare's Final Plays*. London: Methuen.

Knowlson, James (1996) *Damned to Fame: The Life of Samuel Beckett*. London: Bloomsbury.

Kolve, V. A. (1966) *The Play Called Corpus Christi*. Stanford CA: Stanford University Press.

Konstan, David (1998) "Reciprocity and Friendship." In Christopher Gill, Norman Posthelwaite, and Richard Seaford (eds) *Reciprocity in Ancient Greece*. Oxford: Oxford University Press: 279–301.

Kott, Jan (1964) *Shakespeare Our Contemporary*, trans. Boleslaw Taborski. New York: Doubleday. Reprinted 1974, New York: W. W. Norton.

Kott, Jan and Boleslaw Taborksi (1967) "Hamlet and Orestes." *PMLA*, 82 (5): October, 303–13.

Kottman, Paul (2006) "Speaking as One Witness to the Scene: *Hamlet* and the 'Cunning of the Scene.'" Unpublished book chapter.

Lafargue, Paul (1890) *Reminiscences of Karl Marx*. Accessed at www.marxists. org/archive/lafargue/1890/xx/marx.htm#art1.

Lahr, John and Anthea Lahr (eds) (1974) *A Casebook on Harold Pinter's "The Homecoming."* London: Davis-Poynter.

Lamb, Charles and Mary Lamb (1908) *Works in Prose and Verse*, ed. Thomas Hutchinson. London: Henry Frowde for Oxford University Press.

Lamb, Edel (2005) *The Early Modern Children's Playing Companies: Child-hood, Theatre and Identity 1599–1613*, PhD thesis. Belfast: Queen's University of Belfast.

Lanfranco of Milan (1565) *A Most Excellent and Learned Woorke of Chirurgerie . . . Now First Published in Englyshe Prynte by Iohn Halle Chirurgien.* London.

Lanier, Douglas (2003) "Shakescorp Noir." *Shakespeare Quarterly*, 53 (2): 157–80.

—— (2006) "Will of the People: Recent Shakespeare Film Parody and the Politics of Popularization." In Diana Henderson (ed.) *A Concise Companion to Shakespeare on Screen*. Malden MA: Blackwell Publishing: 175–96.

Lefevere, André (2000) "Mother Courage's Cucumbers: Text, System and Refraction in a Theory of Literature" [1982]. In Lawrence Venuti (ed.) *The Translation Studies Reader*. London: Routledge: 233–49.

Lehmann, Courtney and Lisa Starks (eds) (2002) *Spectacular Shakespeare: Critical Theory and Popular Cinema*. London: Associated University Presses.

Leitch, T. (2003) "Twelve Fallacies in Contemporary Adaptation Theory." *Criticism*, 45 (2): 149–71.

Lemnius, Levinus (1576) *The Touchstone of Complexions*. London.

Lesser, Zachary (2004) *Renaissance Drama and the Politics of Publication: Readings in the English Book Trade*. Cambridge: Cambridge University Press.

Levack, Brian P. (1987) *The Formation of the British State: England, Scotland, and the Union, 1603–1707*. Oxford, Clarendon Press

Levenson, Jill L. (ed.) (2000) *Romeo and Juliet*. Oxford: Oxford University Press.

Levy, Harry L. (1941) "Catullus, 5, 7–11, and the Abacus." *American Journal of Philology*, 62 (2): 222–4.

Lewis, Philip (2004) "The Publishing Crisis and Tenure Criteria: An Issue for Research Universities." In Rosemary G. Feal (ed.) *Profession 2004*. New York: Modern Language Association of America: 14–24.

Littleton, Adam (1662) *Solomons Gate*. London.

Loewenstein, Joseph (1988) "The Script in the Marketplace." In Stephen Greenblatt (ed.) *Representing the English Renaissance*. Berkeley CA: University of California Press.

Long, William B. (1997) "Perspective on Provenance: The Context of Varying Speech-heads." In George Walton Williams (ed.) *Shakespeare's Speech-Headings*. Newark, DE: University of Delaware Press: 21–44.

Loomba, Ania (2002) *Shakespeare, Race, and Colonialism*. Oxford: Oxford University Press.

Lowe, Peter (1597) *The Whole Course of Chirurgerie*. London.

Lupton, Julia Reinhard (2005a) *Citizen-Saints: Shakespeare and Political Theology*. Chicago IL: University of Chicago Press.

—— (2005b) "Rights, Commandments, and the Literature of Citizenship." *Modern Language Quarterly*, 66 (1): 21–54.

Lyotard, Jean-François (1977) "Jewish Oedipus." *Genre* X.3: 395–411.

McCarthy, A. (2001) *Ambient Television: Visual Culture and Public Space*. Durham NC: Duke University Press.

McCrea, Scott (2005) *The Case for Shakespeare: The End of the Authorship Question*. Westport CT: Praeger.

McGann, Jerome J. (1997) *The Textual Condition*. Princeton NJ: Princeton University Press.

—— (2001) *Radiant Textuality: Literature After the World Wide Web*. Houndmills: Palgrave.

Machiavelli, Niccolo (1983) *The Discourses*, ed. Bernard Crick, trans. Leslie J. Walker. London: Penguin.

McKenzie, Jon (2001) *Perform or Else: From Discipline to Performance.* London: Routledge.

McKerrow, R.B. (1935) "A Suggestion Regarding Shakespeare's Manuscripts." *The Review of English Studies,* 11: 459–65.

MacLeod, C. W. (1982) "Politics and the Oresteia." *Journal of Hellenic Studies* 102: 135–6.

Mcleod, Donald. (2006) "Research Exercise to be Scrapped." *Education Guardian.* Accessed at http://education.guardian.co.uk/RAE/story/ 0,,1737082,00.htm on March 22, 2006.

McLeod, Randall (1982) "UN *Editing* Shak-speare." *Sub-Stance,* 33: 26–55.

—— (1986) "The Psychopathology of Everyday Art." In G. R. Hibbard (ed.) *Elizabethan Theatre IX.* Toronto: University of Toronto Press: 100–68.

McLuskie, Kathleen (2005) "Shakespeare Goes Slumming: Harlem '37 and Birmingham '97." In Barbara Hodgdon and W. B. Worthen (eds) *Companion to Shakespeare and Performance.* Oxford: Blackwell: 249–66.

McMillin, Scott (1991) *Shakespeare in Performance: Henry IV, Part One.* Manchester: Manchester University Press.

Maguire, Laurie E. (1996) *Shakespearean Suspect Texts: The "Bad" Quartos and Their Contexts.* Cambridge: Cambridge University Press.

Maguire, Nancy Klein (1991) "Nahum Tate's *King Lear:* The King's Blest Restoration." In Jean I. Marsden (ed.) *The Appropriation of Shakespeare: Post-Renaissance Reconstructions of the Works and the Myth.* London: Harvester Wheatsheaf: 29–39.

—— (1992) *Regicide and Restoration: English Tragicomedy, 1660–1671.* Cambridge: Cambridge University Press.

Mahood, M. M. (ed.) (1987) *The Merchant of Venice.* Cambridge: Cambridge University Press.

Maley, Willy (1999) "Postcolonial Shakespeare: British Identity Formation and *Cymbeline.*" In Jennifer Richards and James Knowles (eds) *Shakespeare's Late Plays: New Readings.* Edinburgh: Edinburgh University Press: 145–57.

Manton, Thomas (1685) *Christ's temptation and transfiguration.* London.

Marcus, Leah S. (1988) "*Cymbeline* and the Unease of Topicality." In Heather Dubrow and Richard Strier (eds) *The Historical Renaissance: New Essays on Tudor and Stuart Literature and Culture.* Chicago IL: University of Chicago Press: 134–68.

Marlowe, Christopher (1992) *Tamburlaine the Great,* ed. J. W. Harper. London: A. & C. Black.

Marotti, Arthur (1995) *Manuscript, Print, and the English Renaissance Lyric*. Ithaca NY: Cornell University Press.

Marx, Karl (1865) *Confession*. Accessed at www.marx.org/archive/marx/works/1865/04/01.htm.

—— (1973) *Grundrisse: Foundations of the Critique of Political Economy (Rough Draft)*, trans. Martin Nicolaus. Harmondsworth and London: Penguin/New Left Review.

—— (1979). *The Letters of Karl Marx*, selected and trans. Saul L. Padover. Englewood Cliffs NJ: Prentice-Hall.

Massai, Sonia (2000) "Nahum Tate's Revision of Shakespeare's *King Lears*." *SEL*, 40 (3): 435–50.

Masterson, Thomas (1634) *Arithmetick . . . Newly set forth . . . by Humfrey Waynman*. London.

Maus, Katharine Eisaman (1982) "Arcadia Lost: Politics and Revision in the Restoration *Tempest*." *Renaissance Drama*, 13: 189–209.

Mellinkoff, Ruth (1993) *Outcasts: Signs of Others in Northern European Art of the Late Middle Ages*, 2 vols. Berkeley CA: University of California Press.

Mentz, Steven R. (2003) "The Fiend Gives Friendly Counsel: Launcelot Gobbo and Polyglot Economics in *The Merchant of Venice*." In Linda Woodbridge (ed.) *Money and the Age of Shakespeare*. New York: Palgrave Macmillan: 177–87.

Merlin, Bella (2005) *With the Rogue's Company: "Henry IV" at the National Theatre*. London: National Theatre: Oberon Books.

Metz, Christian (1982) *The Imaginary Signifier: Psychoanalysis and the Cinema*, trans. C. Britton. Bloomington IN: Indiana University Press.

Metzger, Mary Janell (1998) "'Now by My Hood, a Gentle and No Jew'": Jessica, *The Merchant of Venice*, and the Discourse of Early Modern English Identity." *PMLA*, 113: 52-63.

Michelson, Annette (1966) "Breton's Surrealism: The Peripeties of a Metaphor or a Journey through Impossibility." *Artform*, 5.1: 72–7.

Middleton, Thomas (1989) *The Nice Valour* (*c*.1616). In George Walton Williams (ed.) *The Dramatic Works in the Beaumont and Fletcher Canon*, *VII*, gen. ed. Fredson Bowers. Cambridge: Cambridge University Press.

—— and William Rowley (2002) "*The Changeling*." In: David Bevington, Lars Engle, Katharine Eisaman Maus, and Eric Rasmussen (eds) *English Renaissance Drama: A Norton Anthology*. New York: W. W. Norton and Co.

Mikalachki, Jodi (1995) "The Masculine Romance of Roman Britain: *Cymbeline* and Early Modern English Nationalism." *Shakespeare Quarterly*, 46 (3): 301–22.

Milling, Jane and Peter Thomson (eds) (2004) *The Cambridge History of British Theatre, vol. I: Origins to 1660.* Cambridge: Cambridge University Press.

Miola, Robert S. (1984) "*Cymbeline*: Shakespeare's Valediction to Rome." In Annabel Patterson (ed.) *Roman Images.* Baltimore MD: Johns Hopkins University Press: 51–62.

MLA (Modern Language Association) (2002) "The Future of Scholarly Publishing." Report of the Ad Hoc Committee on the Future of Scholarly Publishing. In Phyllis Franklin (ed.) *Profession, 2002.* New York: Modern Language Association of America: 172–86.

MLA (Modern Language Association) (2006) *Report on Evaluating Scholarship for Tenure and Promotion.* Accessed at www.mla.org/tenure_promotion on May 30, 2007.

Moravec, Hans (1988) *Mind Children: The Future of Robot and Human Intelligence.* Cambridge MA: Harvard University Press.

Moura, Vasco Graça (2002). "Álvaro Cunhal e *O Rei Lear*." *Público*, 31 August: 38–9.

Mowat, Barbara (1994) "Nicholas Rowe and the Twentieth-Century Shakespeare Text." In Tetsuo Kishi, Roger Pringle, and Stanley Wells (eds) *Shakespeare and Cultural Traditions.* London: Associated University Presses, 314–22.

—— (1998) "The Problem of Shakespeare's Text(s)." In Laurie E. Maguire and Thomas L. Berger (eds) *Textual Formations and Reformations.* London: Associated University Presses: 131–48.

—— and Werstine, Paul (eds) (1992), *The Merchant of Venice.* New York: Washington Square Press.

Munkelt, Marga (1987) "Stage Directions as Part of the Text." *Shakespeare Studies*, 19: 253–72.

Munro, Lucy (2007) [forthcoming] "*Coriolanus* and the Little Eyases: The Boyhood of Shakespeare's Hero." In Kate Chedgzoy, Susanne Greenhalgh, and Robert Shaughnessy (eds) *Shakespeare and Childhood.* Cambridge: Cambridge University Press.

Murray, Gilbert (1914) *Hamlet and Orestes: A Study in Traditional Types.* New York: Oxford University Press.

Newman, Karen (1987) "Portia's Ring: Unruly Women and Structures of Exchange in *The Merchant of Venice*." *Shakespeare Quarterly*, 38: 19–33.

Nora, Pierre (1997) *Les lieux de mémoire*, 3-vol. edition. Paris: Gallimard.

O'Connor, Marion (2006) "Rachel Fane's May Masque at Apethorpe 1627." *English Literary Renaissance*, 36 (1): 90–113.

Olsen, Thomas G. (1999) "Iachimo's 'Drug-Damn'd Italy' and the Problem of British National Character in *Cymbeline*." *Shakespeare Yearbook*, 10: 269–96.

O'Neill, John P. and Schultz, Ellen (eds) (1986) *Gothic and Renaissance Art in Nuremberg, 1300–1500*. New York and Munich: The Metropolitan Museum of Art.

Orgel, Stephen (2003) *Imagining Shakespeare*. New York: Palgrave Macmillan.

Oz, Avraham (1998) "Extending Within: Placing Self and Nation in the Epic of *Cymbeline*." *Journal of Theatre and Drama* 4: 81–97.

Padmanabhan, Manjula (2001) "Harvest." In Helen Gilbert (ed.) *Postcolonial Drama: An Anthology*. London: Routledge.

Paige, D. D. (ed.) (1951) *The Letters of Ezra Pound*. New York: New Directions.

Palsgrave, John (1530) *Lesclarcissement de la langue francoyse*. [London?].

Panofsky, Erwin (1939) *Studies in Iconology: Humanistic Themes in the Art of the Renaissance*. New York: Oxford University Press.

Paré, Ambroise (1634) *The Workes of That Famous Chirurgion Ambrose Parey*, trans. Thomas Johnson. London.

Parker, Patricia (1989) "Romance and Empire: Anachronistic *Cymbeline*." In George M. Logan and Gordon Teskey (eds) *Unfolded Tales: Essays on Renaissance Romance*. Ithaca NY: Cornell University Press: 189–207.

—— (2002) "Preposterous Conversions: Turning Turk and its 'Pauline' Rerighting," *JEMCS*, 2 (1): 1–34.

—— (2004) "Barbers and Barbary: Early Modern Cultural Semantics." in *Renaissance Drama* (new series 33). Evanston IL: Northwestern University Press: 201–44.

Parolin, Peter A. (2002) "Anachronistic Italy: Cultural Alliances and National Identity in *Cymbeline*." *Shakespeare Studies*, 30: 188–215.

Parry, Graham (ed.) (1991) *The History of Britain: John Milton: A Facsimile Edition with a Critical Introduction* (1670; 2nd edition 1677). Stamford: Watkins.

Pascal, Blaise (1941) *Pensées/ The Provincial Letters*. New York: Modern Library.

—— (1995) [reissued 1999] *Pensées and other Writing*, trans. Honor Levi. Oxford: Oxford University Press.

Paster, Gail Kern (1993) *The Body Embarrassed: Drama and the Disciplines of Shame in Early Modern England*. Ithaca NY: Cornell University Press.

—— (2004) *Humoring the Body*. Chicago IL: The University of Chicago Press.

Patterson, Annabel (1989) *Shakespeare and the Popular Voice*. Oxford: Blackwell.

Paulin, Tom (1983) *Liberty Tree*. London: Faber.

Pavis, Patrice (1988) "From Text to Performance." In Michael Issacharoff and Robin F. Jones (eds) *Performing Texts*. Philadelphia PA: University of Pennsylvania Press.

Pearson, Roberta E. and William Uricchio (2006) "Brushing up Shakespeare: Relevance and Televisual Form." In Diana E. Henderson (ed.) *A Concise Companion to Shakespeare on Screen*. Malden MA: Blackwell Publishing: 197–215.

Penuel, Suzanne (2004) "Castrating the Creditor in *The Merchant of Venice*." *Studies in English Literature*, 44: 255–75.

Pereira, José Pacheco (1999) *Álvaro Cunhal-uma biografia política, Vol.1: "Daniel", o Jovem Revolucionário (1913–1941)*. Lisboa: Temas e Debates.

——(2001) *Álvaro Cunhal-uma biografia política, Vol.2: "Duarte", o Dirigente Clandestino (1941–1949)*. Lisboa: Temas e Debates.

—— (2005) *Álvaro Cunhal-uma biografia política, Vol.3: O Prisioneiro (1949–1960)*. Lisboa: Temas e Debates.

Phelan, Peggy (1993) *Unmarked: The Politics of Performance*. London: Routledge.

Pinciss, Gerald M. (2005) *Why Shakespeare?* New York: Continuum.

Pincombe, Michael (2000) "Cupid and Eliza: Variations on a Virgilian Icon in Plays by Gager, Lyly, and Marlowe." In György E. Szonyi and Rowland Wymer (eds) *The Iconography of Power: Ideas and Images of Rulership on the English Renaissance Stage*. Szeged: Institute of English and American Studies: 33–52.

Pochoda, Phil (1997) "Universities Press On." *The Nation*, 29. Accessed at http://www.brocku.ca/english/courses/4F70/univpresses.html on February 2, 2006.

Pocock, J. G. A. (1975) "British History: A Plea for a New Subject." *Journal of Modern History*, 47: 601–28.

Polan, D. (2006) "Foucault TV." *Flow*, 4 (7): col. 1. Accessed at http://jot.communication.utexas.edu/flow/?jot=view&id=1929 on June 10, 2006.

Poovey, Mary (1998) *A History of the Modern Fact: Problems of Knowledge in the Sciences of Wealth and Society*. Chicago IL: University of Chicago Press.

Power, Carla (2006) "Review of *Henry IV, Parts 1 and 2*." *Newsweek*, June 20.

Pratt, William (1617 edition) *The Arithmeticall Jewell*, London.

Pye, Christopher (2000) *The Vanishing: Shakespeare, the Subject, and Early Modern Culture*. Durham NC: Duke University Press.

Quinn, David Beers (1945) "Sir Thomas Smith (1513–1577) and the Beginnings of English Colonial Theory." *Proceedings of the American Philosophical Society*, 89: 543–60.

Rabelais, François (1994) *Oeuvres completes*, eds Mireille Huchon and François Moreau. Paris: Gallimard, "Bibliotheque de la Pleiade."

RAE (Research Assessment Exercise) (1996) "1996 Research Assessment Exercise: Criteria for assessment." Last accessed at www.hero.ac.uk/rae/rae96.50.html on May 2, 2006.

RAE (2006) "2008 Panel Criteria and Working Methods." Accessed at www.rae.ac.uk/pubs/2006/01/byuoa.asp?u=m on May 2, 2006.

Ramos, Domingos (trans.) (1905). *William Shakespeare, Rei Lear*. Porto: Chardron.

Record, Robert (1594 edition) *The Ground of Arts*, London.

Redmond, Michael J. (1999) "'My Lord, I fear, has forgot Britain': Rome, Italy, and the (Re)construction of British National Identity." *Shakespeare Yearbook*, 10: 297–316.

Regier, Willis with Jeffrey J. Williams (2004) "In Defense of Academic Publishing: An Interview with Willis Regier." *The Minnesota Review*, N.S. 61–2. Accessed at http://www.theminnesotareview.org/journal/ns61/regier.htm.

Rider, John (1589) *Bibliotheca Scholastica*. Oxford.

Roach, Joseph (1996) *Cities of the Dead: Circum-Atlantic Performance*. New York: Columbia University Press.

Robbins, Bruce (1999) "CelebReliance: Intellectuals, Celebrity, and Upward Mobility." *Postmodern Culture*, 9.2: 1–22.

Roberts, Peter (1964) "An Epic Restored." *Plays and Players*, June: 36–7.

Roberts, Sasha (2002) *Reading Shakespeare's Poems in Early Modern England*. Basingstoke: Palgrave Macmillan.

Rosenblum, Joseph (ed.) (2005) *The Greenwood Companion to Shakespeare*, 4 vols. Westport CT: Greenwood.

Rossi, Joan Warchol (1978) "*Cymbeline*'s Debt to Holinshed: The Richness of III.i." In Carol McGinnis Kay and Henry E. Jacobs (eds)

Shakespeare's Romances Reconsidered. Lincoln NE and London: University of Nebraska Press: 104–12.

Rowe, Katherine (2003) "'Remember Me': Technologies of Memory in Michael Almereyda's *Hamlet*." In Richard Burt and Lynda E. Boose (eds) *Shakespeare, the Movie, II: Popularizing the Plays on Film, Television, and DVD*. New York: Routledge: 37–55.

Rubin, Stanley (1974) *Medieval English Medicine*. New York: Barnes & Noble.

Rust, Jennifer (2003) "Wittenberg and Melancholic Allegory: The Reformation and Its Discontents in *Hamlet*." In Dennis Taylor and David Beauregard (eds) *Shakespeare and the Culture of Christianity*. New York: Fordham University Press.

Ryan, Judith (2004) "Publishing and Purchasing: The Great Paradigm Shift." In Rosemary G. Feal (ed.) *Profession 2004*. New York: Modern Language Association of America: 7–13.

Saavedra Fajardo, Diego de (1700) *The Royal Politician*, trans. Sir J. Astry. London.

Sayre, Gordon (2005) "The Crisis in Scholarly Publishing: Demystifying the Fetishes of Technology and the Market." In Rosemary G. Feal (ed.) *Profession 2005*. New York: Modern Language Association of America: 52–8.

Schäfer, Jürgen (1970) "The Orthography of Proper Names in Modern-spelling Editions of Shakespeare." *Studies in Bibliography*, 23: 1–19.

Schechner, Richard (1992) "A New Paradigm for Theatre in the Academy." *The Drama Review: The Journal of Performance Studies*, 36 (4): 7–10.

Schleiner, Louise (1990) "Latinized Greek in Shakespeare's Writing of *Hamlet*." *Shakespeare Quarterly*, 41 (1): 29–48.

Schmitt, Carl (1922) *Political Theology: Four Chapters on the Concept of Sovereignty*, trans. George Schwab (1988 ed.). Cambridge MA: MIT Press.

—— (1956) *Hamlet oder Hekuba? Der Einbruch der Zeit in das Spiel*. Stuttgart: Klett-Cotta. Unpublished translation by Jennifer Rust.

—— (1987) "The Problem of the Tragic," trans. David Pan. *Telos*, 72: 133–51.

—— (1996) *The Concept of the Political*, trans. George Schwab. Chicago IL: University of Chicago Press.

Schneider, Ben Ross, Jr (1995) "*King Lear* in Its Own Time: The Difference that Death Makes." *Early Modern Literary Studies* 1.1: 3.1–49. Accessed at http://purl.oclc.org/emls/01–1/schnlear.html.

Schwyzer, Philip (2004) *Literature, Nationalism and Memory in Early Modern England and Wales*. Cambridge: Cambridge University Press.

Sconce, J. (1995) "Trashing the Academy: Taste, Excess, and an Emerging Politics of Cinematic Style." *Screen*, 36 (4): 371–93.

Scultetus, Johannes (1674) *The Chyrurgeons Store-house*. London.

Seaford, Richard (1994) *Reciprocity and Ritual: Homer and Tragedy in the Developing City-State*. Oxford: Oxford University Press.

Securis, John (1566) *A Detection and Querimonie of the Daily Enormities and Abuses Committed in Physick*. London.

Sedgwick, Eve Kosofsky (1993) "Queer Performativity: Henry James's *The Art of the Novel*." *GLQ*, 1: 1–16.

Semenza, G. (2005) "Shakespeare After Columbine: Teen Violence in Tim Blake Nelson's *O*." *College Literature*, 32 (4): 99–124.

Seneca, Lucius Annaeus (1614) *The Workes of Lucius Annaeus Seneca*. London.

—— (1969) *Epistulae Moralaes ad Lucilium* V. *Letters from a Stoic*, ed. and trans. Robin Campbell. London: Penguin Books.

Shakespeare, William (1971) *The Winter's Tale*, ed. Baldwin Maxwell. Harmondsworth: Penguin Books Ltd.

—— (1984) *The Winter's Tale*, ed. Baldwin Maxwell. Harmondsworth: Penguin Books Ltd.

—— (1986; 2nd ed 2005) *William Shakespeare, The Complete Works*, eds Stanley Wells and Gary Taylor. Oxford: Oxford University Press.

—— (1994) *Macbeth*. Nicholas Brooke (ed.) Oxford: Oxford University Press.

—— (1997) *King Lear*. Arden Shakespeare (3rd series). R. A. Foakes (ed.) London: Thomson.

—— (1997) *Macbeth*. A. R. Braunmuller (ed.) Cambridge: Cambridge University Press.

—— (1997) *The Norton Shakespeare: Based on the Oxford Edition*. Stephen Greenblatt (ed.) New York: W. W. Norton.

—— (2000) *Romeo and Juliet*. Jill L. Levenson (ed.) Oxford: Oxford University Press.

—— (2002) *King Henry IV, Part 1*. The Arden Shakespeare (3rd series), ed. David Scott Kastan London: Arden.

—— (2006) *Hamlet*. Ann Thompson and Neil Taylor (eds) The Arden Shakespeare (3rd series). London: Thomas Learning.

Shannon, Claude E. and Warren Weaver (1949) *The Mathematical Theory of Communication*. Urbana IL: University of Illinois Press.

Shannon, Laurie (2002) *Sovereign Amity: Figures of Friendship in Shakespearean Contexts*. Chicago IL: University of Chicago Press.

Shapin, Steven (1994) *A Social History of Truth: Civility and Science in Seventeenth-Century England*. Chicago IL: University of Chicago Press.

—— and Simon Schaffer (1985) *Leviathan and the Air-Pump: Hobbes, Boyle, and the Experimental Life*. Princeton NJ: Princeton University Press.

Shapiro, James (1996) *Shakespeare and the Jews*. New York: Columbia University Press.

Shaughnessy, Robert (2006) "Stage, Screen, and Nation: Hamlet and the Space of History." In Diana E. Henderson (ed.) *A Concise Companion to Shakespeare on Screen*. Malden MA: Blackwell Publishing: 54–76.

Shell, Marc (1982) *Money, Language, and Thought*. Berkeley CA: University of California Press.

Sher, Antony (1985) *Year of the King*. London: Methuen.

Shumway, David R. (1997) "The Star System in Literary Studies." *PMLA* 112. 1: 85–100.

Shurbanov, Alexander and Boika Sokolova (2001) *Painting Shakespeare Red: An East-European Appropriation*. Newark NJ/London: University of Delaware Press/Associated University Presses.

Sinfield, Alan (1985) "Royal Shakespeare: Theatre and the Making of Ideology." In Jonathan Dollimore and Alan Sinfield (eds) *Political Shakespeare: New Essays in Cultural Materialism*. Manchester: Manchester University Press: 158–81.

—— (2006) *Shakespeare, Authority, Sexuality: Unfinished Business in Cultural Materialism*. London: Routledge.

Sjögren, Gunnar (1983) *Hamlet the Dane*. Lund, Sweden: New Society of Letters.

Sokol, B. J. (1998) "Prejudice and Law in *The Merchant of Venice*." In Stanley Wells (ed.) *Shakespeare Survey*, 51: 159–73.

Sourvinou-Inwood, Christiane (2005) "Greek Tragedy and Ritual." In Rebecca Bushnell (ed.) *A Companion to Tragedy*. Malden, MA: Blackwell Publishing.

Southwell, Robert (1595) *Moeoniae, Or, Certaine Excellent Poems and Spirituall Hymnes*. London.

Speaight, Robert (1964) "Shakespeare in Britain." *Shakespeare Quarterly*, 15: 377–89.

Spencer, Christopher (1965) *Five Restoration Adaptations of Shakespeare*. Urbana IL: University of Illinois Press.

—— (1972) *Nahum Tate*. New York: Twayne.

Spigel, Lynn (1991) *Make Room for Television*. Chicago IL: University of Chicago Press.

Spiller, Elizabeth A. (2000) "From Imagination to Miscegenation: Race and Romance in Shakespeare's *The Merchant of Venice*." In *Renaissance Drama* (new series), 29: 137–64.

Spurgin, Tim (2001) "The *Times Magazine* and Academic Megastars." *The Minnesota Review* N.S. 52–4. Accessed at www.theminnesotareview. org/journal/ns52/spurgin.html on March 28, 2006.

Stallybrass, Peter (2000) "Naming, Renaming and Unnaming in the Shakespearean Quartos and Folio." In Andrew Murphy (ed.) *The Renaissance Text: Theory, Editing, Textuality*. Manchester: Manchester University Press, 108–34.

Stam, Robert (2005) *Literature through Film: Realism, Magic, and the Art of Adaptation*. Oxford: Blackwell.

—— and Alessandra Raengo (2005) *Literature and Film: A Guide to the Theory and Practice of Film Adaptation*. Oxford: Blackwell Publishing, Ltd.

Stanton, Domna C. (2004) "Working through the Crises: A Plan for Action," In Rosemary G. Feal (ed.) *Profession 2004*. New York: Modern Language Association of America: 32–41.

Steedman, Carolyn (2002) *Dust: The Archive and Cultural History*. New Brunswick NJ: Rutgers University Press.

Steinberg, Leo (1983) *The Sexuality of Christ in Renaissance Art and in Modern Oblivion*. New York: Pantheon/October.

Styan, J. L. (1971) *Shakespeare's Stagecraft*. Cambridge: Cambridge University Press.

—— (1977) *The Shakespeare Revolution: Criticism and Performance in the Twentieth Century*. Cambridge: Cambridge University Press.

Sullivan Jr, Garrett A. (1998) "Civilizing Wales: Cymbeline, Roads and the Landscapes of Early Modern Britain." EMLS 4, 2/SI 3: 3.1–34.

——, Patrick Cheney, and Andrew Hadfield (eds) (2005) *Early Modern English Drama: A Critical Companion*. Oxford: Oxford University Press.

Tate, Nahum (1681) *The History of King Lear*. London: Wing STC S2918–77_06, via Early English Books Online.

—— (1975) *The History of King Lear*, ed. James Black. Lincoln NE: University of Nebraska Press. Also Jack Lynch, transcriber, http://newark. rutgers.edu/~jlynch/Texts//tatelear.html

Taylor, Diana (2003) *The Archive and the Repertoire: Performing Cultural Memory in the Americas*. Durham NC: Duke University Press.

Taylor, Gary (1993) "The Renaissance and the End of Editing." In George Bornstein and Ralph G. Williams (eds) *Palimpsest: Editorial Theory in the Humanities*. Ann Arbor MI: University of Michigan Press, 121–49.

—— (2000) "c:\wp\file.txt 04:41 10–07–8." In Andrew Murphy (ed.) *The Renaissance Text: Theory, Editing, and Textuality.* Manchester: University of Manchester Press, 44–54.

Taylor, Mark C. (2001) *The Moment of Complexity: Emerging Network Culture.* Chicago IL: University of Chicago Press.

Taylor, Neil (1994) "Two Types of Television Shakespeare." In Anthony Davies and Stanley Wells (eds) *Shakespeare and the Moving Image: the Plays on Film and Television.* Cambridge and New York: Cambridge University Press: 86–98.

Taylor, Thomas (1612) *Commentarie vpon the Epistle of S. Paul written to Titus.* Cambridge.

Thomas, Thomas (1587) *Dictionarium Latinae et Anglicanae.* London.

Thompson, Ann (1991) "Person and Office: The Case of Imogen, Princess of Britain." In Vincent Newey and Ann Thompson (eds) *Literature and Nationalism.* Liverpool: Liverpool University Press: 76–87.

—— and Neil Taylor (eds) (2006) *Hamlet.* The Arden Shakespeare (3rd series). London: Thomas Learning.

Tiffany, Grace (2003) *My Father Had a Daughter: Judith Shakespeare's Tale.* New York: Berkley Books.

Tillyard, E. M. W. (1944 [1962]) *Shakespeare's History Plays.* Harmondsworth: Penguin.

Tinkle, Theresa (1996) *Medieval Venuses and Cupids: Sexuality, Hermeneutics, and English Poetry.* Stanford CA: Stanford University Press.

Torre, Manuel Gomes da (2002) "Uma Tradução com História e para a História." *Público* (31 August): 39–40.

—— (trans.) (2005). *William Shakespeare, Rei Lear.* Porto: Campo das Letras.

Trapp, John (1657) *A Commentary or Exposition upon the Books of Ezra, Nehemiah, Esther, Job and Psalms.* London.

Tumbleson, Raymond D. (2005) "A Confluence of Crises: Tenure and Jobs." In Rosemary G. Feal (ed.) *Profession 2005.* New York: Modern Language Association of America: 59–63.

Tynan, Kenneth (1950) *He That Plays the King.* London: Longmans, Green & Co.

—— (1964) *Tynan on Theatre,* Harmondsworth: Penguin.

Udall, John (1588) *The State of the Churche of Englande Laide Open.* London.

Ullmann, Walter (1979) "This Realm of England is an Empire." *Journal of Ecclesiastical History,* 30: 175–203.

Uristitius, C. (1596 edition) *The Elements of Arithmeticke,* trans. Thomas Hood, London.

Vaillant-Couturier, Paul (1937) "Jeunesse" [song]. Music by Arthur Honegger. Accessed at http://centenaire.parti-socialiste.fr/article.php3?id_article=329 on June 24, 2006.

Vernant, Jean-Pierre and Pierre Vidal-Naquet (1981) *Tragedy and Myth in Ancient Greece*, trans. Janet Lloyd. Brighton: Harvester Press.

Vidal-Naquet, Pierre (1981) "The Black Hunter and the Origin of the Athenian Ephebeia." In R. L. Gordon (ed.) *Myth, Religion and Society*. Cambridge: Cambridge University Press, 147–62.

Vigo, John (1543) *The Most Exelent Worckes of Chirurgery*. London.

Vitkus, Daniel (2003) *Turning Turk: English Theater and the Multicultural Mediterranean, 1570–1630*. New York: Palgrave Macmillan.

Walford, Leo (2000) "The Research Assessment Exercise: Its Effect on Scholarly Journal Publishing." *Learned Publishing* 13: 49–52.

Waltz, Robin (1996) "Serial killings: 'Fântomas', Feuillade, and the Mass-culture Genealogy of Surrealism." *Velvet Light Trap* 37: 51–7.

Wardle, Irving (1974) "A Director's Approach: An Interview with Peter Hall." In John Lahr and Anthea Lahr (eds) *A Casebook on Harold Pinter's "The Homecoming."* London: Davis-Poynter: 9–26.

Waswo, Richard (1996) "Shakespeare and the Formation of the Modern Economy." *Surfaces*, 6: 217. Accessed May 23, 2006 at www.pum.umontreal.ca/revues/surfaces/vol6/waswo.html.

Waters, Lindsay (2000) "A Modest Proposal for Preventing the Books of the Members of the MLA from Being a Burden to their Authors, Publishers, or Audiences." *PMLA*, 115.3: 315–17.

—— (2001) "Rescue Tenure from the Tyranny of the Monograph." *Chronicle of Higher Education*. Accessed March 16, 2006 at http://chronicle.com/prm/weekly/v47/i32/32b00701.htm.

Wayne, Valerie (2003) "*Cymbeline*: Patriotism and Performance." In Richard Dutton and Jean Howard (eds) *The Poems, Problem Comedies, Late Plays: A Companion to Shakespeare's Works*, Volume IV. Oxford and Malden MA: Blackwell, 389–407.

Webster, John (1623) *The Duchess of Malfi*. London.

Wecker, Johann Jacob (1585) *A Compendious Chyrurgerie Gathered, & Translated (Specially) out of Wecker by Ihon Banester Maister in Chyrurgerie*. London.

Weimann, Robert (1978) *Shakespeare and the Popular Tradition in the Theatre*, ed. Robert Schwartz. Baltimore MD: Johns Hopkins University Press.

Wells, Stanley (1984) *Re-Editing Shakespeare for the Modern Reader*. Oxford: Clarendon Press.

—— (2005) "Current Issues in Shakespeare Biography." In Christa Jansohn (ed.) *In the Footsteps of William Shakespeare*. Münster: LIT Verlag: 5–21.

—— and Gary Taylor (eds) (1986) *William Shakespeare, The Complete Works*, 2nd ed. 2005. Oxford: Oxford University Press.

—— et al. (1987) *William Shakespeare: A Textual Companion*. Oxford: Oxford University Press.

Werstine, Paul (1988) "McKerrow's 'Suggestion' and Twentieth-Century Shakespeare Textual Criticism." *Renaissance Drama* 19: 149–73.

Wharton, T. F. (1983) *Text and Performance: Henry the Fourth, Parts 1 and 2*. Basingstoke: Macmillan.

Wiener, Norbert (1962) *Cybernetics or Control and Communication in the Animal and the Machine*, 2nd ed. Cambridge MA: MIT Press.

Wierzbicka, Anna (1994) "Emotion, Language, and Cultural Scripts." In S. Kitayama and H. R. Marcus (eds) *Emotion and Culture: Empirical Studies of Mutual Influence*, Washington DC: APA: 133–95.

Willems, Michele (1994) "Verbal-Visual, Verbal-Pictorial or Textual-Televisual? Reflections on the BBC Shakespeare Series." In Anthony Davies and Stanley Wells (eds) *Shakespeare and the Moving Image: the Plays on Film and Television*. Cambridge and New York: Cambridge University Press: 69–85.

Williams, George Walton (ed.) (1997) *Shakespeare's Speech-Headings: Speaking the Speech in Shakespeare's Plays*. Newark NJ: University of Delaware Press.

Williams, Jeffrey J. (2004) "Smart." *The Minnesota Review*, N.S.: 61–2. Accessed February 17, 2006 at www.theminnesotareview.org/journal/ns61/williams.htm.

Williamson, Arthur H. (2005) "An Empire to End Empire: The Dynamic of Early Modern British Expansion." *Huntington Library Quarterly* 68 (1&2): 227–56.

Willis, Susan (1991) *The BBC Shakespeare Plays: Making the Televised Canon*. Chapel Hill NC: University of North Carolina Press.

Wilson, Emily (2004) *Mocked with Death: Tragic Overliving from Sophocles to Milton*. Baltimore MD and London: Johns Hopkins University Press.

Wilson, John Dover (1935) *What Happens in Hamlet*. Cambridge: Cambridge University Press (1959 edition).

—— (1943) *The Fortunes of Falstaff*. Cambridge: Cambridge University Press.

—— (ed.) (1946) *The First Part of the History of Henry IV*. Cambridge: Cambridge University Press.

—— and T. C. Worsley (1952) *Shakespeare's Histories at Stratford 1951*. London: Max Reinhardt.

Winkler, John (1985) "The Ephebes' Song: Tragoidia and the Polis." *Representations*, 11: 26–62

Womack, Peter (2002) "Secularizing King Lear: Shakespeare, Tate, and the Sacred." *Shakespeare Survey*, 55: 96–105.

Woodall, John (1617) *The Surgeon's Mate*, London.

Woolf, Virginia (1989) *A Room of One's Own*. New York: Harcourt Brace Jovanovich.

Worsley, T. C. (1959) "Review of *Roots*." *Financial Times*, July 31.

Worthen, W. B. (1997) *Shakespeare and the Authority of Performance*. Cambridge: Cambridge University Press.

—— (2003a) "The Imprint of Performance." In W. B. Worthen and Peter Holland (eds) *Theorizing Practice: Redefining Theatre History*. Basingstoke: Palgrave: 213–34.

—— (2003b) *Shakespeare and the Force of Modern Performance*. Cambridge: Cambridge University Press.

—— (2005) *Print and the Poetics of Modern Drama*. Cambridge: Cambridge University Press.

—— (2007) "Performing Shakespeare in digital culture." In Robert Shaughnessy (ed.) *The Cambridge Companion to Shakespeare and Popular Culture*: 227–47.

Yates, Frances A. (1936) *A Study of "Love's Labour's Lost."* Cambridge: Cambridge University Press.

Yeats, W. B. (1990) *Collected Poems*. London and Basingstoke: Picador.

Zeitlin, Froma (1984). "The Dynamics of Misogyny: Myth and Mythmaking in the *Oresteia*." In John Peradotto and Y. P. Sullivan (eds) *Women in the Ancient World*, Albany NY: State University of New York Press: 159–94.

Zryd, Michael (2006) "The Academy and the Avant-Garde: A Relationship of Dependence and Resistance." *Cinema Journal*, 45 (2): 17–42.

INDEX